MONEY AND MODERNITY

MONEY AND MODERNITY
Pound, Williams, and the Spirit of Jefferson

by Alec Marsh

The University of Alabama Press

Tuscaloosa and London

Copyright © 1998
The University of Alabama Press
Tuscaloosa, Alabama 35487-0380
All rights reserved
Manufactured in the United States of America

∞

The paper on which this book is printed meets the minimum
requirements of American National Standard for Information
Science-Permanence of Paper for Printed Library Materials,
ANSI
Z39.48-1984.

Library of Congress Cataloging-in-Publication Data

Marsh, Alec, 1953–
Money and modernity : Pound, Williams, and the spirit of
Jefferson
/ by Alec Marsh.
p.   cm.
Includes bibliographical references (p. 269) and index.
ISBN 0–8173–0921–7 (alk. paper)
1. Pound, Ezra, 1885–1972—Political and social views.
2. Williams, William Carlos, 1883–1963—Political and social
views. 3. Capitalism and literature—United
States—History—20th century. 4. Williams, William Carlos,
1883–1963—Knowledge—Economics. 5. American poetry—20th
century—History and criticism. 6. Pound, Ezra,
1885–1972—Knowledge—Economics. 7. Jefferson, Thomas,
1743–1826—Influence. 8. Modernism (Literature)—United
States. 9. Economics in literature. 10. Money in literature
I. Title. PS3531.082Z746 1998 811'.5209358—dc21
97–45459

British Library Cataloguing-in-Publication data available.

For George Kearns and Jim Livingston

CONTENTS

PREFACE

In bringing together the discourses of poetry, economics, and the history of ideas, I find myself writing cultural history—half history, half a guide to what Ezra Pound called, with a wink, "Kulch." For Pound this Kulchur was something America manifestly lacked. Or rather, culture was something he felt the pseudocultural apparatus of finance capitalism had suppressed in the United States. According to Pound, true American culture, expressed by Thomas Jefferson and his ideological descendants among the Populists, had been relegated to what his friend William Carlos Williams in a crucial essay called "the American background." There an abortive, truly American "primary" culture waited for the flimsy superstructure of finance to collapse from its own unreality, bringing down with it the simulacrum of "secondary culture," which Williams defined as "the culture of purchase, the culture of effigy" (*SE* 147) that had coopted American civilization.

I see Pound and Williams as latter-day Jeffersonians rather than Populists because I want readers to understand that their American political background—or more accurately their ideological affinity—constitutes a positive position and is not simply reactionary or antimodern. Although they share a certain nostalgia for lost authenticities that manifests itself as a yearning for an agricultural and therefore quasi-natural world, they, unlike their contemporaries the Southern Agrarians, are not looking to turn back the clock. Rather, they both undertake Jeffersonian analyses of modern capitalism, which accept the inevitability of modernity. Their Jeffersonian critique of progress stands above all for a fairer, more democratic distribution of the fruits of industrial labor. It seeks to democratize capitalism by reorganizing its benefits. This critique explains the two poets' extraordinary interest in money, because through money the distributive effects of capital and capitalism—profits, goods, and wages—are measured. It is generally true that Jeffersonians feel that, if the control of money could be returned to "the people," then the control of capitalism would take care of itself. So in reading Ezra Pound and William Carlos Williams as latter-day Jeffersonians, I am placing them in a long tradition of American political and economic dissent.

ACKNOWLEDGMENTS

I THANK Muhlenberg College for a generous summer research grant that enabled me to work on this book. I am extremely grateful to the National Endowment for the Humanities for funding a 1994 seminar at the Brunnenburg that was led by Tim Redman and Vincent Sherry, who encouraged me to pursue this project. There I met Burt Hatlen and Ellen Keck Stauder, who convinced me that I had something to say.

Ever since she first invited two honeymooning pilgrims to tea, Mary de Rachewiltz has been an inspiration and the embodiment of all that is best in the tradition. Without her insights and dedication to her father, Pound scholarship could all too easily lose itself in a dark wood. Hildegard Hoeller and I are most grateful for her friendship and hospitality.

My interest in Ezra Pound was sparked long ago by great teachers at Bennington College, Phebe Chao and Stephen Sandy. At Rutgers University, George Kearns and James Livingston showed me what scholarship was as they patiently oversaw the sprawling dissertation from which this work grew. I respectfully dedicate this work to them. I am indebted to many others there as well: to Bruce Robbins for his helpful reading, to Barry Qualls, to Daniel Harris, and especially to Richard Poirier for the brilliant seminars that formed my sense of Emerson, Pragmatism, and Robert Frost. His influence underlies much of the intense conversation that makes Rutgers such a lively place. Thanks to Jim Albrecht, Claire Berardini, Anthony Bernardo, Rebecca Brittenham, Lyall Bush, Bob Coleman, David Evans, Regina Graemer, Lisa Honecker, Jonathan Levin, Matthew Kearney, Ray Klimek, Jonathan Nashell, Alan Parker, Wendell Pies, Mark Richardson, Mark Scott, Joe Thomas, and many others. Most of all, thanks to Hildegard Hoeller for the intensest conversation of all.

I am grateful to my colleagues in the English Department at Muhlenberg. I owe much to the warm friendship and inspired teaching of Larry and Margie Hass, who kindly took me on as a student in philosophy, and to Mark Edmundson, who encouraged me. Conversations with the young poet David Killeen and his outstanding undergraduate thesis *Paterson* clarified much of my thinking about that difficult poem.

I am grateful to Leon Surette for reading an early draft of Chapter 3. His rigorous and patient commentary has made this a much better book. I remain indebted to him, even where we disagree, and look forward to continuing a lively correspondence.

Thanks to Glen MacLeod, who once gave a fledgling scholar a break, and to Debra Ratner, who a long time ago made me believe that anything was possible.

Permissions

Quotations from *Pragmatism and the Political Economy of Cultural Revolution, 1850–1940* by James Livingston, copyright © 1994, are reprinted courtesy of The University of North Carolina Press. Used by permission of the publisher.

From *The Poetry of Robert Frost*, edited by Edward Connery Lathem, copyright 1936, © 1956 by Robert Frost, © 1964 by Lesley Frost Ballantine, copyright 1928, © 1969 by Henry Holt and Company, Inc. Reprinted by permission of Henry Holt and Company, Inc.

Quotations from Wallace Stevens, *Collected Poems* copyright © 1954 by Wallace Stevens and *Opus Posthumous* copyright © 1957 by Elsie Stevens and Holly Stevens are reprinted by permission of Alfred A. Knopf, Inc.

Ezra Pound

I gratefully acknowledge New Directions Publishing Corporation and Faber & Faber Ltd. for permission to quote from the following copyrighted works of Ezra Pound:

The ABC of Reading. All rights reserved.
The Cantos. Copyright © 1934, 1937, 1940, 1948, 1956, 1959, 1962, 1963, 1966, and 1968 by Ezra Pound.

Acknowledgments

William Carlos Williams

Acknowledgments

ABBREVIATIONS

Ezra Pound

References to Ezra Pound, *The Cantos,* show the canto number followed by a colon and a page number and refer to the eleventh edition (New York: New Directions, 1989).

C	*Confucius*
CWC	*The Chinese Written Character as a Medium for Poetry*
EPS	*"Ezra Pound Speaking": Radio Speeches of World War II*
GB	*Gaudier-Brzeska*
GK	*Guide to Kulchur*
JM	*Jefferson and/or Mussolini*
LE	*Literary Essays*
PD	*Pavannes and Divagations*
P/W	*Pound/Williams*
P/Z	*Pound/Zukofsky*
SL	*Selected Letters*
SP	*Selected Prose*
SR	*Spirit of Romance*

William Carlos Williams

A	*Autobiography*
AG	*In the American Grain*
CP1	*The Collected Poems, Vol. 1, 1909–1939*
CP2	*The Collected Poems, Vol. 2, 1939–1962*
EK	*The Embodiment of Knowledge*
I	*Imaginations*
IWWP	*I Wanted to Write a Poem*
P	*Paterson*

Abbreviations

RI	*A Recognizable Image: William Carlos Williams on Art and Artists*
SE	*Selected Essays*
SL	*Selected Letters*
SS	*Something to Say: William Carlos Williams on Younger Poets*

MONEY AND MODERNITY

INTRODUCTION

THE MODERNIST POETS William Carlos Williams (1883–1963) and Ezra Pound (1885–1972) were latter-day Jeffersonians strongly marked by the Populism of the late decades of the nineteenth century. Much of their Modernism is, like Jeffersonianism, both a reaction against modernity and the pursuit of an alternative claim against the form and fruits of progress. The poets' Jeffersonianism made them sharply aware of the social contradictions of modernization, and this committed them—in different ways—to a highly politicized, often polemical poetry that criticized finance capitalism and its institutions—notably banks—in the strongest terms. It seemed to commit them as well to the so-called agrarian values of small producers and proprietors, the values of those who, like poets, are self-employed and engage in craftwork. Much of Williams's and Pound's writing is an attempt to find a better, more flexible description of this apparently anachronistic position.

In his important unsympathetic treatment of the "agrarian myth" in America, Richard Hofstadter spoke of the "dominant themes of Populist ideology": "The idea of the golden age; the concept of natural harmonies; the dualistic version of social struggles [between debtors and creditors]; the conspiracy theory of history; and the doctrine of the primacy of money" (Hofstadter 1955 62).[1] These themes shape Ezra Pound's *Cantos* and control important aspects of Williams's poetry.[2] In effect, these themes constitute a kind of aesthetic ideology for the two poets.

Fear of a global conspiracy of finance is a mark of the populistic Jeffersonianism that provided the intellectual justifications for "agrarian" ideology in America. Jeffersonianism and its Populist manifestations, then as now (as, for instance, in the work of the late Christopher Lasch),[3] remain in reaction against the "financial revolution" of the seventeenth century, which was a crucial step in the creation of capi-

1

talism and hence of modernity itself (McDonald 1976 161–62). For this reason money takes on extraordinary, almost totemic importance in Jeffersonian thinking.[4]

Pound once defined the epic as "a poem including history" and added, "I don't see that anyone save a sap-head can now think he knows any history until he understands economics" (*LE* 86). But his is a peculiarly Jeffersonian economics that works like an "Ariadne's thread," leading us through the maze of history into the labyrinthine *Cantos* and beyond to Williams's collagist *Paterson*. Indeed, it is their economic determinism that makes Pound and Williams most modern and most like other intellectuals of their time. Few contemporary historians would argue with this assertion because the most influential American historians of the Modernist moment, Frederick Jackson Turner, J. Allen Smith, Charles A. Beard, Vernon Parrington, and the popular Claude Bowers, were all firm believers in economic determinism. All had been formed by the political experience of Populism, and all were to some degree consciously Jeffersonian.[5]

Williams and Pound met at the University of Pennsylvania just after the turn of the century. Pound was a very young undergraduate, Williams a medical student in the days when medical school was undertaken in lieu of an undergraduate education. They became close friends and corresponded until the end of their very different lives. While Williams spent his life as a physician ministering to the ethnic working poor of Rutherford, New Jersey, Pound lived as an expatriate bohemian in Europe. Temperamentally, they could hardly have been more different. Pound was contentious, literary, aggressively cosmopolitan; Williams self-consciously tried to escape the literary, to move past history into the local, into the mysteries of place, where he would ultimately assert that there were "no ideas but in things." What they shared was a certain belief in the redemption of American civilization in and through poetry.

Neither poet made any money. They found little that was progressive about progress except in the arts: technological innovation was not erasing poverty but exacerbating it. Western civilization seemed bent on perfecting the art of war while warring against art. Williams and Pound were poets, not social reformers, but their vision of social justice, which is not significantly different from a sense of reality, necessarily informed their sense of poetry. Both men were convinced that the financial system caused wars and poverty, that it was a destructive power that systematically warred on life by promoting false values. The antibank polemic that marks their work is rooted in the Populist reaction[6] to what we might call the second financial revolution of the final decade of the nineteenth century,[7] when many citizens of all political stripes became deeply concerned about the role played by the "monied interests" and "the trusts" in financial crises and the corruption of American political life.

In the 1890s, as the two poets were growing up, not only the radicalized farmers of the People's Party but figures as diverse as the patrician historian Brooks Adams, the money agitator William "Coin" Harvey, and the Christian Democrat William Jennings Bryan believed that the country was in the grip of an international financial conspiracy. They agreed that a clique of financiers and usurers was attempting to corner all the gold in existence for the purpose of enslaving the world through perpetual indebtedness. Such is the thesis of Harvey's influential bimetallist tract *Coin's Financial School* (1894), and his sensationalistic conspiracy novel of that year, *A Tale of Two Nations* (1894), as well as of Adams's *Law of Civilization and Decay* (1898) and Bryan's great "Cross of Gold" speech at the Democratic Convention in Chicago in 1896. A sense of conspiracy is a commonplace in labor tracts of the period, like the Knights of Labor publication *The Voice of Labor* (1888), in which a series of Labor Knights inveigh against the "money users" and the policy of bankers to keep money scarce, debt perpetual, and labor in conditions near slavery. Conspiracy theory reached an apocalyptic crescendo in the "Omaha Platform" of the People's Party in 1892.

> The national power to create money is appropriated to enrich bondholders; a vast public debt, payable in legal tender currency, has been funded into gold bearing bonds, thereby adding millions to the burdens of the people. Silver, which has been accepted as coin since the dawn of history, has been demonetized to add to the purchasing power of gold by decreasing the value of all forms of property as well as human labor; and the supply of currency is purposely abridged to fatten usurers, bankrupt enterprise, and enslave industry. A vast conspiracy against mankind has been organized on two continents, and it is rapidly taking possession of the world. If not met and overthrown at once, it forebodes terrible convulsions, the destruction of civilization, or the establishment of an absolute despotism. [Quoted in Unger, 38]

The struggle between the politics of the debtor classes and the creditors came to a head in the presidential election campaign of 1896. Bryan's candidacy absorbed the political "insurgency"[8] of the People's Party (the Populists), the Greenback Party, the Free-Silverites, Knights of Labor, Henry George's Single-Taxers, and other dissident groups, all of whom considered themselves Jeffersonians, into the political mainstream represented by the Democratic Party. United on the "money question" and determined to bring money back to the people somehow, the Democrats with their 1896 campaign smashed against the rock of the financial establishment and nearly overwhelmed it. As the Bryan candidacy has been considered the high-water mark of insurgent Jeffersonianism,[9] so Bryan's defeat has been seen as a crushing blow to the more radical elements of the Jeffersonian critique of modern American culture and political life. A fragile coalition at best, the Democrats could not sustain the struggle.

"The new American," Henry Adams mused as he looked back on that troubled time, "whether consciously or not, had turned his back on the nineteenth century before he was done with it; the gold standard, the protective [tariff] system, and the laws of mass could have no other outcome, and, as so often before, the movement, once accelerated by attempting to impede it, had the additional, brutal consequence of crushing equally the good and the bad in its way" (*Education* 349). Events overtook the "money question": "the needs of business had outgrown the bullion theory of money and credit was taking the place of a metallic currency," Vernon Parrington decided (*Main Currents* 3:270–71). The Jeffersonian version of the next phase of capitalism suggests that by the turn of the twentieth century, the financiers had accepted the notion that a monopoly of credit was more profitable than a monopoly of gold.

The Populist rendition of Jeffersonian ideology that had organized itself around the issue of "the money question" shared common features with an agrarian mythic tradition that went back through the period of antibank agitation in the Jacksonian period to Jefferson. Jeffersonians had a horror of debt, which Jefferson associated with death.[10] Since Jeffersonianism is an ideology of the debtor classes more than anything else, the Populists, like earlier Jeffersonians, stood for cheap money and opposed usury, banks, Wall Street, and the institutions of the creditor class. Debtors, they argued, were almost universally members of the "producing classes," including farmers, small capitalists, and, implicitly, artists. Finance capitalism, with its "trusts," corporations, stock market, and banks, was in Populist terms no more than the ideology of the money-using class and its predatory super-structure, associated for obvious reasons with Alexander Hamilton, Jefferson's historic adversary and the founder of the American financial system.

Pound's and Williams's interest in the "money question" has a special relevance for the "modernist" style of their poetry because it involved them in similar (though not identical) theoretical efforts to reconcile poetic and economic theory at the linguistic level and not just through criticism of capitalism or society. The money question prepared them to see money as another form of representation much like a limited form of language. If the solution to the economic crisis lay in the conundrum of money, it was therefore wrapped up with the problem of speech. The power of money was, in fact, money's power to utter the otherwise inchoate wishes of social, political, and economic power that far exceeded the traditional poet's linguistic and literary resources.

Those resources were, according to Pound and Williams, anchored in the continuities of cultural traditions that capitalism works unceasingly to alter for monetary profit. Both men believed that a financial elite dazzled by the exaggerated values imputed to money was blindly and destructively wielding power. As they saw it, the role of the modern poet was to restore true aesthetic, ethical, and moral values, an undertaking that entailed agitation in verse for a practical political program bent on defining exactly what money was and what it was not. The Social Credit movement offered a comprehensive program for achieving this goal, and through the 1930s both Pound and Williams were active Social Creditors.

Social Credit has, of course, been badly maligned as a crackpot, reactionary, anti-Semitic, and even proto-Fascist movement. But Social Credit's critique of industrial capitalism is sound as far as it goes; it is no more proto-Fascist in and of itself than Marxism is proto-Stalinist. Like Marxism, like Guild Socialism, Social Credit can be turned to authoritarian ends. Authoritarianism is a temptation within political movements of all kinds, and so it is not especially revealing to analyze Social Credit in such terms.

Part of my purpose is to show how Pound's denunciations could become authoritarian dicta that were consistent with both Communism and Fascism. His *Cantos,* which seem at times to announce allegiance to fascistic authority, give it in such idiosyncratic fashion as to confound the authoritarian fantasy of social control. In fact, I will insist that Pound's services to Fascism are incoherent in any but an American context. Pound knew as much and attempted to contextualize his politics in his quirky *Jefferson and/or Mussolini* (1935), a book not nearly as odd or "un-American" as its title suggests. The ideological animus that resulted in Pound's faith in Mussolini taps a rich cultural tradition, and an unlikely one, in Jeffersonianism. In short, Pound's "fascism" can be better understood as a belated case of American Populism.

For readers of Pound, this study will be one of several recent attempts to provide a context and a genealogy of the poet's political and economic ideas. Robert Casillo's exhaustive study of Pound's anti-Semitism, *The Genealogy of Demons* (1988), Wendy Stallard Flory's *The American Ezra Pound* (1986), Peter Nicholls's *Ezra Pound: Politics, Economics, and Writing* (1984), and Tim Redman's *Ezra Pound and Italian Fascism* (1991) are four such works. While I often find myself agreeing with these scholars, I differ from them in stressing the roots of Pound's thinking in American Populism and the Jeffersonian ideology that informs it. Pound's anti-Semitism and unorthodox "left Fascism" derive from and are, in fact, a temptation within this quintessentially American worldview. One can find parallels for Pound's descent into hatred and racism in the careers of the Georgia Populist Tom Watson and the poet Edgar Lee Masters. The myth of the American farmer freeholder that is the legacy of Jefferson can descend very easily into a shrill nativism, because a "Jeffersonian" distrust of finance capitalism can readily become a septic anti-Semitism. Nor must we look for foreign sources for Pound's interest in fertility cults on the one hand and hatred of financial manipulation on the other. Unlike Casillo, who has constructed an intricate "genealogy of demons" for Pound's hatreds from Continental anti-Semitism and Nazi mysticism and who wants to show "that Pound attacks the Jews for mainly non-economic reasons" (Casillo 36), I want to argue that Pound's anti-Semitism is largely consistent with American Populist prejudices—prejudices that defined the land itself as the source of cultural value and the source of identity for the male freeholder. In this sense, if Pound's anti-Semitism must be linked to Continental thought, it resembles Heidegger's bigotry much more than it does Alfred Rosenberg's.

For Pound, the anti-Semitism that eventually linked Jews to financial manipulation was not originally race hatred. Rather, like Edgar Lee Masters, Pound linked the Jews to puritanical Hebraism, to sexual repression and other forms of social hypocrisy in opposition to the "healthy" example of Greece. "Protestantism as factive and organized," Pound noted in an article in Eliot's *Criterion*, "may have sprung from nothing but pro-usury politics" (*SP* 243). This Hebraism/Hellenism dichotomy, familiar in Anglo-American literary discourse since Matthew Arnold, became connected with the nebulous (but nevertheless dangerous) Populist hatred of "eastern Jews," "operators," and "Wall St. swindlers." It is the same unreasonable hatred that could lead Henry Adams, an otherwise sensitive observer, to assume that his fellow Yankee, the financial manipulator and railroad magnate Jay Gould, was Jewish, as he did in *Chapters from Erie*.[11]

In my narrative, William Carlos Williams remains the counterforce to anxieties about the status of the individual in a corporate age that are revealed in the populistic anti-Semitism that infected his friend. Because he remained in the United States, Williams benefited from American pragmatism—especially the work of John Dewey. Like Williams, Dewey was also a latter-day Jeffersonian who "sought to adapt Jeffersonian idealism to the corporate-industrial age" (Bullert 11). An open-minded Deweyan pragmatism is especially evident in Williams's epic poem *Paterson*, and it rescues the poet's critique of capitalism from the often cryptic, sometimes evil chatter that badly damages the latter half of Pound's *Cantos*.

Taking his cue from Dewey's short essay in the *Dial* called "Americanism and Localism" (1920), Williams pursued the economic ramifications of corporate capitalism in a local setting, which was epitomized for him by the decrepit industrial city of Paterson, New Jersey. In Paterson, Williams saw the compressed struggle between industrialization and democracy. This moral, political, and economic struggle is reflected in *Paterson*, a poem profoundly informed by the Populist's moral critique of financial, corporate capitalism. Through the pragmatism of Dewey, Williams was able to see a way out of the otherwise unavoidably reactionary antiindustrialism that eventually crippled Pound's critique.

Pragmatism taught Williams that we cannot go back to the past. We cannot deny history. Pragmatism allowed Williams to maintain a constructive position as a poet and a social critic. The struggle of poet against capital, the struggle I like to imagine as the struggle of *poesis* against production, was not a fight to the death but a battle for definition. In affirming the wreck of Paterson, in picking its bones to make an epic, Williams celebrates the staying power of what must be called "indigenous," local, or even ahistorical values, which form a kind of human landscape persisting in the wreck of the corporate vision. These values, sustained by "invention," a favorite Deweyan term, offered Williams a vantage that could contain the mess of Paterson in history rather than cast it out. To put the matter another way, where Pound found it necessary to reject much of modernity in the name of social justice, Williams declared that we must embrace it, in all its filthiness, if we are to control it.

Williams's pragmatism and his attempt to comprehend the modern corporation and its social relations—that is, modernity itself—in a poem, is, I think, a point of importance for any student of American history. Going beyond Pound's own pathbreaking poetic exposé of the military-industrial complex in his Cantos of the 1930s (see especially Canto 38), Williams uses Dewey's pragmatic method to invent a "corporate" poem. *Paterson* reflects, critiques, and mirrors but never endorses the corporation. Williams is able to understand how a corporate aesthetics—especially visible in newspapers—offered a poetic way to understand the new ascendancy of corporate capitalism in the early decades of the twentieth century. The "reconstruction of corporate capitalism"[12] made use of pragmatic possibilities glimpsed by Williams very early—they are implicit in "The Wanderer" of 1914—which came to him via Whitman, himself a Jeffersonian protopopulist.[13] Like Pound, Williams made a critique of corporate capitalism that was initially informed by the tradition of American Populism—the historical political manifestation of the collision of Jeffersonian ideology and corporate capitalism.[14] Like Pound, Williams was attracted to the Social Credit movement. Following in the Populist tradition, Williams believed that reform of the monetary system, not social revolution, was the answer to the prolonged dreary crisis in capitalism that underlay the Great Depression and the wars of the twentieth century.

This book discusses the ways in which two poets used Jeffersonianism to interpret modernity—which is to say modern capitalism—and the ways in which their corresponding sense of social justice brought them together, and then drove them apart, under the postrepublican signs of Pragmatism and Fascism. I do not mean to suggest that we must choose between Williams and Pound or between Fascism and Pragmatism. Instead I mean to explain how the terms of the two writers' choices were established and the aesthetic implications of those choices.

I have not attempted to make systematic book-by-book readings of the two epic poems *The Cantos* and *Paterson,* nor do I narrowly focus on the writers' treatment of Jefferson or Hamilton as characters in these poems. Rather, I have tried to give representative readings from moments in these works and other poems that show Jeffersonianism informing the writing and the poetical stance of the two poets.

In order to make sense of the economic issues that "the money question" addresses, the first half of this study is mostly historical, devoted to defining and tracing Jeffersonian economic ideas and their aesthetic implications from the early United States to the "corporate age" of the twentieth century. This procedure seemed advisable because both Williams and Pound were engaged in an effort to rewrite American history from a Jeffersonian perspective—as were the principal historians of their day.

The latter half of this work concerns itself with some of the many implications of a Jeffersonian stance in Pound's and Williams's poetry. On the whole, these poems are radical—even revolutionary—in their politics, their economics, and their sharp critique of American finance capitalism and the hollow "culture of effigy" it has produced. By clarifying Williams's relationship to Dewey and thus to pragmatism in the final chapters, I hope I have suggested how Williams was able to find something to affirm in the mostly bleak picture of America presented by the city of Paterson. Pound, starting with Jeffersonian premises nearly identical to those of his college friend, found himself driven beyond Western civilization altogether, especially after the defeat of Italian Fascism. Lacking knowledge of pragmatism, Pound looked east and ingeniously tried to reestablish Confucian economic morality and social order in a world that seemed more than ever defined by its ad hoc, flexible, "pluralistic" arrangements—arrangements that Pragmatism, virtually alone among philosophical approaches, was prepared to accept and put to use.

1

JEFFERSONIAN ECONOMICS
Debt and the Production of Value

THE DISCOURSES OF political economy and aesthetics are inextricable. As John Guillory has recently shown,[1] "the problem of aesthetic judgement was as essential to the formation of political economy as the problem of political economy was to the formation of aesthetics" (Guillory 303). Thus, for the same reason that there can be no meaningful politics divorced from economics, politics cannot be divorced from aesthetics.

Just as any economic philosophy needs to decide what is valuable and what is not, so every aesthetic must discriminate between that which is beautiful, or at least meaningful, and that which is not; Jeffersonianism is no exception. To determine how this aesthetic is organized, I must explore the ideological implications of Jeffersonian economics, which have always been mythologized in American history as a symbolic struggle between Jefferson and Hamilton. The struggle between the differing political, economic, and aesthetic legacies of these two men provides a framework for understanding much of Pound's and Williams's writing. Their work is energized and made more meaningful by the poets' obvious strain in their confrontations with this uniquely American ideological antagonism.

Briefly, what is the struggle about? First, both positions are clearly fraught with what we now call postcolonial anxieties about cultural as well as political independence. These anxieties cluster around the theme of debt, both monetary and cultural. Jeffersonianism creates a positive program for debtors, regardless of whether they are rich or poor in real property—or in cultural capital.[2] By contrast, Hamiltonianism is a creditor's philosophy. As it happens, the financiers associated with the Hamiltonian view have also been instrumental in the importation of cultural capital from abroad to the United States. Yet

11

many American artists and writers have been embarrassed into silence by the social prestige of the best European masterwork that money can buy. "Morgan bought freely out of a conservative if rich imagination," Williams wrote. "But if he could have seen the field of art with the radical eye with which, perhaps, he saw the field of finance the result would have been to place America in an advanced position in the start superior to any" (*EK* 120). Williams means an advanced *cultural* position, but the tycoons, no matter how well intentioned, have tended to treat art like capital, which means that they have their eye on sound, and therefore "conservative," artistic investments. While financiers like Ford Frick or J. P. Morgan paid fortunes for European art, American artists, "doing modern work" (120), were struggling for recognition literally around the corner. And the same was true for American writers, who, to invoke Emerson, longed to discover their "original relation to the universe," to American particulars and Americanness.

This chapter deals with debt and value. It is about the Jeffersonian attempt to capture and redefine the meaning of debt and its moral consequences for the citizen and the artist. First I explore the relationship between Jefferson and Hamilton's understanding of debt and its political, aesthetic, and moral implications for the American experiment. The second part of the chapter deals with the site of value. In it I show how the Jeffersonian version of capitalism reflects a belief in use values rather than exchange values, "worth" as opposed to "value." Following the beliefs of the French Physiocrats, Jeffersonians see land and man as working in partnership, not in some subject/object relation. That is, Jeffersonians believe that wealth is partly "natural," an expression of the natural fertility of the soil on real property cultivated by an independent freeholder.

Hamiltonians—in this matter simply modern capitalists—believe that money (or credit) is, for all practical purposes, the same as wealth; they believe in value in exchange.[3] Jeffersonians can never fully accept this proposition. They argue that money merely represents prices, and prices, which are determined by markets and the cost of money, can never accurately reflect true or natural value. For the Jeffersonians, the unreliability of markets and prices indicates structural problems that lie at the heart of Hamilton's financial system. Specifically, Jeffersonians believe that a clique of bankers fixes prices, manipulating the value of money by controlling the amount of money in circulation. For this reason the early Jeffersonians felt that inflationary paper money (they were particularly wary of banknotes) was merely the "sign" of value. Following some dubious logic, they assumed that metal coin was the adequate "symbol" of value—that it naturally embodied labor—although they constantly searched for ways to make paper signs cognate with the value of the things they stood for. Later, during the period of Populist money agitation, in an attempt to increase the media of exchange, the Jeffersonians championed silver and paper money as against the "god of gold." In all cases, as the ideology of the debtor classes, Jeffersonianism is "distributionist," that is, it wants to broaden access to money, either by increasing its quantity or by increasing its velocity of circulation. As Hamiltonian thinking is the justification of creditors, Hamiltonians are always interested in controlling and limiting access to the media of exchange; Hamiltonians want to keep money relatively scarce so as to increase its value, or its buying power.

Equally important for our purposes, the Jeffersonian emphasis on natural value, labor, and use values is obviously relevant for poets, who have little interest in resisting an atavistic belief in the worth of "natural" word magic and who often have trouble finding a market for their work. Is poetry valueless because it often cannot find buyers? No poet could sustain himself if he or she believed that the value of one's work is determined by the market. These are good reasons why Pound and Williams were attracted by the Jeffersonian critique of capital, and especially the objection to money as the arbitrary measure of value.

This line of thinking brings us to the Physiocratic roots of Jeffersonian thinking about value. Jefferson, Hector St. John (Michel-Guillaume-Jean de Crèvecoeur), and the "Jeffersonian" French political economist and moral philosopher Destutt de Tracy were all familiar with Quesnay's Physiocracy. The "natural" relationship between man and nature implied by the Physiocratic approach results proposes the man/nature relationship as a marriage, often imagined as the male freeholder's monogamous relationship to his female property, which responds to his virtuous "husbandry" as a giving wife. Significantly, we can find such Physiocratic imagery in famous poems by Pound and Williams, for example in Pound's Canto 45 and at the climax of Pisan sequence in Canto 82 and at moments in *Spring and All* (1923) and "To a Poor Old Woman."

This seemingly abstruse economic argument has implications for human freedom, because the freedom to stay out of debt is crucial for independent selfhood. Debt, in fact, is treated as a life-and-death matter by Jefferson; at bottom, Jeffersonianism is war on debt. Using the writing of Crèvecoeur, we can see how the American experience of "beginning the world" via homesteading echoes the revolutionary struggle to get out of debt and how the westward expansion of the country tended to recreate the same dependent debtor/creditor relationships that in part structured the American War of Independence. The relationship of the colonies to London was reproduced in the relationship of midwestern farmers to eastern banks in New York, Boston, and Philadelphia. The writings of Pound and Williams can be read as the continuation of the American War of Independence at the cultural level.

If, to the despair of many readers, Pound's *Cantos* and Williams's *Paterson* lack any clear narrative, they do have a clear agenda. They are partly Jeffersonian jeremiads and partly experimental structures through which Jeffersonianism can be renovated and modernity reshaped in such a way as to allow for a truly American independence.

Jefferson, Hamilton, and the Bounds of Virtue

Jeffersonianism is a dissenting ideology; idealistic and easily scandalized, in American life it has preferred to take the role of prophet in the wilderness. Its heroes, Jefferson, John Taylor, and Andrew Jackson (and retrospectively, a revised Lincoln), have all been mythologized as pure men of the West come to Washington to "chase the money-changers from the temple" and restore government and moral purity to the people.[4] The contributions of other great Jeffersonians, especially James Madison but also Martin Van Buren, who do not conform to this mythic paradigm (despite Pound's best efforts on behalf of Van Buren), have therefore remained relatively obscure. In American poetry, both Walt Whitman and Pound (notably in his letters) self-consciously cultivated western personae as poetic "roughs" in order to tap this strain of republican virtue. So did Williams, who late in life delighted to think that he'd scandalized a Harvard Phi Beta Kappa assembly with a poem called "The Desert Music" about the seamy delights of Juarez.[5]

Republican virtue is associated with the American farmer because he is imagined to be largely free of toxic social and commercial relations. "The substantial and genuine virtue" of "those who labor in the earth" that Jefferson praised is "suffocated" by the oddly unnatural temptations of human contact, of commerce with the world. For this reason John Taylor, who worked in his fields at the head of his slaves, can embody republican virtue, while certain doctrinaire types, like Pound, can regard Benjamin Franklin, a self-made but entirely urban figure, as "slithery" (*SP* 118).

As Jefferson wrote, the incorruptibility of the cultivators and husbandmen who till the earth

> is a precarious affair, for others haven't their virtues. It is the mark set on those, who not looking up to heaven, to their own soil and industry, as does the husbandman, for their own subsistance, depend for it on the casualties and caprice of customers. Dependance begets subservience and venality, suffocates the germ of virtue, and prepares fit tools for the designs of ambition. This, the natural progress and consequence of the arts, has sometimes been retarded by accidental circumstances: but generally speaking, the proportion which the aggregation of the other classes of citizens bears in any state to that of its husbandmen, is the proportion of its unsound to its healthy parts, and is a good-enough barometer whereby to measure its degree of corruption (Jefferson 290–91).[6]

The ideological density of this much quoted passage makes it clear why it has become the locus classicus for generations of Jeffersonians. "Virtue" is natural, a seed to be nurtured, "husbanded," conserved, and protected from the "suffocating" weight of "dependance, subservience and venality"—all terms describing the corruptions of a mercantile economy replete with markets and manufacturing concerns. "The natural progress of the arts," which means the fatal progress of manufacture, moves like the advance of age towards the gradual and inexorable corruption of the mass of mankind, who more and more bear the "mark" of Cain. Already in the 1780s Jefferson sees the intrusion of manufacture and commerce as inevitable. As Drew McCoy has pointed out, "The Jeffersonian vision grew out of an attempt to reconcile classical republicanism with more modern social realities and American conditions" (McCoy 10). Fully aware of these conditions, Jefferson understands that any attempt to "retard" the "natural" progress of what amounts to history itself cannot succeed.

As we shall see, Jefferson's idealism is colored by a classical pessimism absorbed from the Roman poets and their Whig popularizers. The decline and fall of Rome laid out the path of republican virtue to decadent venality. Thus the "natural" decline and fall of the Roman Republic, first into Caesarism and then into an increasingly rotten Empire that deserved its destruction, underlies the parlous state of the "virtuous husbandman," who, like pastoral Abel, is always threatened by the Cain-like, artificial, predatory, and therefore modern, ephemeral, and fictional "progress of the arts."

These are arts in the worst sense; they verge on the diabolical. These have nothing to do with the fine arts, or even with artifice; they are the arts of "ambition" and specifically of buying and selling, of trade and finance, which prey on the independence of the husbandman and incorporate him into a web of obligations that will destroy his "virtue," his independent selfhood and manhood, and make him dependent, a child or a slave.

To the Jeffersonian, all obligations threaten to become debts and all economic activity that involves the transfer of money becomes "venal." Jefferson's use of the word "venality," a word with the same roots as "vend," implies that to sell is to be for sale. Through a false etymology linking venal to "venereal," there is also a sexual implication, a link to prostitution, which Jeffersonian writers like to evoke by alluding to the physical ravages of syphilis. Jefferson himself says that the proletariat ("the mobs of the cities") who have sold themselves for wages add "just so much to the support of pure government as sores do to the strength of the human body" (Jefferson 291).[7] The problem of sale was always, from the Jeffersonian point of view, intractable.

If selling amounts to selling oneself, then commerce is indeed a disease, but a disease, like aging, that is a fact of even the most stringent republican existence. The Jeffersonians accept this fact but remain "acutely aware of the moral dimension of economic life" (McCoy 7). They don't want to abolish what Thoreau called "the curse of trade" (Thoreau 378) but to ameliorate its unavoidable evils. Trapped in an increasingly commercial world, the Jeffersonians see themselves as fighting a holding action, resisting the intrusion of the market into the relationship between man and nature and also between man and his human nature, his sanity or cleanness-of-mind.

This sanity, as Pound points out, is, to a large degree, mental clarity. Mental clarity might be defined as the ability to distinguish what is meaningful from what is not, "to see clearly" and to read and write accurately. It is also the ability to make moral choices. The relations of commerce and of finance obscure the moral view by inserting fictions into transactions between people. Hence Jeffersonians have frequently found it rhetorically necessary to reconstruct Jefferson's corruption barometer to probe the body politic for signs of moral collapse.

In *Walden*, for example, Thoreau[8] speaks of a "Realometer, that future ages might know how deep the freshet of shams and appearances had gathered from time to time." This gauge would be set on some "hard bottom" we could call "reality," underlying church, state, poetry, philosophy and religion (Thoreau 400). Economy doesn't appear on Thoreau's list, but he clearly means everything we can conceive as political economy and aesthetics.

Pound took "usury" as his unit of measure and pegged his "realometer" to the rate of allowable interest on loans. A typical statement reveals a rhetorical stance and social anxiety indistinguishable from Jefferson's.

> You can probably date any Western work of art by reference to the ethical estimate of usury prevalent at the time of that work's composition; the greater the component of tolerance for usury the more blobby and messy the work of art. The kind of thought which distinguishes good from evil, down to the details of commerce, rises into the quality of line in paintings and into the clear definition of the word written. [*SP* 90][9]

The "quality of the line" is something an artist of the Italian Renaissance might have termed its *virtú*, just as the ability and courage to say exactly what one means is the sign of virtue in a person.[10] In either case, Pound's diagnosis is the same as Jefferson's: "commerce," the art without virtue, corrupts.

These very similar quotations have an explicit aesthetic agenda that is closely related to the preoccupation of American artists with originality or, looked at another way, to the burdens of cultural debt to England and Europe. "Original" is another way of saying "pure," which, in its moral form, is "virtue." Virtue carries with it echoes of *vir* as in "virile," or manly. Likewise, "the original relation to the universe," for which Emerson longs in *Nature*, is the wish to be free of cultural debt, to free himself from the "filial system of property" (Emerson 26). It is the same as Williams's wish to "enter the new world naked" (*CP1*

183), declared in *Spring and All* (1923), and reflects the same postcolonial anxieties. This wish inevitably embroils American poets in issues of political economy and aesthetics, especially "the money question," because money is to the economy as words are to language: money is the signifier of value and the bearer of desire. Money, in short, is like a language: it is the script we use to spell out our American identities. What is wanted, then, is a language free of history and a currency free of debt. Americans want to start over.

The problem of modernity is a problem of history as well. That is to say, the threat that complex social and commercial relations present to a philosophy of radical individualism, implicit in an industrial society, accounts for the characteristic defensive stance of Jeffersonianism and for much of its potentially reactionary and heavily mythologized aesthetic. Not for nothing was Jefferson's party first simply known as the "antis." The Jeffersonians were not only "anti-Federalist"; from the beginning, they were defensive about their republican virtue and the purity of their political vision. The Jeffersonian version of the United States sought to limit the powers of finance because to its proponents finance capital represented British imperialism.[11] At the same time, however, Jeffersonians recognized the need for the potential liberating power of a national, self-sufficient sort of capitalism, which they addressed in much the same ambivalent fashion as they did the federal government. The Jeffersonian slogan that the best government is that which governs least applies in effect to the financial side of capitalism—it is a necessary evil. In both cases the Jeffersonians hoped to conserve a minimally capitalistic, agrarian polity based on personal relationships.

The Federalist party of Hamilton, by contrast, sought the free play of capital and financial power in a "pragmatic" mercantile society that frankly reproduced the principal features of English finance in the United States (Elkins and McKitrick 103). Above all, Hamilton sought to empower the creditor class. The central figure in his economic universe is not the freeholder but the merchant, the archetypal figure in the "financial revolution" (Elkins and McKitrick 111).

The Financial Revolution, manifest by the latter half of the seventeenth century, encompasses the transition from a precapitalist economy to a capitalist one, the end of spiritual authority over economic life, and the transfer of power from the landowning aristocracy to the middle classes. It is a vital part, perhaps even the determining component, of what Karl Polanyi called "the great transformation," which inserted the market into all areas of human society, altering social relations from personal to economic ones by creating markets for both land and labor and destroying the more stable, village society of fixed social relations and obligations (Polanyi 163, 178). Clearly, this transformation threatened and altered the moral foundations of the self, substituting, among other things, the rule of law for the rule of God. The Financial Revolution promoted the importance of contract and law over tradition, religion, kinship, privilege, and honor. Eventually, it created new forms of paper property: bonds, stocks, futures contracts, and insurance as well as new institutions to produce and exchange such property: banks, joint-stock companies, trusts, corporations, and funds. In important ways, the Financial Revolution was the triumph of a written economy over an economy of the spoken word: the contract succeeded prayer and the pledge, laws succeeded royal prerogative, and paper money succeeded specie. All of these new formations resulted in a palpable extension of governmental and social power over the actions of individuals. If the invention of the modern state limited the individual caprice of the monarch, it also asserted itself over the hitherto unwritten responsibilites, duties, and pleasures of citizens.

From its intellectual antecedents in French Physiocracy to the endemic "money radicalism" that was a persistent issue in American political discourse until it was driven below the surface by the founding of the Federal Reserve Bank in 1913, Jeffersonianism has worked to undo this Financial Revolution (McDonald 1976 161). The peculiar radical conservatism of Jeffersonianism lies in its reaction to the corrosive effects of these depersonalizing developments on both man and the state. In Forrest McDonald's jaundiced view, the Jeffersonians

> proposed to restore a pristine and largely imaginary past in which life was rural, relationships were personal, the gentry ruled as a natural aristocracy, the main corpus of the citizenry was an honest yeomanry, commerce and craft-manufacturing existed only as handmaidens to agriculture, standing armies and privileged monopolies and fictitious paper wealth were all unknown, and government was limited—limited to an essentially passive function as impartial arbiter and defender of the existing social order, and limited by the unwritten but inviolable Constitution, dividing power among three separate, distinct, and coequal branches. In other words, the Jeffersonians' ideo-

logical forebears were reactionaries, swimming against the tide of history, for the world aborning was the depersonalized world of money, machines, cities, and big government. [McDonald, 1976 161–62]

McDonald's observation about an "unwritten" Constitution is shrewd, for Jeffersonians are suspicious of texts. "Where is our constitution to be found?" Jefferson asked rhetorically of a correspondent in 1816. "Not in our constitution certainly, but in the spirit of our people" (Jefferson 1397). Indeed, Jefferson's relative separation from the Constitution gives Jeffersonianism much of its ideological appeal and justifies its reflexive demonization of Hamilton: "the Prime snot in ALL American history" as Pound rudely remarks in Canto 62 (62:350). Because he was on diplomatic service in France, Jefferson could not take any direct part in the creation of the Constitution of the United States, neither through direct contributions to the *Federalist* nor as a participant in the constitutional debates. Though he warmly approved of the *Federalist,* his initial reaction to the Constitution itself was ambivalent; he objected strongly to the lack of a Bill of Rights and wrote Madison that the advantages of incumbency were such that the routine reelection of presidents would lead to a virtual monarchy (Jefferson 914f.).

In Jeffersonian circles, the Constitution has been considered fatally compromised by Jefferson's absence, while the Declaration of Independence is touted as his alone and he gets full credit for insisting on the Bill of Rights. Hamilton, on the other hand, actively engaged himself in the constitutional debate and is the principal author of the *Federalist.* While experience later taught Hamilton to believe that constitutions were "frail and worthless fabrics" (quoted in McDonald 1979 96), he understood the usefulness of constitutional practice—the rule of law—as providing that *"equality* of political rights exclusive of all *hereditary* distinction"* (quoted on 109) necessary to modern political economy. This for Hamilton was the "essence of republicanism" (109) because it meant that property could be founded in written laws, not the incestuous tangle of blood relations. "The rock on which Alexander Hamilton built his church," writes Arthur Schlesinger, Jr., "was the deep-seated conviction that society would be governed best by an aristocracy, and that an aristocracy was based most properly and enduringly on property" (Schlesinger 12). Hamilton believed in a paradoxical capitalist aristocracy, supreme in property but uncomplicated by heredity, a system where the ties of blood became the ties of gold.

For Hamilton, money answers all of the questions aristocracy as an institution never needed to answer. In his career, Hamilton displayed the same pragmatic attitude toward the convenient power of monetary and social fictions that he revealed in the process of creating the Constitution. I use the term "pragmatic" deliberately here, for Hamilton's position is ancestral to one strand of American Pragmatism. Hamilton appears to have simply been unmoved by political ideals and the idealism necessary for the visionary democracy that would increasingly animate Jefferson and the Republican opposition. Hamilton wanted to get things done, and he saw very clearly that his objects were facilitated by the magical properties of paper. This statement does not mean that Hamilton saw himself as simply creating conditions that would allow him to buy into the aristocracy; rather, in Napoleonic fashion, he regarded himself as paving the way for the ascendancy of a new aristocracy of talent—in this case a financial aristocracy based not on heredity but on financial and legal skill.[12]

Hamilton's sense of a Constitution was therefore importantly different from Jefferson's. What Jefferson hoped would be a legal foundation of the rights of the governed against the tyrannical powers of government Hamilton saw as the authorization of financial power against both the old prerevolutionary elite and the new threat of a democratic majority.

The U.S. Constitution was designed, the historians of "conflict" once argued, to protect existing property effectively from the perils of a democratic redistribution.[13] With the Federalist ascendancy in the young republic, Hamilton's kind of aristocracy—a "textual" aristocracy of financial power rather than blood and land—legitimated itself very quickly. This development was especially threatening to the entrenched planter society of the southern states, which produced the great theorists of American republicanism: Jefferson, James Madison, and John Taylor of Caroline. They feared the upstart Federalists and saw that the new financial

> aristocracy's greatest source of strength lay in its success in cloaking "fictitious" property—bank paper and stocks—with the prestige of honest private property. By pretending to protect land and labor from redistribution from below, the [financial] aristocracy was en-

abled to maintain its own institutions of redistribution from above. [John] Taylor desperately fought this unnatural alliance. "If the fruit of labour is private property, can stealing the fruit from labour, also make private property? By calling the artillery property, which is playing on property, the battery is masked. Tithes and stocks, invented to take away private property, are as correctly called private property as a guillotine could be called a head." [Schlesinger 24–25]

The new triumph of paper, of lawyers, merchants, and financiers of the big eastern cities, effectively forced the established planter aristocracy to side with those smaller landowners who are always oppressed by the moneyed classes. Their agrarian ideology, derived (the Jeffersonians argue) equally from French Physiocracy, Whiggish oppositionism, and American experience, stood for the sanctity of real property, the special virtues of tilling the soil, a definition of wealth as the "fruit of labor"—that is, as actual produce and real property rather than money—a corollary belief in "plain talk" (a guillotine is not a head) and "self-evident truths," a strong distrust of governments, a horror of debt, and thus a concern with distributive economics. Jeffersonianism evolved from these elements, creating a new and positive program for the debtor classes.

By contrast, the financial apparatus that Hamilton imported to the United States as secretary of the treasury was not new; it was the old English system. His was a threefold vision. First he needed to control the national debt, or rather, he needed to redefine it in the English mercantile sense as a potential asset, not as a destabilizing liability. Second, in place of the Bank of England, Hamilton proposed and created a Bank of the United States. Once established, the Bank made possible the third and final phase of Hamilton's plan, his visionary Society for Useful Manufactures, a giant industrial complex in Paterson, New Jersey, designed to reproduce the productive power of the Manchester mills. The financial purpose of the Society was to provide an investment opportunity for the very same people who had bought up the bonds that were to pay off the debt and who therefore had an interest in the Bank of the United States: the creditor class.

Hamilton's system was built perforce on the public debt. When he joined Washington's new government in 1789, the United States had no credit, no cash, and a debt of approximately $76 million (McDonald 1979 148). Hamilton's genius was his recognition that debt, properly conceived and handled, was wealth, because the basis of wealth was credit, not gold.

As secretary of the treasury, Hamilton capitalized the public debt by creating a sinking fund, which allowed him to sell the debt in the form of government bonds. In so doing he bonded the interests of the investors to the fortunes of the fledgling federal government. In a passage that Jeffersonians until the time of Ezra Pound would quote with scorn, Hamilton wrote: "A national debt, if it is not excessive, will be to us a national blessing" (quoted in Schlesinger 11). This "national blessing" would, by Jeffersonian lights, be a blessing to only a tiny creditor class, while the rest of the country indirectly paid interest on the national debt to this already wealthy group in the form of higher taxes.[14]

The details of Hamilton's achievement are of less interest here than its ideological implications, which strongly suggested (1) that an elite group of creditors was equivalent to the nation, (2) that an industrial economy and the class divisions it exacerbated was not only necessary but just, and (3) that appearances, obligations, desires, and symbols, in the form of credit, debt, and the salable paper instruments—texts—that represented them were the true basis of economic life. These implications were not to be confined to political economy but reverberated through the American sense of independence to find expression in our national literature.

Jeffersonian Economics: The Site of Value

Hamilton and Jefferson obviously had very different ideas about wealth. Wealth plainly means more than money, yet following Adam Smith, many would say that it is "purchasing power." Smith says that wealth is "the power of purchasing: a certain command over all the labor, or over all the produce of labor which is in the market" (A. Smith 134). This is the source of Marx's "labor theory of value." Smith approaches the problem—and it is nothing if not problematic—in two ways. He notes that there are two kinds of value: "value in use" and "value in exchange" (131).[15] He notes that "things which have the greatest value in use, have frequently little or no value in exchange; and, on the contrary, those which have the greatest value in exchange have frequently little or no value in use"; water and diamonds are cases in point (131–32). According to Smith, the only value that might encompass these two extremes of commodity is the value of labor. Ricardo accepts this hypothesis, and so does Marx.

The value of labor or its produce is determined on the market, Smith says, in exchange. Labor in the marketplace is thus transformed into a commodity and becomes indistinguishable, economically speaking, from what it produces. Labor, like other primary ingredients, is reckoned a "cost" of production. It follows, then, that labor taking place outside the marketplace cannot be valued. Following Lewis Hyde, we may say that such unpaid labor has "worth" but not "value." Thus the labor of the grandmother—cooking and cleaning, washing, and tending the grandchildren—has no economic "value" although (or even because) its social "worth" is beyond price (Lewis Hyde 60).

In distinguishing the Jeffersonian vision of capitalism from the Hamiltonian, we must recognize that the Jeffersonians are more concerned with "worth" than with "value." They want to rescue use values from exchange values, while the Hamiltonians want to mix them up, making all use values exchangeable. Jeffersonian economics tends toward ethical ideals that cannot be valued in money; Jeffersonians value things with "natural" worth that cannot be expressed in monetary terms. These are often "priceless" abstractions like "life, liberty and the pursuit of happiness" that lie beyond the boundaries of monetary relationships. The notion of "freehold" property, the Jeffersonians' ideal form of ownership, expresses a self-sufficiency and relation to nature whereby money plays a minimal role in facilitating exchanges without ever determining social relations.

Hamiltonianism, by contrast, prefers value to worth and when it can will try to transform worth into value in part because value can be measured and, once measured, can be exchanged. The possibility of accurate measurement is a crucial assumption of a Hamiltonian, or financial, view of capitalism. Money, numbers, statistics, and trends, all of the tools of modern economics and modern speculation, are based on the Hamiltonian assumption that the relationship between economics and society is "pragmatic"[16] rather than idealistic, rational rather than communal, exchangeable rather than customary, culturally constructed rather than natural.

At its most rational the Hamiltonian position can sound like cold Benthamite utilitarianism. Hamilton's "Report on Manufactures"

(December 5, 1791) argues that one of the advantages of a manufacturing system "is the employment of persons who would otherwise be idle," a provision that sounds excellent until we hear him note approvingly that "in general, women and children are rendered more useful, and the latter more early useful, by manufacturing establishments, than they would otherwise be. Of the number of persons employed in the cotton mills of Great Britain," Hamilton continues, "it is computed that four sevenths, nearly, are women and children, of whom the greatest proportion are children, and many of a tender age" (*Works* 4:91). It is striking that these facts are deployed *in favor* of manufacturing. From this icily rational, radically utilitarian perspective, money—commodified, anonymous, ubiquitous—is the only measure of the value of labor. Indeed, it is the only measure of all value. Usefulness can be expressed only in exchange, in the market, not in the precapitalized economy of hearth and home. Worth, in this view, is not the business of political economy.

The legacy of statements like Hamilton's is one reason why the United States is considered to be a capitalist country. The implication is that capitalism is a monolithic ideology. We may owe this oversimplification to the Marxist commonplace that capitalist development moves inevitably from early to late and from agricultural to industrial modes of production as productive forces create and empower first the bourgeoisie and later the proletariat. Marx's emphasis on production in the formation of class and capital, which became his followers' obsession, may have prevented him from sufficiently exploring capital's signification, namely the representation of capital and labor, wealth, and value through the elaborate social fiction of money.[17] I do not mean to imply that the man who called money "the God of commodities"[18] was unaware of the problematics of money (in fact he was acutely aware of its quasi-magical powers); I mean only that Marx's cure for the evils of capitalism does not involve the reform of money, because for him, labor, and not finance, is the key to the relations of production (that is, power relations and also value) under capitalism. For Marx, labor is the only term large enough to encompass the total relations between humankind and nature. "Capital is, among other things," he wrote, "also an instrument of production, also objectified, past labor. Therefore capital is a general, eternal relation of nature" (1975 27). Consequently money, which is the principal way in which past labor is objectified, becomes the measure of labor and labor as the measure of value. Here Marx follows the "classical" economists David Ricardo and Adam Smith. These thinkers underestimate the all but linguistic power of monetary signification and the powerful fictional propensities of finance capital.

The American money radicals would have only half agreed with Marx that money should be "the measure of value which is immanent in commodities, namely labour-time" (Marx 1977 188), as is required by the labor theory of value; they would have argued that commodities also have intrinsic values. The Jeffersonian critique of money reveals that, in practice, money did not really work in Marx's carefully considered way. Instead of standing for actual wealth and real things produced by real labor, money was simply being issued by banks as a way of controlling the real values produced by others. Pound, in what is a typically American money radical's statement of the case, insists that we focus on "the problem of issue." He notes that political solutions to monetary problems pay "attention to outlet, no attention to source"; we still don't understand where money comes from: "Who issues it? How? (87:583–84).[19] Like so many linguistic theorists, the Jeffersonians have been alternately troubled by the seeming arbitrariness of monetary value and their wish that money, like language, should somehow be "natural" or that money should correspond in some intimate, intrinsic way to real things in nature and the world (see Michaels 154–55).

A rich example of this kind of Jeffersonian thinking on political economy and money is Destutt de Tracy's *A Treatise on Political Economy* (1817). This book was first published in America at Jefferson's instigation; he commissioned an English translation that he himself corrected and revised for publication.[20] A letter from Jefferson that serves as a kind of foreword to the work places it firmly near the center of what would later be called Jeffersonianism. He writes, "The merit of this work, will, I hope, place it in the hands of every reader in our country. By diffusing sound principles of Political Economy, it will protect the public industry from the parasitic institutions now consuming it, and lead us to that just and regular distribution of the public burthens from which we have sometimes strayed" (no page number).[21] The "parasitic institutions" in question are clearly the Bank of the

United States and more generally the excessive costs of the federal government and its debts.

Chapter 6 of Destutt de Tracy's book is "On Money." He argues forcefully against paper money and for a silver currency because "gold is too rare, the other metals too common" (79). His argument for silver (the "people's money," as later Free-Silver agitators would have it) is balanced by an attack on paper money. Paper money leads inevitably, Destutt de Tracy argued, to inflation, anarchy, and tyranny. A witness to the French Revolution writing in 1810, he saw how Napoleon financed imperial wars by printing paper money. Destutt de Tracy quotes with gusto the phrase of the Physiocrat Mirabeau: "All paper money is a phrensy [sic] of despotism run mad" (94).

To Destutt de Tracy, paper money is nothing more than the perfect way to adulterate the currency.[22] Where kings and governments once alloyed their coinage to avoid paying their debts by putting less and less silver into each coin, paper money absolved them from using any metal at all (86–87). Destutt de Tracy claims that only metal (silver) has any real value; paper is just the valueless sign of it. Silver is value because it is "useful" and because it represents the labor value put into its extraction and distribution, for labor is "the first and only cause of all value" (86). In this sense, Destutt de Tracy is a thoroughly classical economist.

Paper money is invidious because "it is founded on the false idea that money is but a sign, while [money] is value and a true equivalent for which it is given" (xxi). By arguing that money is value, Destutt de Tracy means that it embodies values *already in existence*; for example, that silver embodies the cost of its own extraction. Insofar as a piece of paper may stand for a certain sum of money in the possession of a "solvent person," it is also *like,* or as good as, the actual silver: "we are as sure of having it when we wish, as with the money we are sure of having a dinner when we shall be hungry. It is this which induces us both to say, that this paper is the same thing as the silver—But this is not exact; for the paper only promises, and the silver alone is the value itself" (87).

Paper money becomes a political problem when governments (and also banks) start printing it as a way of meeting their obligations. In France, the government had at first issued money against expected revenues from its monopolies and its rents or "sometimes on a sinking fund, which cannot fail to produce marvelous effects" (88). (This statement must have struck Jefferson, who was highly dubious about Hamilton's marvelously effective sinking fund.) Such money is not "real money" but what would later be called "credit money." And since not everyone will take such money in lieu of silver, people must be forced to do so by law (89). Thus, in Destutt de Tracy's experience, paper money policies encourage tyranny and reckless "enterprizes, either of war, politics or administration" (89).

Destutt de Tracy's work sheds light on what at first seems inconsistent in Jeffersonian money radicalism. The early Jeffersonians were simultaneously for and against paper money just as they were later for "hard money" at the same time that they were dead set against a gold standard. The real issue was the control of credit. In the absence of any native gold or silver deposits, Jeffersonians wanted a paper currency without the threat of despotism from either the government or a clique of bankers. As an example both of Jefferson's interest in the matter of paper money and of its ongoing importance for latter-day Jeffersonians like Pound, who quoted it often and made it part of his "Introductory Text Book" (1938), note the following passage from a Jefferson letter of 1816: "and if the national bills issued be bottomed (as is indispensable) on pledges of specific taxes for their redemption within certain and moderate epochs, and be of *proper denominations* for *circulation*, no interest on them would be necessary or just, because they would answer to every one of the purposes of the metallic money withdrawn and replaced by them" (Pound's emphasis, *GK* 354). Because it is tied to taxation and borrowing, the administration of the national credit thus remains an immediate problem for liberty.

First, who decides how *much* money should be in circulation? If there is too little money, people cannot pay their debts; too much money, on the other hand, sucks out the value of things. Does money belong to the state? to the bankers? Or does it belong to all the people, including the laboring classes who actually produce the wealth that paper money signifies? These questions are apparent behind Jefferson's "Opinion on the Constitutionality of a National Bank" (1791, Jefferson 416–21), and despite the rejection of Jefferson's opinion, they have never been fully resolved.

Yet without their own precious metals, Americans at the turn of the nineteenth century faced a chronic shortage of money that could be made up only with paper. As the country expanded westward, the need for a circulating medium of some sort became one of the main impulses behind the phenomenal appeal of Andrew Jackson—he succeeded in the money-poor West because he promised to "put money in the pants of the people" (as Pound put it) and to democratize the central banking system, which had failed to distribute money into the new western regions of the country. One of the reasons Jackson was so feared by Easterners (whose monetary wants were relatively well supplied) is that he promised to increase the currrency, thereby threatening to devalue the money Easterners already had.

Destutt de Tracy's analysis also helps us understand an apparent contradiction in the turn within Jeffersonianism to the Populists' Free-Silver agitation in the latter half of the nineteenth century. The Populists were for Free Silver (quite in accordance with Destutt de Tracy) *and* paper money. Under the gold standard (imposed in 1873), gold was perceived as the whip that despotic bankers wielded over the producing classes, because debts could be stipulated for repayment in gold only. In response, the Populists argued for a paper currency that was legal tender for all debts, public and private. They wanted what they called "real money" based on the credit potential of an industrialized economy. They argued, in effect, that the fulfillment of an industrial economy and an increase in the power of the central government meant that it could print money against the gigantic new credit that these developments implied. The gold standard, by controlling the terms of debt, confined the currency to a radically narrow basis derived from mercantile analyses of labor power. This standard benefited the banking class but could not account for the radical transvaluation of all values achieved by steam, coal, and steel (Brooks Adams 342–51).

The problems with these simultaneously paranoid and utopian claims about money have everything to do with the importance for Jeffersonians of America as a frontier society, a place in which the paradigmatic social and economic act is "to begin the world" (Crèvecoeur 272)—indeed, to begin it again and again. The frontier makes for an economy that appears always to be enacting beginnings; first in the clearing of land for agriculture and next in the clearing of farms for industry. "The Occident is based on the homestead," Pound would later claim over Rome Radio, " . . . the civilization of the whole Western world comes up from the soil, and from the personal responsibility of the man who produces things from it" (*EPS* 176). Yet despite the actual experience of creating wealth from the ground up, these new operations generally find themselves in debt to the more established parts of the economy. Since they are capitalized by borrowing against the future success of homestead, farm, or factory, the world cannot be begun completely anew—one enters the new world not naked but encumbered by debts; the present is mortgaged to the past. Since debts can be paid only with money, money and access to it become all important, and those that control it can easily be regarded as tyrants.

Because throughout our history debt has been the fundamental economic reality for the mass of people, the significance of getting out of debt has taken on mythic proportions. It is hardly too much to say that the ongoing war of independence for most Americans, regardless of time or place, is the struggle to get out of debt. Moreover, in its social and geographical structure debt in American history has tended to reproduce our colonial experience. Just as the American colonies were indebted to England, so the southern and western sections of the United States have been indebted to the eastern financial establishment. The American money radicals, Jeffersonians all, consequently saw the value of money as being fixed by the banks, not by their own labor, and they experienced debt as oppressive colonialism.

"These Englishmen are strange people" Crèvecoeur wrote in *Letters from an American Farmer* (1783), "because they can live upon what they call bank notes, without working, they think that all the world can do the same. This goodly country would never have been tilled and cleared with these notes" (Crèvecoeur 48).[23] The midwestern farmer of the nineteenth century might have said exactly the same thing about his New York bankers. The labor of the American farmer creates leisure for the creditor class, which, while "wealthy" in the traditional sense, does not actually produce anything. The creditors' "strangeness" is their seemingly effortless ability to transform paper into goods—the food and necessaries that keep them alive without labor. Meanwhile, solely through his labor, almost in spite of the money system, the American farmer actually creates "a goodly country." Labor translates waste into worth (value in use), while the financiers operate in the "strange" and estranging world of value in exchange that is a market economy. This attitude toward finance and markets helps explain why Crèvecoeur, who was not sympathetic to the American Revolution, could remain a friend and correspondent of Thomas Jefferson.

Prices obviously express the value of things—and value is usually so expressed—but Jeffersonians found prices inadequate to their experience. Because of the difficulties of getting goods to market, prices did not always reflect the value of labor at a given time, as Marx would have it (1977, 188f.). Without markets, produce cannot be transformed into commodities and the prices that measure their exchange value. It is axiomatic that goods that cannot find a market have no value because they are not useful (the farmer has more than he needs for his own purposes) and they cannot be exchanged. Yet these goods remain a sign of labor—somebody sowed and reaped, threshed, and bagged the grain that cannot find a use or a buyer.

This problem has obvious relevance for poets, who for the most part have had great difficulty in selling the products of their imaginative labor.[24] Because there is a very small market for the poet's output, it is difficult for him to become a seller.[25] It is easy to see, then, why our unpopular modern poets should concern themselves with what otherwise seems like a fairly abstruse economic question, the labor theory of value and the problems it entails for commodities, their prices, and the much deeper question with which artists are always concerned: the question of their own value. That is, how can artistic labor be fairly assessed in terms of money?

Is this just a modern problem? Emerson opens his essay on Swedenborg by claiming for poets the key role of "producers," "who, from the intellectual kingdom, feed the thought and imagination with ideas and pictures which raise men out of the world of corn and money, and console them for the short-comings of the day, and the meannesses of labor and traffic" (Emerson 661). Economists may not call poets producers, but as Emerson's imagery makes clear, he believes that poets do indeed produce; they "feed the thought and imagination." How poets are to be recompensed for their work except by adulation is, however, unclear. In a world where economists have no way of accounting for artistic production, true poets, as opposed to hacks and commercial writers who produce commodities responsive to popular demand, must rescue their labor from the marketplace so that they can maintain their integrity regardless of prices.[26]

One can see why it is tempting for poets to believe that prices, not demand, prevent them from disposing of their work. They further assume, as Emerson does in the opening of "Swedenborg," that poets and poetry are automatically "dear to men," that literature has natural value for which there is a kind of natural demand. Therefore it is understandable that unpopular writers like Pound and Williams want to separate price from demand instead of assuming, as economists usually do, that price is the pure effect of demand. Poets know that their productions cost time and labor and therefore should have some monetary value. No doubt this is one reason why the Jeffersonian position concerning money was so attractive to our poets. As producers, and, insofar as they hoped to make money from their productions, would-be capitalists, it was easy for Pound and Williams to agree with indebted farmers that prices must include the costs of borrowing money and that creditors tax society at large to collect their debts while contributing nothing to the general welfare. From the producers' point of view, it was only some capitalists—the finance capitalists—who produce nothing.

Despite their purely fiduciary relation to the production process, the financiers appeared to be able to determine the value of labor through their control over the distribution of funds. The Jeffersonians began to suspect that as the rate of interest charged on loans was the principal determinant of price, so, more deeply, it also determined value. In the relative absence of markets, the worth of labor could not find its way into the price equation. Value, in essence, was not produced so much as dictated, determined more or less arbitrarily by a clique of moneylenders. Under these conditions, money was not the measure of value at all but instead the exercise of a tyrannical distortion of values. In this view, money is the hegemonic language of the creditor class.

Capitalism was therefore not itself oppressive. Indeed insofar as it favored the producer, Jeffersonians believed it to be liberating. The real enemy was finance capitalism, a perversion of capital that was distant, unproductive, and unresponsive to local conditions, which undermined and parasitized the integrity of life and labor, prematurely and inexorably sucking away its value and refusing to recognize its worth. At its most radical, the Jeffersonian critique of finance capital is quite literally imagined as the struggle of life against death.

For Jefferson, death is the power of the past extending its obligations over the living. Jefferson can sound like a Modernist writer in his embrace of the present: "The Earth belongs to the living not to the dead," he argued, speaking against long-term debt—words partly quoted by Pound in *Jefferson and/or Mussolini* (1935 116). This formula is not so very different from Pound's modernist slogan "make it new." Williams also constantly cited Jefferson as his authority for the renewal of letters: "Jefferson said, Liberty to be preserved requires a revolution every twenty years. By taking language as real and employing it with a full breadth and sweep, letters frees it from encroachments and makes it operative again" (*EK* 20).[27] As we can see from the full passage by Jefferson below, Williams's allusion has an economic subtext. "Perpetual debt," Jefferson believed, was contrary to the laws of nature because

> the earth belongs to the living, not to the dead. The will and the power of man expire with his life, by nature's law. Some societies give it artificial continuance, for the encouragement of industry; some refuse it, as our aboriginal neighbors, whom we call barbarians. The generations of men may be considered as bodies or corporations. Each generation has the usufruct of the earth during the period of its continuance. When it ceases to exist, the usufruct passes on to the succeeding generation, free and unincumbered, and so on, successively, from one generation to another forever. . . . Or the case may be likened to the ordinary one of a tenant for life, who may hypothecate the land for his debts, during the continuance of his usufruct; but at his death, the reversioner (who is also for life only) receives it exonerated of all burthen. [TJ to Eppes, June 24, 1813, Jefferson 1280–81]

Debt is the "artificial continuance," or what Williams called the "encroachments," of death on life. It creates what Blake called "death-in-life," the pseudo, or simulated, "flourishing," which Crèvecoeur, in the passage cited below, noticed in the prosperous-seeming farms in his neighborhood, which were in fact, "cankered" with the disease of debt. Jefferson observes that this mode of indebtedness is tolerated in "some" (read "Federalist") societies, to encourage "industry," presumably capitalist enterprises financed by bank credit.

Crèvecoeur provides us with a perfectly Jeffersonian statement of the case.

Flourishing as we may appear to a superficial observer, yet there are many dark spots which, on due consideration, greatly lessen that show of happiness which the Europeans think we possess. The number of debts which one part of the country owes to the other would greatly astonish you. The younger a country is, the more it is oppressed, for new settlements are always made by people who do not possess much. They are obliged to borrow; and, if any accidents intervene, they are not enabled to repay that money in many years. The interest is a canker-worm which consumes their yearly industry. Many never can surmount these difficulties. The land is sold, their labors are lost, and they are obliged to begin the world anew. [Crèvecoeur 273]

One might point out that, in the bigger picture, the farmer's labor is not "lost" but is "objectified" in coin and appropriated by creditors who have "alienated" his labor from him; from a certain purely economic perspective, this statement is undoubtedly true. The experience of foreclosure is more absolute, however. The bankrupt experiences the loss of his labor and all he has worked for as the loss of the world itself. He must feel that he has been sold out by words on a piece of paper. These words, which seemed to promise him the freedom to live and prosper, as long as he could turn his labor into money to be returned to his creditors, have revealed themselves to be a contract selling him into servitude. He is a capitalist betrayed by finance capital. The debtor finds that he has been working for the bank, not himself. He also sees that the merely monetary value of a debt cannot measure the worth of the creation of a world that, always more than the sum of total labor put into it, is property itself, or "reality."

Debt is, in this sense, a metaphysical problem, one not to be solved through any "pragmatic method." "The practical cash value" (James 1977 380), which William James chose as his metaphor for truth, is also the reality of debt. "Cash value" is, in this sense, an illusory, radically limited quantification of being in the world, which has the effect of denying or alienating true worth, a far more comprehensive but politically embattled version of reality. Debt decisively undermines, not the fact, but the meaning of production. It thus puts in question the integrity of experience and the evidence of the senses. Debt imposes arbitrary rules that effectively determine both the value of value and the reality of reality.

Like its financial counterpart, cultural debt also generates an aesthetic of the unreal. "Men are driven to their fates by the qualities of their beliefs," Williams wrote. He meant that if our beliefs are derivative, if "the culture of immediacy, the active strain, which has left every relic of value which survives today," is overwhelmed by moneyed culture, as he believed, then "the success of [this] unrelated, borrowed, the would-be universal culture which [has been] imposed on men to impoverish them" will end up "disenfranchis[ing] their intelligences" (*SE* 148–49).

Williams's formula is not only Jeffersonian but Physiocratic in its anxiety about the "universal" money culture and his linkage of independence to an unalienated relation to reality, to things, and, finally, also to nature and property. Recall how John Taylor of Caroline equated the "fruits of labor" with private property, not commodities. The market is incidental and, to the extent of its influence coercive and corrupting, because it challenges economic and personal independence. Marx's "social relations of production" are, for Jeffersonians like Taylor, intrusive fictions in what to him appears as an individual struggle, an essentially private, monogamous, and "natural" relationship between a man and his land.

The Legacy of Physiocracy

Physiocracy was the brainchild of the French physician and philosophe François Quesnay and the lesser known Marquis de Mirabeau, who, as Ronald Meek puts it, "played the role of Engels to his master's Marx" (Meek 1963 15). Well versed in it through his extensive reading in political economy and his personal acquaintance with many prominent Physiocrats, Jefferson was "a devoted adherent" to its principles (Fox-Genovese 11).

To the Physiocrats, all wealth came directly from the earth. The source of wealth was land; wealth itself, called the "net product," was agricultural produce. "Agriculture was the supreme occupation, not only because its produce was primary in the scale of wants and always in demand, but also—and mainly—because it alone yielded a disposable surplus over net cost" (Meek 1963 20). Farmers were the sole productive class. " 'Productive' to [the Physiocrats] meant, essentially, productive of a net product. Manufacture and commerce, they contended, were by contrast 'unproductive' and 'sterile' " (20). As for finance, Quesnay wrote that Physiocracy was not to be confused with "the trivial and specious science of financial operations whose subject-matter is only the money stock of the nation and the monetary movements resulting from traffic in money, in which credit, the lure of interest . . . bring about nothing but a sterile circulation which only in exceptional circumstances can be of any benefit" (Kuczynski and Meek 21–22). Pound was uncannily in the Physiocratic tradition when he wrote in 1914: "The artist is one of the few producers. He, the farmer and the artisan create wealth; the rest shift and consume it" (*LE* 222). For the Physiocrats and their ideological descendants, like Pound, the entire apparatus of capitalism and finance was not superfluous but simply sterile. It only manipulated an already existing wealth, never augmenting its value.

Physiocracy came under criticism from Marx because it was not yet what he called "political economy" proper, that is, it did not recognize the labor theory of value, nor, and most important, did it fully understand private property as capital (Marx 1975 342). He noted with disapproval that to the Physiocrats, "the land is still regarded as a part of nature which is independent of man, and not yet as capital, i.e. as a moment of labour itself. Rather, labour appears as a moment of *nature*" (Marx's emphasis, 344). This insight is helpful in understanding the attitude toward land and agriculture found in Jefferson and Crèvecoeur[28] and reverberating still in the poems of Pound and Williams. By the Physiocratic (and Jeffersonian) account, the farmer, or husbandman, was unalienated from nature; indeed he was quite literally working in full partnership with it. The whole point of this kind of economic thinking was, in effect, to conserve what Emerson and Williams would both call this "primary" relationship between man and nature.

It is striking that the word "husband" originally meant an "economist," or manager of a household, as it has always meant farmer and, of course, a married man. Like a marriage, the institution of property extends beyond the ceremony of sale that entitles the husbandman. Like marriage, property attains its worth by means of a personal relationship that has developed over time and through laborious husbandry. As Crèvecoeur shows, for the man at least, this relationship replaces the solitude of nature with the abundance of selfhood.

The instant I enter my own land, the bright idea of property, of exclusive right, of independence, exalt[s] my mind. Precious soil, I say to myself, by what singular custom of law is it that thou wast made to constitute the riches of the freeholder? What should we American farmers be without the distinct possession of that soil? It feeds, it clothes us; from it we draw even a great exuberancy, our best meat, our richest drink; the very honey of our bees comes from this privileged spot. [Crèvecoeur 54]

The relationship of this farmer to his land is not one of typically alienated capitalistic exploitation. He addresses the soil as he might his wife, with the intimate "thou," and the soil responds not with commodities for sale but with nourishing gifts for his use and enjoyment. It is no accident that Crèvecoeur's narrator/farmer apparently acquired this attitude following the birth of his first son (53). The "riches of the freeholder" have nothing to do with money. Instead they reward the husbandman with an "exuberancy," a fertility that exceeds selfish-sufficiency and becomes a true sufficiency of self, or independence.

Crèvecoeur's American Farmer is truly independent, because we know that the property was bequeathed to him by his father unencumbered by debts (52–53). As we can see, the issue of debt is closely tied to the issue of liberty, because liberty is independence. And independence is connected both to reality and, consequently, to an "exaltation" of self. This exaltation is nothing less than the power of life over death, of production over sterility.

By the Jeffersonian account quoted earlier, our relationship to the world is usufructory. No doubt, the use of the term "usufruct" by Jefferson records the influence of Physiocracy on his thinking. A portmanteau word combining *usus*, "use," and *fructus*, "enjoyment, or fruit," the dictionary tells us that usufruct, a legal concept, refers to the right of enjoying all of the advantages of a thing that belongs to another as far as is compatible with the substance of the thing not being destroyed or injured. As Jefferson notes with approval, this relation to the world is shared by virtually all aboriginal peoples; it is "natural." Possession of the earth is not absolute but usufructory, a temporary gift that, like air and water, comes with life and remains in perpetual reversion to the living.[29] According to one commentator, usufruct is the best translation of the Physiocratic sense of wealth, which they rendered as *jouissance* or *utilité* (Beer 141). We have seen that for the Physiocrats wealth was agricultural produce, but more broadly the Physiocratic notion of wealth referred to "things which satisfy in a direct manner the general human demand for food, raiment and shelter. It is much nearer to nature's gifts and the bodily needs of man than that which the urbanized man conceives as the substance of wealth" (141). This definition is virtually identical to the "riches of the freeholder" that Crèvecoeur apostrophizes in the passage quoted above.

The usufructory concept survives in what I regard as the monogamous ownership relation between land and "her" farmer and is therefore inscribed in the Jeffersonian sense of self. If we recall John Taylor's equivalence between the fruits of one's labor and private property, we get the particular flavor of his use of "private," which suggests something like a kinship created by the mutual laboring of the land and farmer together rather than the merely legal power to alienate the land for his own profit. Such a sale would be like a divorce. Speculation in land is a kind of labor that can yield no fruit—only money.

The poets understand this point. In *Spring and All* (1923), Williams likens the farmer to the artist, in "the artist figure / of the farmer":

> in deep thought
> is pacing through the rain
> among his blank fields, with
> hands in pockets,
> in his head
> the harvest already planted [*CP1* 186]

The farmer and poet are both "composing antagonist[s]" engaged in a private struggle to create. The compositional situation is envisioned here as a private meditation between farmer and "blank fields," metaphorically the poet and blank paper. If we take this situation as paradigmatic for Williams and we translate it, via the Jeffersonian sense of husbandry, into a kind of marriage, a creative partnership, then we are ready to see why the later Williams, in *Paterson*, sings that "Divorce is / the sign of knowledge in our time" when he notices "a bud forever green / tight-curled, upon the pavement, perfect / in juice and substance but divorced" (*P* 18). Divorce is, in effect, the modern condition in the alienated urban world of commodity relations where all and everything is for sale and nothing, apparently, can bear fruit.

The significance of "fruit" as a key term for Williams suggests the deep ideological affinity between him and Physiocracy, evident in "To a Poor Old Woman" (1935), one of Williams's best-known poems.

TO A POOR OLD WOMAN
munching a plum on
the street a paper bag
of them in her hand

They taste good to her
They taste good
to her. They taste
good to her

You can see it by
the way she gives herself
to the one half
sucked out of her hand

Comforted
a solace of ripe plums
seeming to fill the air
They taste good to her [CP 383]

Why is the woman "poor"? Intentionally pointing to her economic status, Williams lets his poem bear on economics. This seemingly simple poem achieves ideological resonance when considered physiocratically. It is about wealth and poverty, it is about enjoying the fruits of the earth. Here good taste tastes good, and the old woman, who is poor in money, is "comforted, solaced," and, for a moment, made wealthy by the jouissance in the fruit. Note that she "gives herself" to the fruit in eating; the fruit reciprocates by being itself. Its value does not need to be quantified. This is an experience of wealth prior to the money economy and more powerful because it can actually give solace as bought things cannot.

Clearly, the fruit is like a poem, which, as "the embodiment of knowledge," Williams compared to an apple (EK 59) because it has "roundness" (76) and because it is complete in and of itself. The poem is "all of a piece, knowledge presented in the form of pure writing which is made of the writing itself" (73). The poem, like an apple or plum, presents itself as "primary" value.

The old woman, then, is not poor but rich in the moment of her solace. She is rich too, in her giving, which, pointedly, is not labor and which can be gained not by labor but only by desire. In this moment she becomes part of nature, in direct contact with it.

No poet has been more obsessed with debt than Pound. He even invented a name for his obsession, "Usura," which stands for a kind of debt complex—a tangle of obligations to the past that the poet—especially the epic poet of *The Cantos*, the "poem including history"—needs both to acknowledge in the name of history and to resist in the spirit of originality, of "making it new." For Pound, Usura is the problem of debt conceived as sin. In his most famous canto, Canto 45, the great chant against Usura, Pound's imagery harkens to tropes deeply embedded in the American discourse on debt and thus to Physiocratic views.

Canto 45 is an indictment of usury not just as a crushing rate of interest on loans but more deeply as "a charge for the use of purchasing power, levied without regard to production; often without regard to the possibilities of production" (45:230). Pound's brief is not directed narrowly at institutionalized loan-sharking but targets some metaphysical evil in indebtedness. Usury proper is only a technical aspect of the radical evil addressed in the body of the poem and called Usura. By turning usury into usura, Pound turns the problem of debt into a life-and-death matter in ways that are unmistakably Jeffersonian.

In the body of the poem Pound makes claims that also echo persistent Jeffersonian tropes of debt.

> with usura, sin against nature,
> is thy bread ever more of stale rags
> is thy bread dry as paper,
> with no mountain wheat, no strong flour
> with usura the line grows thick
> with usura is no clear demarcation
> and no man can find site for his dwelling. [45:229]

These charges, that debt is a sin against nature, that it interferes with the freehold and male freeholder ("no man can find site for his dwelling"), at the same time promote agricultural production and natural fertility. The issue of fertility is more than agricultural. It spills over into the sexual realm, where usura "slayeth the child in the womb" and causes sexual dysfunction. "It stayeth the young man's courting / It hath brought a palsy to bed" (82:230). At stake is the covert connection between virtue, sexual potency, and virility, something about which I will have more to say later in this book. As we can see, when Pound also claims that "Azure hath a canker by usura" (230) he engages a tropic connection between usury and venereal disease used by Jefferson and Crèvecoeur. Pound ends the canto by making a connection between debt and death that is central to Jeffersonian thinking: "Corpses are set to banquet / at behest of Usura." The dead feast while the living eat bread dry as paper—a simile that we can now read as covertly antifinance. In fact, Pound expresses the same astonishment and outrage that Crèvecouer did before him, when he wondered at English creditors "living on" banknotes. This perversity is underwritten by the structure of debt, which views obligations to the past as more important than life in the present and mistakes paper values for real wealth.

It appears that a knowledge of Jeffersonian ideology can give readers of Pound or Williams powerful interpretive leverage. Jeffersonianism supplies the subtextual narrative structure to which our poets constantly refer and on which they constantly draw for poetic energy, for tropes, and for the themes that drive their poems. In the following chapter I will use three aspects of the Jeffersonian aesthetic to explicate their work. Each aspect becomes a lens that clarifies and intensifies the meaning of various poems, or moments in poems that otherwise seem telegraphic and obscure.

2

THREE ASPECTS
OF THE JEFFERSONIAN
POLITICAL AESTHETIC

I<small>F</small> J<small>EFFERSONIANISM</small> <small>LOOKS</small> back to a nonindustrial, agrarian form of capitalism as its economic ideal, then in an agricultural landscape dotted with republican freeholds where manufacture, like government, is tolerated as a necessary evil, citizens are imagined to live unalienated lives in touch with things. In such a world there could be no history—this world is, in fact, an escape from history, literally a New World—and all citizens live in a condition of virtuous liberty. Since such a world never existed, and could not exist historically, we may call this an aesthetic vision and not simply an economic, or political, one.[1]

The Agrarian Myth

As my introduction notes, the aesthetic vision became a central part of what Richard Hofstadter has called "the agrarian myth." This myth, he argues, was not necessarily the view held by farmers themselves but rather was promulgated by "the articulate people who wrote about farmers and farming—the preachers, poets, philosophers, writers and statesmen" who were "drawn irresistibly to the noncommercial, nonpecuniary, self-sufficient aspect of American farm life. To them it was an ideal. 18th century writers like Thomas Jefferson and Hector St. John de Crèvecouer admired the yeoman farmer not for his capacity to exploit opportunities and make money but for his honest industry, his independence, his frank spirit of equality, his ability to produce and enjoy a simple abundance" (Hofstadter 1955 23).

As we have seen, the not so implicit moral of this tale insists that the republican freeholder "speaking a populist dialect [is] the paradigm of the moral personality" (Livingston 1992 9), which links the complex nostalgias of modernism to Jeffersonian ideology.[2] It is not surprising, then, that we can find this same ideal articulated in Pound and Williams and even the contemporary agrarian essayist and poet Wendell Berry;[3] every presidential aspirant pays lip service to it. The agrarian myth serves as a key with which to unlock much of what otherwise seems buried, vague, and willfully difficult in Pound and Williams's poetry.

The themes that structure Williams's *Paterson* and much of Pound's *Cantos* can be found in Richard Hofstadter's typology of the "dominant themes of Populist ideology." They are worth repeating: "The idea of the golden age; the concept of natural harmonies; the dualistic version of social struggles [between debtors and creditors]; the conspiracy theory of history; and the doctrine of the primacy of money" (Hofstadter 1955 62).[4]

If I am right, we should be able to find these themes at work in the poetry of Pound and Williams. Take this passage from book 2, part 3 of Williams's *Paterson* (1948), called "Sunday in the Park," a book that may be read as a reply to Alexander Hamilton's disparaging retort to an incipient Democrat: "Your people, sir, are a great beast!" Here, "the great beast" (*P* 46, 54, 80) has been disporting itself in the park, which is all the free space the utilitarian regime of Hamiltonian factory discipline allows for or can imagine. The speaker, Dr. Noah Faitoute Paterson, the transparent persona of Dr. William Carlos Williams himself, meditates on the rivalry of the poem with the economic superstructure that conditions the modern American imagination.

> That the poem,
> the most perfect rock and temple, the highest
> falls, in clouds of gauzy spray, should be
> so rivalled . that the poet,
> in disgrace, should borrow from erudition (to
> unslave the mind): railing at the vocabulary
> (borrowing from those he hates, to his own
> disenfranchisement) .
> —discounting his failures .
> seeks to induce his bones to rise into a scene,
> his dry bones, above the scene, (they will not)
> illuminating it within itself, out of itself
> to form the colors, in the terms of some

back street, so that history may escape
the panders
. . accomplish the inevitable
poor, the invisible, thrashing, breeding
. debased city [P 80–81]

This passage is a record of the poet's struggle to write his poem within the confined imaginative space, "the Park," allowed by those he hates—those who, following Hamilton, have seized the meaning of America. Resistant, the poet "seeks to induce his bones to rise into a scene . . . (they will not.)" Why not? Why is he "disenfranchised" and "in disgrace"? Who are these people he hates, who want to prostitute history?

Consider this passage in light of Hofstadter's fivefold summation of agrarian ideology:

1. The idea of a golden age. Subsumed here under the sign of "history," the poet complains that the soul of the republic has been corrupted by interested parties equally commercial and criminal, hence "panders" who will sell the body of history as though it were its spirit. The role of the poet is to rescue history by faithfully "illuminating" the back streets, the "poor, . . . invisible, thrashing, breeding, city." Or, read ideologically, this passage is about democracy perverted by capital, the Jeffersonian ideal under the Hamiltonian regime that is America in 1948.
2. Natural harmonies. These are represented by "the poem," which is "the most perfect rock and temple," fusing nature and the highest aspirations of man to "the highest / falls"; thus connecting the poem to the waterfalls at Paterson, the natural wonder that caused Hamilton to plan his model industrial city on the site. It is this city, "debased" by commerce, not the "city on a hill" that "rivals" the poem and disturbs the natural harmony.
3. The dualistic nature of social struggles between debtors and creditors. This agon is inscribed in this passage as the poet's struggle with "erudition" that he must "borrow" from those he therefore "hates." This position of debt is reflected in his feeling of "disenfranchisement" or lack of citizenship. Typically for Williams, this is expressed in unflattering (though veiled) allusions to T. S. Eliot, whom Williams regarded as a kind of Benedict Arnold of modern

poetry.[5] Thus, the "dry bones" of Eliot's "Ash-Wednesday" (1930) find their way into *Paterson*, where, *pace* Eliot, they cannot be induced to rise into a scene because Williams's scene is not a scene composed in terms of Anglican Christianity. It is not a religious scene at all but an economic one, composed "in terms of some / back street" where the poor are constrained to live not for their sins but because of economic injustice. The city is not morally "depraved" but economically "debased," like bad coin.

4. The conspiracy theory of history is most evident in this passage from its tone. Williams asks, Who benefits from the disgrace of the poet, the slavery of the uneducated mind, and the invisibility of the poor? Later in *Paterson* he will name these as "the special interests" who "restrict knowledge" and perpetuate class division and struggle (*P* 34).

5. The doctrine of the primacy of money is admittedly only dimly present in this passage in the resonance of words like "debased" and the theme of debt. But the term "debased" functions here as a term of value. Williams's characteristic concern is not simply right and wrong; like Pound he is concerned about the adulteration of value, the perversion of the ideal. The most stunning passage in *Paterson* is the hymn to the "beautiful thing"—the poor and abused young African-American woman—who the poet believes "like all desired women have had each / in the end / a busted nose" (*P* 128). Beauty marred and debased by poverty, ignorance, and violence, like the city of Paterson, like the United States itself, lies at the heart of Williams's vision. *Paterson*, Williams told Edith Heal, concerns the theme of "pollution," is "about the conception of the filth in the world" (*IWWP* 79). Williams is determined to rescue beauty from corruption and to nurse it tenderly back to health from its ordeal at the hands of the real, "the guys of Newark and Paterson" (*P* 127) (or Washington for that matter) who destroy beauty for their own vanity and profit, that it

> live afterward marked up
> Beautiful Thing
> for memory's sake
> To be credible in their deeds [*P* 128]

These deeds are deeds of capitalistic excess, which use the power of money to inscribe the domination of nature by capital. The result is the poverty of Paterson, deformed and debased by the money force of economic determinism. We can now see that "debased" refers back to the debauched language of exchange, which therefore exacerbates the preventable social antagonisms that inspire the Jeffersonian critique of modernity.

Hofstadter's agrarian myth is surprisingly useful in elucidating this typical moment in *Paterson*. The myth speaks to the defensive stance that marks Williams's epic from the beginning, when it is presented to us as "a reply to the greek and latin with the bare hands" (no page number), a stance that might now recall Emerson's "embattled farmers" at Concord bridge and that certainly suggests a poet compelled to answer some threatening literary demand based on "classic," European standards with inadequate and homemade weapons (Emerson 1994 125).

Yet *Paterson* is also "a gathering up; a celebration" (*P* 2) precisely because it proposes a democratic and (as I will argue later) pragmatic answer to the tyrannical excesses screened by the classical ideal of art. Always defensive yet doggedly celebratory, Jeffersonianism in Williams's writing becomes a kind of common sense to which he refers complicated or contradictory problems. It becomes the unspoken basis for an entire aesthetic.

Here is another example of the agrarian myth, this time operating subtextually in Williams's prose. In a provocative little essay called "French Painting (Its Importance, a Definition, and the Influence Upon Modern Writing Traceable to It)," we find three propositions:

1. The artist['s?] "idea" is not to limit, not to constrict, but not to fly off into "universals," into vapors, either. That is what it is to be an artist with his material before him. It is to be a kind of laborer—a workman—a maker in a very plain sense—nothing vague or transcendental about it: that is the artist—at base. [*EK* 23]

This statement recalls a more famous one in Williams's "Introduction" to *The Wedge* (1944): "Let the metaphysical take care of itself, the arts have nothing to do with it" (*CP2* 54). Williams's irritability over abstractions and high-flown philosophical claims reveals a populistic *resentment* against any universalizing system of truths that mystifies the plain sense of things by promoting esoteric learning over "hands-on" or "real-life" experience sanctified by labor. The "base," the bottom, essence, or foundation of art and poetry is the direct relation between material and labor. This direct "primary" relation is the basis for Jeffersonian democracy.

Here is Williams's second proposition:

2. The basis being—that one can come up through to excellence in the arts—as to an intelligent use of his life—anywhere—at any time—tho' with variations—and this is a liberal understanding of the word and an American one. [EK 23]

The way in which Williams is able to move from an implicit artistic base to a democratic "basis" is certainly Jeffersonian in its implications. There is a pluralistic idealism at work; the move from base to basis reveals that a narrative of artistic self-reliance is equated with the Jeffersonian dream of self-sufficiency and thus with a democratic confidence that "variations" are as important as universals.

Williams links this dream of freedom to a sense of locality derived via Dewey from the Jeffersonian exaltation of the freehold as the basis of an independent self:

3. (last bit) It is because we confuse the narrow sense of parochialism in its limiting implication, that we fail to see the complement of the same: that the local in a full sense *is* the freeing agency of all thought, in that it is everywhere accessible to all: not in the temple, of a class, but for every place where men have eyes, brains, vigor, and the desire to partake with others of that same variant in other *places* which unites us all—if we are able. [Williams's emphasis, *EK* 23]

Place is defined here by what it isn't—it is *not* of the "temple" of learning or any particular religious affiliation, *nor* is it "of a class." Place is where we happen to be now; any place where our senses and our will are active. It is where "we" (not "they") live, and it forms the material for our imaginations. Fine. But why the catch? Why the doubt expressed in the pendant "if we are able"? Clearly, Williams believes that people who see themselves as declassed and outside the temple must struggle to maintain their place. Place is maintained *against* something—some agency—that wants it for its own. This agency, in the Jeffersonian formulation, is "the money-using class," "big money," or "special interests,"[6] who have no particular place of their own (except perhaps the "city"), who don't seem to work in any recognizable way, and who must therefore not be truly American in the Jeffersonian sense.

Just as with Williams, one can put the agrarian myth to work on almost any page of Pound's massive *Cantos* to reveal much of the unspoken agenda in his poem. Although Pound has much to say on these Jeffersonian matters that is quite clear—Jefferson is a figure in the poem, and he called himself a Jeffersonian[7]—the agrarian myth can unlock unexpected meanings in many of the less obviously polemical moments throughout the poem, such as the Cantos' lyrical and "Chinese" moments.

Confucianism is rooted in the agrarian experience of China, so it is not surprising that Confucian ethics and agrarian virtue should be linked in Pound's mind: "turn conversation toward justice" he says in Canto 99, in what is a kind of free translation of Confucius, "keep mind on the root / Ability as grain in the wheat-ear / Establish the homestead" (99:718). In the "Seven Lakes Canto," Canto 49, Pound sets the Jeffersonian fear of debt in a Chinese landscape: his lines, "State by creating riches shd. thereby get into debt? / This is infamy, this is Geryon" modulate into a timeless "Oriental" scene:

Sun up; work
sundown; to rest
dig well and drink of the water
dig field; eat of the grain
Imperial power is? and to us what is it? [49:245]

The questioning of imperial power by the peasant speakers suggests their understanding that the basis of society, politics, and economy is their work in the fields. They express a belief in an agrarian version of the labor theory of value. Imperial power passes, and dynasties come and go, but the peasant and the land—the permanent sources of all value—remain. One reason debts are "infamous" is because they attack the agrarian basis of value by asserting the power of abstract financial arrangements, privileging the artificial times and seasons of payment schedules over the rhythms of nature. Usura creates conditions where "the peasant does not eat his own grain" (51:250).

Luxury and Austerity

"Will you tell me how to prevent riches from becoming the effects of temperance and industry?" John Adams wrote Jefferson with exasperation. "Will you tell me how to prevent riches from producing luxury? Will you tell me how to prevent luxury from producing effeminacy intoxication extravagance Vice and folly?" (JA to TJ, December 21, 1819, Cappon 551). One of the most thoroughly documented discourses of the American revolutionary and Federalist period is that of luxury.[8] The decline and fall of Rome haunted the American revolutionary imagination. In founding a republic, Americans hoped to avoid the pitfalls of empire; yet as John Adams makes clear, they saw the vices of empire as the inevitable fruit of republican success. The problem of luxury goes to the heart of the American experiment. Gordon Wood writes, "The Americans' compulsive interest in the ancient republics was in fact crucial to their attempt to understand the moral and social basis of politics" (Wood 50).

In many ways Americans' identification with a virtuous Roman republic helped justify their rebellion against the British Empire they regarded as corrupt. England's luxury and vice was a Whig commonplace in the eighteenth century. The writers who prepared the ideological ground for the American Revolution made a habit of quoting Roman writers like Cicero and Tacitus, who had in their own day "contrasted the corruption and disorder they saw around them with an imagined earlier republican world of ordered simplicity and arcadian virtue" (Wood 51). Indeed, the very victory of the American revolutionaries suggested the rot in the moral fiber of the British Empire and stood as a warning about any grandiose imperial visions of an American future. American interest in ancient republics was proportionate to Americans' anxieties about the powers of the empire from which they had just become independent. A belief in "the austere simplicity of the Roman Republic" seasoned "the ideology of the Revolution" (Elkins and McKitrick 48).

"The Americans' view of antiquity was highly selective, focusing on decline and decadence" (Wood 51); it was an anxious view. The moral maintenance of the republic required constant vigilance. American political discourse then as now was permeated with the fear of moral corrosion by luxury and vice. The remedy called for is an "austere simplicity" in all things, which became as synonymous with republican virtue as it had with religious virtue in an earlier period. Often enough, however, the fear of decadence has led to a distrust of the arts altogether, a puritanism and stiff Billy Sundayism that has historically put American artists on the moral defensive. Subliminally, all Americans and American artists still hear the gripe of John Adams to Jefferson: "Every one of the fine Arts from earliest times has been inlisted [sic]] in the service of Superstition and Despotism" (December 16, 1816, Cappon 503).

The politics of austere simplicity clearly implies an aesthetics, which is unmistakably reproduced in the aesthetic pronouncements of Pound and Williams and their war against artistic decline. Like the American revolutionaries, they founded their own artistic morality on a narrative of liberation from a decadence—in this case the aestheticism of the late nineteenth century. An early statement by Pound seems firmly in the austere republican tradition:

> As to Twentieth century poetry, and the poetry I expect to to see written in the next decade or so, it will, I think, move against poppy-cock, it will be harder and saner, it will be . . . "nearer the bone." It will be as much like granite as it can be, its force will lie in its truth, its interpretive power. . . . it will not try to seem forcible by rhetorical din, and luxurious riot. We will have fewer painted adjectives to impede the shock and stroke of it. At least for myself, I want it so, austere, direct, free from emotional slither. [*LE* 12]

Much of the aesthetic of imagism (c. 1913), with its "direct treatment of the thing" and admonition "to use absolutely no word that does not contribute to the presentation" (*LE* 3), partakes of a republican austerity. When Pound sent HD's first poems to *Poetry*, he praised them for being "Objective—no slither; direct—no excessive use of adjectives, no metaphors that won't permit examination. It's straight talk, straight as the Greek!" (*SL* 11). Greek is the language of probity and directness—the opposite of slithery: "A civilization was founded on Homer, civilization not a mere bloated empire," Pound claimed (*LE* 21).

One can understand Pound's identification with John Adams (and his identification of Adams with Confucius) in the tone of these remarks from "How To Read" (1929), an article published in the *New York Herald Tribune*. Pound asks whether literature has a function in "the republic." "It has," he decides (*SE* 21). Here's why.

It has to do with the clarity and vigour of "any and every" thought and opinion. It has to do with maintaining the very cleanliness of the tools, the health of the very matter of thought itself. Save in the rare and limited instances of invention in the plastic arts, or in mathematics, the individual cannot think and communicate his thought, the governor and legislator cannot act effectively or frame his laws, without words, and the solidity and validity of these words is in the care of the damned and despised *litterati*. When their work goes rotten—by that I do not mean when they express indecorous thoughts—but when their very medium, the very essence of their work, the application of word to thing goes rotten, i.e. becomes slushy and inexact, or excessive or bloated, the whole machinery of social and individual thought and order goes to pot. This is the lesson of history and a lesson not yet half learned. [*SE* 21]

Pound's evocation of the "damned and despised *litterati*" suggests an ambivalence, one shared by many Americans, about the moral status of the artist. Yet Pound also understands that when artists are suspected of encouraging decadence, they are usually suspect for the wrong reasons—because their ideas are new, unsettling, "indecorous," even revolutionary. Pound's point is that the words themselves, the "tools"—not the ideas they convey—must be "clean." His prescription for verbal health is not the puritanical idea of censorship but the artistic ideal of form. The form/content distinction is crucial for Pound and for Williams in order to establish a position for the artist that is compatible with the ideal of a republic.

It is illuminating that the first time we encounter the voice of Thomas Jefferson in *The Cantos* he is asking a French correspondent to find him "a gardener / Who can play the french horn." For "The bounds of an American fortune / Will not admit the indulgence of a domestic band of / musicians" (21:97). Terrell comments that Pound is presenting Jefferson as a kind of renaissance man (Terrell 87), but it also seems clear that Pound is rehearsing the question of art's place in an austere republic. Where, "within the bounds of an American fortune," is there a place for the artist except as a figure who is an artist in his spare time? Jefferson cannot even think of employing a musician who is a gardener on the side—that is beyond republican bounds and hints of decadence.

The flip side of Jefferson's cultural dilemma is indicated somewhat later in the canto where Pound invokes the legend of Midas. The reader

will remember that Midas rescued the drunken god Silenus, father
of Pan. When granted a wish in return for his good deed, the king
foolishly asked that everything he touched turn to gold. In Pound's
poem we hear the voice of Silenus as "the old man sweeping leaves: /
Damned to you Midas, Midas lacking a Pan" (21:99). Juxtaposed with
the passage about Jefferson's request for laborers who are also artists,
we might conclude that Pound wants us to understand Midas's choice
as the fate of the American plutocrats who have chosen gold over art.
They are damned to a destructive system of merely monetary value,
where the spirit of Pan as manifested in the arts, and the Dionysian
side of human nature is officially absent, repressed.

I offer as another example the opening of Canto 58, a poem that
couldn't seem further from our Jeffersonian concerns and that yet,
when regarded through the lens of republican austerity, seems an example of "Orientalism"—that is, a displaced and exoticized parable of
the history of the United States and, one might add, Mussolini's Italy,
which Pound saw as a potential Jeffersonian republic (*JM*).

> Sinbu put order in Sun land, Nippon, in the beginning
> of all things.
>
> where were DAI till Shogun Jorimoto
> These Dai were of heaven descended, so saying.
> Gods were their forebears. Till the Shogun
> or crown general put an end to internal wars
> And DAI were but *reges sacrifoli* after this time
> in Miaco, with formalities
>   wearing gold-flowered robes.
> At each meal was a new clay dish for their service
> "Descended from Ten Seo DAISIN
>   that had reigned for a million years."
> All these lords say they are of heaven descended
> and they ran into debt to keep up appearance
> they were there busy with sciences, poetry, history
> dancing, in Miaco, and music, playing at jeu de paume and
> escrime
> with a garrison to keep watch on 'em
>   and to keep 'em from interfering with business.
>   [58:316]

This, like virtually all of the Cantos in the "Chinese" sequence (Cantos 52–61), is, in the guise of a Confucian parable, really a republican

warning against decadence and debt. The Confucian speaker sounds like the founding fathers on luxury, while the signature growl of Pound himself sounds distinctly "Amurk'n" note in the last two lines. This admonition could be construed as a revolutionary republican critique of a decadent aristocracy, which as sacrificial kings, have the form but not the substance of power. "Dress 'em in folderols / and feed 'em with dainties, / In the end they will sell out the homestead" (99:719), the poet concludes in another canto. The message of Canto 58 is indistinguishable from his message in "How to Read" above, concerning the cleanliness of the verbal tools, and Pound's Confucian ethics would have seemed very familiar to Jefferson and Adams:

> The men of old wanting to clarify and diffuse throughout the empire that light which comes from looking straight into the heart and then acting, first set up good government in their own states; wanting good government in their own states, they first established order in their own families; wanting order in the home, they first disciplined themselves; desiring self-discipline, they rectified their own hearts; and wanting to rectify their hearts, they sought precise verbal definitions of their inarticulate thoughts (the tones off by the heart); wishing to attain precise verbal definitions, they set to extend their knowledge to the utmost. This completion of knowledge is rooted in sorting things into organic categories (*Confucius* 30–31).

The emphasis on order in this passage from Pound's translation of the *Ta Hsio* explains his use of the "Shogun" in Canto 58—an odd figure to find in a poem I am claiming to be Jeffersonian in outlook. The Shogun can be construed as the figure of Mussolini, however, as Mussolini was, in Pound's mind, a paragon of Jeffersonian (and Confucian) rectitude in action. This link between the two men, which prompted Pound's notorious book *Jefferson and/or Mussolini* (1935), is a peculiarity of the poet. Read through the anxieties of those other "men of old," the founding fathers of the United States, this Shogun is a figure of Caesar and the evils of Caesarism, one who cordons off an enfeebled aristocracy from the "business" of plunder to which the State is now devoted.[9]

In this fragment of a canto, we can see the class struggle organized along Jeffersonian debtor/creditor lines, although here the debtors are a decayed aristocracy rather than the typical farmer/freeholder. The ethical lesson lies in the ominous military garrison that guards the decadent aesthetes who have squandered their birthright and have run hopelessly into debt. We can be sure that the arts and sciences they pursue are insufficiently serious, part of their need to keep up luxurious appearances. These Dai can write no epics, no "poem including history" (*ABCR* 46). Lacking order in themselves, they must be ordered from without.

If anything, Williams's poetic practice goes beyond Pound's belated republican austerity. "Tract" (1917) is just that, a tract against luxury and pomp. The speaker proposes to teach his "townspeople / how to perform a funeral" for they have the potential to do it better than the "troop" of what seem to be foreign "artists," much like Pound's implicitly foreign "litterati." "You," the speaker insists, "Have the "ground sense necessary" (*CP1* 72) to perform the rite correctly, which means in a republican spirit of sharing and class collaboration, not misguided pomp. Williams didactic poem begins with a "design for a hearse."

> For Christ's sake not black—
> nor white either—and not polished!
> Let it be weathered—like a farm wagon—
> with gilt wheels (this could be
> applied fresh at small expense)
> or no wheels at all:
> a rough dray to drag over the ground [*CP1* 73]

The sumptuous hearse recast into a farm wagon is an American allegory, a reassertion of a republican austerity over luxury. "Tract" continues and intensifies its attack on luxury by advocating a mild sort of revolutionary violence. The driver with his silk hat must be brought down, made "low and inconspicuous! I'd not have him ride / on the wagon at all—damn him— / the undertaker's understrapper!" Finally, Williams closes with an offer of republican solidarity between the truer artist, the poet, and the people—that is to say, with an image of the commonwealth:

> . . . Go with some show
> of inconvenience; sit openly—
> to the weather as to grief
> Or do you think you can shut grief in?
> What—from us? We who have perhaps
> nothing to lose? Share with us

share with us—it will be money
in your pockets
            Go now
I think you are ready [*CP1* 74]

The right kind of art should be an aid to republican virtue, not its enemy. Thus Williams allows for the possibility that the postrevolutionary hearse could have gilded wheels (which could be applied at "small expense"—within the bounds of an American fortune) and that the mourners could be permitted to make some "show / of inconvenience." With the same form/content distinction that Pound stresses in "How to Read," Williams makes it clear that his attack is not on the feelings of the mourners. Their "grief" is not under scrutiny, only their way of expressing it. Nor is Williams arguing for an artless transparency of "weather," which is the province of nature, not the artist. Rather he wants to clear a space for a new kind of austerity (not severity), to restore a lost republican authenticity.

Yet what fascinates me about "Tract" is not so much its allegiance to an aesthetic of austerity, which is obvious, but its gestures toward the modification of that austerity by art. The poem attempts to find a ground from which a republican art might be possible. A radically austere aesthetic is no aesthetic at all—art would simply be suppressed or classed as something else, sermons or religious tracts, for example. But the poem is about establishing a republican artistic position. It is not antiart but only antiluxury.

Concrete Measures

Clearly, Pound and Williams were engaged in what we would now call "cultural criticism," and this criticism extends to their poetry and into the poems themselves, including the way they are laid out on the page. These poems are designed to provide a means by which to measure American life against American ideals—the true ideal of democracy and the false ideal of success, especially commercial and monetary triumph. Both poets were obsessed with the term "measure," about which they each said many obscure and tantalizing things. Williams's enigmatic notion of the "variable foot" continues to baffle his critics, tending to provide us with a term flexible enough to supplement any particular reading but insufficient to provide a fixed point of definition. This ambiguity seems to have been intentional on Williams's part; that we can have no fixed measure is, perhaps, his point. Pound's fascination with measure seems, at first, much more frankly about money than Williams's and it has been easy for critics to ignore it as part of Pound's "cranky" economic side. He constantly reminds us that money is "a measured claim" on goods and services. But there is also a linguistic, poetic aspect to Pound's interest in measure. What both Pound and Williams call measure is the linguistic and monetary negotiation between fantasy and reality, the abstractions of Hamiltonian finance versus a Jeffersonian rootedness. Conversely they also measure Jeffersonian idealism against Hamiltonian practice, which is another way of saying that they enact the American ideological dilemma.

Williams claimed that "the *subject matter* of the poem is always phantasy—what is wished for, realized in the 'dream' of the poem—but that the [poetic] structure confronts something else" (*SE* 281, Williams's emphasis). He saw "the poem as a field of action." In a lecture of that name written in 1948, in the midst of *Paterson,* he observes of the poet in the industrial age, "The one thing that the poet has not wanted to change, the one thing he has clung to in his dream—unwilling to let go— . . . is structure. Here we are immovable. But here is precisely where we come into contact with reality. Reluctant we waken from our dreams. And what is reality? How do we know reality? The only reality that we can know is MEASURE" (*SE* 283). Williams seems to be trying to explain to himself the relation between his dream for the poem and its historical "reality." Eventually, Williams would resolve the problem through his concept of the triadic line and the obscure "variable foot"—a democratic claim that measure "gives resources to the ear which result in a language which we hear spoken around us every day" (WCW to Richard Eberhart, May 23, 1954, *SL* 327).

Williams persistently links his claim to Einstein's theory of relativity (*SE* 283, 337–40) and to what he sees as a welcome moral relativism implied by Einsteinian physics. This relativism is neither absolute nor amoral. It has real, if loose, limits; it is democratic and various; it has something in common with what William James in his *Principles of Psychology* called the "re-instatement of the vague" (James 1977 45).[10] Like James, Williams is sensitive to the transitive nature of language—

its inexact, provisional perversity, the way that "language works against our perception of truth" (James 1977 34).

Commenting on James, Richard Poirier remarks that his stress on the transitional rather than substantive nature of language implied a "grammar [that] would make us aware that the relations between things are as important to experience as are the things themselves. It is necessary to stay loose. [James's] ideal grammar leads to his politics, and not the other way round. The grammar he proposes is already anti-imperialist, anti-patriarchal, while never becoming directly focused on political or social structures" (Poirier 1992 152). James's transitive grammar is, it seems to me, a kind of prose equivalent of Williams's variable measure.[11] While aware of the political implications of a "vague" James-like measure, Williams is Jeffersonian, as James is not, because he wants to use his "variable foot" to focus on political and social structures—specifically democracy's relation to finance capitalism. One conclusion Williams draws from his attention to politics is that there can be no such thing as "free verse": "No verse can be free, it must be governed by some measure, but not by the old measure. . . . We have to return to some measure but a measure consonant with our time" (*SE* 339). The linking of measure to government and of government with the modern historical situation is telling. It is tempting to suggest that Williams is pondering the contemporary relevance of the Jeffersonian adage that the best government is that which governs least, but a more fruitful connection might be with pragmatism, especially Dewey's variety, because Dewey, like Williams, is constantly trying to historicize both his mode of inquiry and American political institutions.

Stephen Cushman, who has written a thorough book-length study of measure in Williams,[12] finds, finally, that "at the core of Williams' search for measure lies the American pragmatic effort to reconcile freedom with limitation" (Cushman 137)—a conclusion that points indirectly but inescapably to an attempt by the poet to measure the encompassing American ideological struggle between the "natural harmonies" of Jeffersonian republican idealism and the "economic realities" associated with its antagonist, the Hamiltonian ideology of the financial establishment. In "The Poem as a Field of Action," Williams argued that his radical prosody was "trying . . . not only to disengage the elements of a measure [so as to reveal its structure] but to seek (what we believe is there) a new measure or a new way of measuring that will be commensurate with the social, economic world in which we are living as contrasted with the past. It is in many ways a different world from the past calling for a different measure" (*SE* 283). Why? Because

> with the industrial revolution, and steadily since then, a new spirit,— a new *Zeitgeist* has possessed the world, and as a consequence new values have replaced the old, aristocratic concepts—which had a pretty seamy side if you looked at them like a Christian. A new subject matter began to be manifest. It began to be noticed that there could be a new subject matter and that that was not in fact the poem at all. Briefly then, money talks, and the poet, the modern poet has admitted a new subject matter to his dreams—that is, the serious poet has admitted the whole armamentarium of the industrial age into his poems. [*SE* 282]

The turn here toward economics is striking. The industrial age has made economics a proper subject for poetry, and because "money talks," money has actually emerged as the principal competitor of poetry in a contest to win the public imagination. "The creative mind is jealous of wealth." Williams mused, "It would rival a [J. P.] Morgan and make his field, finance, seem insignificant" (*EK* 120). Artists are jealous because money, in a very real sense, dominates the modern imagination and shapes it to monetary modes of valuation. The great financiers "like to feel themselves kings, as they are (in their category) and to enhance the illusion they purchase works of art, the effects of the great of the past whose crowns of light they think to borrow. But let American purchasers especially recognize that they are not even comparable, much less to the great artists but not even to the great patrons" (*EK* 121). The result of a thoughtless importation of European cultural capital to enhance the monarchial, and thus un-American, fantasies of tycoons resulted in a borrowed, indebted, imaginatively foreclosed culture. As a result, Williams noted:

> A servile copying of Europe, not Jefferson's, became the rule. And along with it a snobbism from which or from the effects of which very few escaped. The secondary split-off from what, but for fear, had been a single impetus, finally focused itself as personal wealth in America, important since it is wealth that controls the mobility of a nation. But dangerous since by its control it can isolate and so render real values, in effect, impotent. [*SE* 146]

It is money, not poetry, that shapes modern dreams. Since money defines value through scarcity, not abundance, the result is isolation and the wasteland mentality, the aesthetic of exhaustion and sexual dysfunction that characterized the modernism of Eliot (a bank clerk once) that Williams despised. Money, Williams saw, unconsciously echoing Emerson, is the language of a "secondary culture, secure in wealth" (*SE* 153). Such is the "mystical power represented by money" that the "actual, the necessity for dealing with a condition as it existed," that Williams called "primary culture," seemed to become "unecessary" (*SE* 151). Well before Baudrillard, Williams saw the result as a simulacrum, noting that "a culture of purchase, a culture of effigy has become predominant," and "the primary cultural influence, embraced by the unfortunately impoverished native, came to a stop" (*SE* 147).

It is the duty of the poet to reverse this disastrous course and to resume the American War of Independence by going native. That is, the American poet must find a native measure with which to counter the ubiquitous measure of money. Money takes us away from what exists because it is unable, in Williams's Jeffersonian formulation, to make adequate or disinterested claims against reality. It is too abstract, too mechanical in the way it divides up the world, and too much a tool of the money-using classes to take the full measure of American existence.

Williams thought that American poetry should and could measure itself against native realities, the primary culture, provided it abandoned the false measure—specifically iambic pentameter (*SE* 281, 337)—that he connected with the undemocratic financial system we had inherited (thanks to Hamilton) from Europe. In "On Measure—Statement for Cid Corman" (1954), Williams compares traditional metrics to "Euclidean" mathematics, which he complains are inadequate to new realities.

> Our lives also have lost all that in the past we had to measure them by, except outmoded standards that are meaningless to us. In the same way our verses, of which our poems are made, are left without any metrical construction . . . , any new measure by which they can be pulled together. We get sonnets etc., but no one alive today . . . seems to see anything incongruous in that. They cannot see that poems cannot any longer be made following the Euclidian measure, "beautiful"

as this may make them. The very grounds for our beliefs are altered. We do not live that way any more; nothing in our lives, at bottom, is ordered according to that measure; our social concepts, our schools, our very religious ideas, certainly our understanding of mathematics are greatly altered. Were we called upon to go back to what we believed in the past we should be lost. [*SE* 337]

With a few exceptions, Williams felt that poets had failed to take up the implications of contemporary philosophy, mathematics, and physics into the structure of the poem. With typically Jeffersonian defensiveness, Williams argued in *Paterson* that "the special interests" restrict "Knowledge / of the avenues of information— / So that we do not know (in time) / where the stasis lodges." They "perpetuate the stasis and make it / profitable" (*P* 33–34). The poet's job is to expose the knowledge racket. His tool will be the radical reinvention of measure, a measure that will embody the new knowledge of our new time and local landscape.

For this reason, much of *Paterson* can be read as a polemic for a new, ideologically Jeffersonian measure. Book 2 of *Paterson* begins as a kind of treatise on meter. In the "Sunday in the Park" section Williams begins:

```
Outside
             outside myself
                            there is a world,
he rumbled, subject to my incursions
—a world
             (to me) at rest,
                     which I approach
concretely—              [P 43]
```

Williams can approach this world concretely through this open structure, a structure that has a kind of flex suitable for a rough and broken terrain. The park here is Garret Mountain (not some English garden, Williams seems to implicitly claim) but rather "the Park / upon the rock, / female to the city // —upon whose body Paterson instructs his thoughts / (concretely)" (*P* 43). Paterson teaches himself to have new thoughts by poetically measuring the female terrain that is American reality for him. It is the body, not the ideal, of the poem that is important. Echoing Whitman's "Crossing Brooklyn Ferry," Paterson/Williams finds

> himself among the others,
> —treads there the same stones
> on which their feet slip as they climb,
> paced by their dogs! [*P* 44]

Their feet slip, not his. Not bound to the metronome as are the others who follow mechanical, not dynamic, measures,[13] Paterson, who in an early gesture toward the "triadic line" has imagined himself as a three-legged dog, finds himself

> —over-riding
> 　　　　the risks:
> 　　　　　　　pouring down!
> For the flower of a day!　　　[*P* 44]

He has "arrived breathless" (44)—and I would suggest that the spaces between these phrases are supposed to measure that breathlessness, which is a kind of physical liberation from the regularly measured ideal breathing of traditional English poetry. The poet can now afford to look "back (beautiful but expensive) to / the pearl-grey towers" (44) of the Manhattan skyline, visible from the summit. As he makes clear later in the poem, these towers represent the beautiful but expensive and ultimately sterile temptations of finance (*P* 165)—the anti-Hamiltonian gesture is reflexive. A good Jeffersonian, Williams "Re-turns / and starts, possessive, through the trees" (*P* 44).

For all his Jeffersonianism, Williams was neither naive nor jingoistic about the notion of a national culture; "because a thing is American or related to the immediate conditions it is not therefore to be preferred to the finished product of another culture," he wrote in "The American Background" (1934) (*SE* 154). Rather, "It is a question of give and take. If there is no equation, no comparable value to be set beside the first, adding or subtracting, multiplying or dividing, the thing stands alone and must stand impotent. America *might* produce work of value to Europe" (my emphasis, *SE* 154–55). We *might* be able to create cultural productions comparable to those of Europe *if* we had something comparable to set beside theirs.

The "first" culture to which Williams refers is the "primary cultural influence" that has been repressed by the simulated, secondary culture imported from abroad. Williams's conception of measure, then, is consistently historicized: he wants a measure that reflects contemporary historical, social, and economic realities. Furthermore, this measure is hypostatized into an equation—like a scientific theorem. In effect, meters are theorems that reflect their time and place. Writing to Sherry Mangan, a fellow poet,[14] Williams noted how "the meter is a word"—that is, it carries significant meaning as words do. One could go further and say that the meter works as the metaphysical frame for a poem, determining its meaning. "What I think happens to you, Williams wrote,

> as it does to us all! is that you have let a conventional (outdated) meter and worn out movement in the poetic line choose your words for you. This is important. This is what Gertrude Stein has struggled against.
> . . .
> Now as I have said, this meter is a "word." It is the binding[,] the [tyranny] with which the past saps away our sense and our courage. The antithesis of this is the serious purpose of poetry—quite apart from what any one poem happens to say. It is to break this lazy, supine leaning on the past that we "create" anything. That we re-realize the world. That we create ourselves. Thus, to lie back on the soft fatty breast of the past is the very opposite of what you should be doing" ["Letter to Mangan"]

"The fatty breast of the past"! A world of anxieties about originality, independence, and manhood rest in that metaphor. How to free oneself from that matronly breast? Clearly, through the creation of new metrical structures. Since a truly American language remains to be invented, not what one says but how one says it will determine whether a new and American poetry is possible. Poirier has noted how American writers grudgingly acknowledge that "language itself remained the one unavoidable cultural inheritance, the one forever demanding Old World institution, that could not be dispensed with. However, a felt need to dispense with it" became "unremitting, not to be assuaged" (Poirier 1992 134). Williams, who in this regard is very much in the tradition that Poirier calls "Emersonian," felt that an American language could be discerned through the development of a new measure adequate to the landscape or mindscape of the New World.

Undoubtedly, Williams felt hindered in this project because he saw American culture in a colonial, not a freely commercial, relation to European cultural production. The point was not to moan about the situation but to produce work that would make Europe (and Euro-enculturated America) sit up and take notice, work that would change the relationship and reverse the flow of cultural influence. This aim could be accomplished, he thought, only by taking the proper measure of his native place, by replacing the European metronome with something variable, dynamic, slippery, relative—but for all of that, also physical and concrete.

Moving on to Pound, one sees that in *Guide to Kulchur* (1937) Pound found it useful to juxtapose a discussion of Charlemagne's "just price" with Flaubert's "just word" (*GK* 47–49). Pound insists on the linkage between verbal accuracy and money as an accurate measure, as "a measured claim." A passage from a letter to C. H. Douglas complaining about the muddled vocabulary typical of economics vividly illustrates this linkage:

CLEAR TERMINOLOGY
T E R M I N O L O G Y

distinction between meanings of different words.
capital not same as PROPERTY
partaggio, not same as usura.
money not same as credit.
money a measured claim. Claim is one thing
            measure is another
These damn blokes make econ/ unreadable . and help the enemy
            [EP to C. H. Douglas, July 22, 1936, Beinecke Library]

In his economic tracts, Pound would define money as a "certificate for work done" (*SP* 212). He asked: "Can we say that perfect money consists in true certificates of goods extant?" (*SP* 206). Either way we can see that money (as opposed to credit) is supposed to stand for something concrete, something real, something accomplished. Pound defined "credit as the future tense of money" (*SP* 278, 315), so money itself ought always to be in the present tense; it should be in a strict correspondence with what actually exists. (It would follow that debt is the past tense of money—it is a claim in the present against what was in the past—death encroaching on life.) There is a connection here to Williams's need for a measure of the concrete present. The link between their theories of measure is the Jeffersonian fear of abstraction— especially the abstractions of finance and the entanglements of debt— but also the fear of "the enemy," apparently those who corrupt us by enforcing cultural indebtedness and obfuscating categories. What is

wanted is a system of terms, both linguistic and economic, that will
enable us to stay in "contact" with reality without entangling us in a
hell of ambivalences.

In his scattered remarks concerning the use of poetic measure,
Pound is best remembered for the Imagist principle "to compose in the
sequence of the musical phrase, not in sequence of a metronome" (LE
3)—a principle that Williams had in mind in the lines from Paterson
quoted above. Pound also said, "I believe in an 'absolute rhythm,' a
rhythm, that is, in poetry which corresponds exactly to the shade of
emotion to be expressed. A man's rhythm must be interpretive, it will
be, therefore, in the end, his own, uncounterfeiting, uncounterfei-
table" (LE 9). Even in these very early remarks, when Pound speaks of
poetic measure, monetary analogies intrude. Pound suggests that a
man's rhythm depends on his character (another monetary analogy),[15]
which allows him to suggest the image of counterfeiting. The true poet
deals in true coin. True coin must be an accurate measure of the reality
of emotion or shades of emotion.

"No intelligent man will be content to treat economics merely as
economics," Pound wrote in Eliot's Criterion in 1935 (SP 250). When
he speaks of monetary measure, he means poetry as well. This connection can help us make sense of some moments in the difficult late cantos, notably those inspired by the historical work of Alexander Del
Mar, whose History of Monetary Systems (1895), written during the
height of Populist money agitation, underwrites these lines from
Canto 97:

> "Salzburg alone struck full weight."
> The 1806 Prussian notes
>   ran 90 years,
> Octonary sun-worshipping Baltic.
> 371 $^1/_4$ grains silver in Del's time
> as I have seen them by shovels full
>   lit by gas flares.
>   One wd/ suppose Theresa's 390,
>   but were, apparently, 353 and a fraction,
> at Salzburg 5 more, or supposedly 361, or
> "Window-dressing" as Bryan admitted to Kitson [97:687]

No explication can make these lines (some might call them notes) less
than forbidding. I will not attempt to suggest that this passage

"works" as poetry to any common reader. Nonetheless it makes sense. The obsession with measure shown here in Pound's repetition of the ratios between gold and silver coinage in several nineteenth-century currencies speaks of his need to devise a poetic measure consonant with monetary measures. More exactly, Pound sees the problem of monetary measure as another manifestation of the same problem as poetic measure.[16] In fact the whole procedure of making poetry out of the activity of taking notes from reading Del Mar suggests a kind of verbal ratio, as though Del Mar's silver prose were being recoined as Pound's golden poetry. Like Williams, Pound thought there ought to be a discernible ratio between words and things or between values and their signs. For Pound however, this ratio, like the ratios between gold and silver coins that specified exactly how many grains of silver equalled a certain unit of gold, is neither some natural fact nor some usefully vague, pragmatic, approximation it requires legislation. Pound's memory of William Jennings Bryan's remark to Arthur Kitson that bimetallism is just "window-dressing"[17] reveals that Pound is interested in reviving not a poetic gold standard but "sound money"; that is, he is interested in creating a sound measure of value, and, more broadly, of reality.

Del Mar's *History* serves for Pound as a metaphysical text and not just an economic text. The historian's compilation of currency ratios reminds Pound of the arbitrary nature of money. His childhood memory of seeing silver dollars shoveled into the furnaces of the Philadelphia Mint for recoining are proof that the mark on the metal is important, not the metal itself. It is not just the metal content but the stamp on the coin that creates value, that makes it exchangeable. In another moment in the same Canto Pound recalls how "in 1914 british sovreigns [sic] / poured into the Philadelphia mint in great quantity / and were promptly restamped with eagles" (97:684).

These late cantos implicitly refer to measuring systems that only the poet has the will to legislate. For "When King's quit [legislating value], the bankers began again," Pound notes with distress, with their "CONtinuous effort to have it"—that is, the units of monetary measure, and therefore the rate of exchange—"different somewhere or other" (97:686). Pound means that interested parties, "the enemy," wangle and fudge what should be sovereign, even sacred, standards for their personal profit. Currency trading consists precisely in creating, maintaining, and profiting from fluctuations in monetary values. In the absence of "kings" or other disinterested parties with the proper terminology and the true knowledge of what words mean, and therefore of what measures of value are, only the poet can articulate proper measures of value. "All value comes from labour and nature" (*SP* 264) Pound observed physiocratically, but the units of measure, like language itself, must, of course, be man-made. Hence the importance of the poet, master of measure.

Pound (and Williams in a slightly different way) assert that poesis takes precedence over production. They recognize, that is, that economic systems are fundamentally ethical systems. As a domain of knowledge, economics ought to acknowledge its canons of value instead of pretending that it simply describes them. What economies mean cannot be separated from what they do. By the same token, poetry must be rescued from a sterile aesthetics of "beauty" and used to measure reality—that is, social and economic justice.

Pound's quasi-mathematical presentation of monetary ratios suggests a sense of measure markedly different from Williams's "pragmatic" flex or variableness. But we would be wrong, I think, to draw conclusions about Pound's poetic practice from what looks like ideological dogmatism. The tone of the lines from Canto 97 suggests a looseness and ease not unlike that of Williams. The difference is that the terrain traversed by Pound's verse is the pages of Del Mar's book, not the American landscape. Perhaps, since Pound is a prisoner as he writes his poem, this observation is not so very surprising, but we can say that Pound's poetry dramatizes the act of reading in a way Williams's does not. The contact that Pound seeks, or at least that of which he speaks in his verse, is contact with the written, rather than the spoken word.

What are we to make of this unexpected affinity between two "high Modernist" writers and their Enlightenment forebears? What are the implications for Modernism? One way to answer this question would be to argue that literary Modernism, as such, does not exist—that it is, at best, an austere mode of writing that attempts to recover an eighteenth-century "purity" of expression from beneath the blobby, luxurious, excesses of the nineteenth century. This, surely, is the project on which Pound and Williams—and so many other Modernist writers—saw themselves embarked. Twentieth-century Modernism, then, is most obviously a matter of rhetorical surfaces, a paring down, a carving away, a flattening, the substitution, as Pound put it, of the austere and direct, for "rhetorical din and luxurious riot" (*LE* 12).

It should by now be clear that this austere, yet flexible, aesthetic is politically overdetermined. The literary Modernism of Pound and Williams is underwritten by an alternative account of modernity. It has been convenient to label such an account reactionary. More accurately it is a different interpretation, a highly critical analysis of the fruits of so-called Western so-called civilization. We know that Pound and Williams in particular were not reactionaries in part from their willingness to test their poetry and thinking against economics, the dominant social science of the century, a discourse so suddenly secure in its premises that it felt ready to drop its historical qualifier, the very unscientific adjective "political."

3

THE VIRTUES OF DISTRIBUTION
A Genealogy of Poundian Economics

Ezra Pound's unorthodox economic views have long formed an obstacle between him and his readers. Despite repeated attempts by critics—notably Earle Davis in *Vision Fugitive* (1958) and Leon Surette in *Light from Eleusis* (1979)—to explain his economics, the impression persists that Pound was a "money-crank." Pound does often sound like a crank when he tackles economic subjects, and his Fascism and anti-Semitism undoubtedly have much to do with the rejection of his economics, but they are not the same thing. As Surette points out, Pound became interested in the money question before Fascism existed, and his radical anti-Semitism did not fully manifest itself until the early 1940s (Surette 1979 92). "Social Credit," the economic program invented by Major C. H. Douglas with which Pound's name is most often linked, has been associated with anti-Semitism for the good reason that Douglas himself was an anti-Semite, but Social Credit itself is not essentially a racist program. The American Social Credit Movement founded by the literary critic Gorham Munson, with which William Carlos Williams was involved, is explicit in its rejection of anti-Semitism.

It is much more useful to see Pound's economics as infused with the spirit of Jefferson than it is with that of Mussolini, just as it is more useful to think of his economic beliefs as, on the whole, ahead of their time than it is to see them as simply naive or mistaken. The "unorthodox" basis of Pound's economics, the recognition of underconsumption in the face of Say's Law of Markets and the quantity theory of money, are now acknowledged to be correct. His valorization of the producer and the concomitant rejection of finance capitalism show the poet to be a Jeffersonian—a dissident but hardly discredited economic position.

68

Distribution Versus Production

Broadly speaking, the reforming zeal of the Jeffersonian money radicals like Pound, unlike that of the Marxists, focuses on the problems of distribution, not on production. As literary theory and historical discourse are currently conceived, it is perhaps important to address this difference of emphasis in Marxist terms. In the preface to the *Critique of Political Economy* (1859), Marx describes the crucial role in history of economics in general and production in particular:

> In the social production of their existence, men enter into definite relations, which are independent of their will, namely relations of production appropriate to a given stage in the development of their material forces of production. The totality of these relations of production constitutes the economic structure of society, the real foundation, on which arises a legal and political superstructure and to which correspond definite forms of social consciousness. The mode of production of material life conditions the general process of social, political, and intellectual life. It is not the consciousness of men that determines their existence but their social existence that determines their consciousness. At a certain stage of development, the material productive forces of society come into conflict with the existing relations of production or—this merely expresses the same thing in legal terms— with the property relations within the framework of which they have operated hitherto. From forms of development of the productive forces these relations turn into their fetters. [Marx 1975 425]

These developments, which Marx called the "the guiding principle of my studies," led inevitably to the "era of social revolution" (425–26). This passage is worth quoting at such length because it contains so much of what we think of as "Marxist"—especially the shaping role of the relations of production on the "social structures" that determine the consciousness of society. Through the available modes and relations of production we produce ourselves and this constitutes the "social production" of (our) existence. We are then, produced by historical forces.

Marxism, in theory and practice, has laid great stress on this word "production." This emphasis is an artifact of Marx's own historical position in the nineteenth century: he was forging his ideas when capital formation and accumulation were put into relief by the new productive forces unleashed by the factory system and steam power. Production itself, however, is but half of an industrial economy. Modes and relations of distribution (sometimes too easily equated with exchange) are equally important. While the followers of Marx continued to emphasize the pivotal role of production, they ignored the determinative character of distribution, which was, apparently, to solve itself in the fulfillment of the social revolution and the centralization of "all instruments of production in the hands of the State (Marx and Engels 104).[1] In their *Manifesto*, Marx and Engels correctly identified the primary existing threat to the regime of capital as "the epidemic of overproduction" (86). Overproduction, the phenomenon of goods unable to find a market, is, of course, a problem of distribution (Livingston 1994 53–55).

As the nineteenth century wore on, periodic crises resulting from gluts of goods did indeed cause a series of depressions and great social instability, just as Marx had predicted. But capital proved far more adaptable than Marx had imagined. The invention of the private corporation in midcentury "provided capitalists with a more flexible and far-reaching instrument than earlier forms of ownership" (Trachtenberg 4). The corporation submerged the identity of the capitalist in a powerful legal fiction, whereby a body—that is, a corpus—of owners is treated as a single entity; an entity, moreover, with no individual liability in law. Second, the corporation can sell shares in itself, a privilege previously limited to certain government monopolies. The effect was to create a pervasive new order of "fictional" property and a new financial market in this new paper. This new form of capital was, equally, a new mode of distribution; a mode peculiar to finance capitalism. As Alan Trachtenberg has argued in *The Incorporation of America*, the new corporate form was greeted uneasily and was resisted by folks of the Jeffersonian persuasion in the name of America itself; the corporation was perceived by Jeffersonians as a "misappropriation" (7) of the meaning of America. The struggle over the corporation was, finally, a struggle over reality (8). More precisely, this was a struggle over the distribution of reality, for the incorporation of America extended financial fictions where they had never been before.

By the twentieth century, stocks and bonds had become generally available. But this extension of the market was not, as might be thought, its democratization. On the contrary, as more smaller investors donated their savings to the financial markets, so the financial market began to control ordinary lives.[2]

To further understand the line of economic dissent called Jeffersonianism, it may usefully be regarded as concerned with the problems, the frictions, and even the metaphysics of the modes and relations of distribution as they become complicated by the evolution of capitalism—especially finance capitalism. Historically, the Jeffersonian critique of capitalism is revealed in a variety of schemes (some quite utopic) to improve and democratize distributive forces by reforming what we might call the modes of distribution—principally money.

The nineteenth-century Jeffersonian protest movements, like the Knights of Labor, the Populists, and Henry George's "Single-Taxers" were all, in part, responses to the monopolistic practices of the railroads, which sought to exert absolute control over the distribution of produce through the manipulations of freight rates. Henry George, arguably the most important economist America has ever produced, was, when a young newspaperman, radicalized by the refusal of the telegraph company owned by the railroad trusts to wire stories critical of railroad machinations. The experience crystallized his awareness of the effect of monopoly on distribution—in this case not only of goods but also of information.[3] His later formulation of the land problem in *Progress and Poverty* (1879) and his lifelong political agitation for economic justice worked through distributive reform, through a revision of the status and taxation of landed property. If he says little about production it is because, unlike Marx, he believes that if distribution is made equitable many of the problems of production will cease to be problems. Twenty-one years younger than Marx but, like him, concerned with the problem of poverty amid plenty, George could already write (in 1879, the year C. H. Douglas was born):

> The cause which, in spite of the enormous increase of productive power, confines the great body of producers to the least share of the product upon which they will consent to live, is not the limitation of capital, nor yet the powers of nature which respond to labor. As it is not therefore, to be found in the laws which bound the production of wealth, it must be sought in the laws which govern distribution. [George 154]

If George is not "classically" Jeffersonian in dismissing the "limitation of capital"—the scarcity of money, or credit—as a principal cause of economic inequality, he confirms the Jeffersonian position by implying that (in Marxist terms) the surplus value of the social product is appropriated by finance capital—in George's example, the landlords. The essence of the problem is not profit but rent—both rent on land and rent on money in the form of interest. Clearly, rent is a charge for distribution because it is a charge for access to the opportunities of capital.

To sum up, we can capture much of the economic stance of the Jeffersonians if we replace Marx's emphasis on "production" with the word "distribution." As a test, using the same example from Marx quoted earlier, we get the following formulation:

> In the social *distribution* of their existence, men enter into definite relations, which are independent of their will, namely relations of *distribution* appropriate to a given stage in the development of their material forces of *distribution*. The totality of these relations of *distribution* constitutes the economic structure of society, the real foundation, on which arises a legal and political superstructure and to which correspond definite forms of social consciousness. The mode of *distribution* of material life conditions the general process of social, political and intellectual life. It is not the consciousness of men that determines their existence, but their social existence that determines their consciousness. At a certain stage of development, the material *distributive* forces of society come into conflict with the existing relations of *distribution* or—this merely expresses the same thing in legal terms—with the property relations within the framework of which they have operated hitherto. From forms of development of the *distributive* forces these relations turn into their fetters. [Marx 1975 425]

A moment of reflection on the differences between this confected passage and Marx's actual words serves to indicate the very different direction of Jeffersonianism. First, it is important to see that the passage still makes sense—indeed much the same sense that it made before. That it does so reveals the intimate relation between production and distribution. The difference between Marxist and Jeffersonian positions is one of emphasis. An emphasis on distribution addresses only the effects of production; Marx's own emphasis, on production itself, is more radical because seizing control of the means of production is seen as the key to all property relations, which themselves are but the distributive effects of capital.

The Jeffersonian position seeks to preserve the stability of property relations by removing them from the arena of capital and thus of exchange, and by reforming the modes of distribution. It insists that all that is needed is control over the means of distribution and argues that such control can be legislated. The common features of this strand of Jeffersonian dissent, from Jefferson himself, through George and Douglas to Pound, is threefold.

First, control over the distribution of credit, for the flow of money is the key to the flow of goods and services. Banks take the place of the capitalist as the source of social injustice. Second, free trade: the Jeffersonians take a *laissez faire* attitude toward foreign trade. They are against all tariffs and protectionism, since these amount to the unnatural protection of mercantile profits, while hindering access to the foreign markets so important for agricultural surpluses. Third, the Jeffersonians share with the Marxists a strong antipathy to monopolies and, like them, they see the monopolistic tendency as integral to capitalism. Unlike the Marxists, however, the Jeffersonians see the parallel monopolistic tendency in politics not as an artifact of capitalistic productive modes but as something in human nature. They see mankind as naturally possessive; they do not regard acquisitiveness as bourgeois false consciousness; they do not even consider it bourgeois. In Hofstadter's striking phrase, the Jeffersonians are biased toward a "democracy in cupidity rather than a democracy of fraternity" (Hofstadter 1948 xxxvii). As this acquisitive tendency must be countered politically with checks and balances, so in economics it must be addressed through a commitment to distributive justice. This view helps explain the characteristic Jeffersonian perception that society consists of debtors and creditors, that is, a perception that "classes" are defined by the relations governing the distribution of money, not the production of real wealth.

These are but general positions. There is no real Jeffersonian idea of a "social being" as there is in Marx; the whole concept of the individual and his relation to society is, of course, utterly different. Where Marx saw history as "the history of class struggles" (Marx and Engels 79) and these classes as composed of "social beings" who are not recognizable in any meaningful *political sense* as individuals, the Jeffersonian vision is predicated on a radical individualism which, nonetheless, and somewhat paradoxically, is able to cohere in the spirit of class collaboration—not by "ironing out class struggle" (Gorham Munson's phrase) in the Fascist manner but by transcending it. This spirit is expressed in theory by the democratic notion that every individual has an equal share in the state.

The Federal Reserve and Corporate Liberalism

Many of the demands made by the Populist Jeffersonians found their way into respectable Progressive ideology of the first decades of the twentieth century (Hofstadter 1955 131–34). Progressivism eventually became bipartisan, realizing itself in the platform of the Progressive (Bull Moose) Party of Theodore Roosevelt and in the ideals of the "Reform" Democrats led by Woodrow Wilson, who promised "the application of Jeffersonian principles to our present day America" (Goldman 170).

The most significant application of these principles as they bear on the "money question" took a perversely Hamiltonian form in the Federal Reserve System. Created in 1913, controlled neither by a group of bankers nor by Congress, the Federal Reserve Board in Washington, a putatively nonpolitical body, oversaw a system of twelve regional Federal Reserve banks that remained under private control. The central Board would decide overall banking policy, and the member banks could advise, but could not vote on decisions (Greider 277). The system was a hybrid institution at best, and Wall Streeters and Populists alike decried the compromise (278–79).

The Federal Reserve has been called "the prototype for the modern liberal state" (Greider 280). It is in many ways the epitome of what Martin Sklar calls "corporate liberalism":[4] "The Fed would pursue large public objectives, but it would also serve private economic interests. It was exactly the mixture of purposes—protecting private profit and the public interest at the same time—that was the hallmark of modern liberal institutions" (Greider 280). In the long run this arrangement had the effect of removing the "money question" from political debate and repressing the deeper aspects of the money issue—the meaning of money—an error Ezra Pound hoped to redress by encouraging Eustace Mullins's populistic exposé *The Secrets of the Federal Reserve* (1952), which has found its way into the reading of the American right wing.[5] After 1913, however, most Americans stopped worrying about what money was and who benefited from the way it was defined and distributed. Instead they tried to be grateful for the relatively flexible monetary policies of the Federal Reserve. The Fed's most important explicit purpose by its own account was "to give the country an elastic currency," to "help counteract inflationary and deflationary movements, and to share in creating conditions favorable to a sustained, high level of employment, a stable dollar, growth of the country and a rising level of consumption" (Federal Reserve 1). The Federal Reserve was designed to avert crashes, depressions, and periods of inflation and to provide a more stable business climate. It did so by controlling the "price of credit" (85) through the interest rate, which operates like a valve to control the supply of money available to borrowers.

This functional endorsement of the quantity theory of money suggests the degree to which Populist money agitation had educated the nation about how money works. If money is cheap—that is, available at a low rate of interest—it should also be plentiful, following the logic of supply and demand. When money is plentiful, prices rise, and producers get more for their produce. Scarce money is reflected in higher interest rates, and its higher cost *makes all other prices fall* even if the quantity of commodities on sale stays the same. This is in accordance with the quantity theory of money, "the historic theorem which holds that prices, the volume of trade being given, will vary in direct proportion to the supply of money" (Galbraith 1987 34). It is interesting that in orthodox English economic circles this proposition was still a radical heresy until the Great Depression of the 1930s made economists like Keynes believers in it. Yet in the United States, the 1892 "Omaha Platform" of the People's Party had called for "a national currency, safe, sound and *flexible,* issued by the general government only" (my emphasis, quoted in Unger 1964 40).

The quantity theory of money seemed to explain a fact of economic life to which farmers have historically been especially sensitive, since their seasonal cash flow requires them to borrow against the harvest in spring and pay off loans in the fall. In spring, money is tight in agricultural areas because farmers borrow in preparation for planting. The law of supply and demand dictates that interest on such loans will be as high as the market will bear. Over the summer, interest on the loans remains constant, while crop prices may fluctuate or fall, even if the weather is kind, reducing the profits on grain or stock at harvest time.[6]

It is obvious that such a situation puts creditors at a great advantage over producers unless they are restrained by a system of values that prizes production of actual goods (and, in this case, the perpetuation of small farms) over the production of paper profits. It is also clear that under such conditions the price of a commodity, like wheat, will also reflect the cost of borrowing money. It follows that prices of goods are to an important degree determined by the price of money—a conclusion that runs quite counter to the ideal of a "free market," in which prices are determined by supply and demand in the marketplace itself.

"The quantity theory of money," Leon Surette explains, "amounts to the proposition that the price of goods and services is a function of their costs, the supply, the demand for them, *and* the supply of money" (Surette's emphasis, 1986 87). Money under such circumstances represents not real wealth—that is, goods—but power. It is the sign not of abundance but of the coercion of scarcity. Those who controlled the supply of money effectively controlled the market for goods. As Surette points out, quantity theory today "seems self-evident, but in the 1930's it had to overcome the massive influence of Ricardo, who held a commodity theory of money" (87–88), which assumed that gold was the only "real" money and that its value, like that of other commodities, reflected the costs of its extraction and production. There are many problems with this now discredited orthodoxy even if we regard gold as the only real monetary form, but in actuality paper money—which the Populists called "credit money"—obviously accounts for the bulk of the monetary supply. With the collapse of the gold standard even the pretense that money is a commodity has been dropped, and today no one pretends that money has any other basis than credit.

An early believer in the quantity theory of money, Pound insisted that Americans (and by extension all producers) should "DIVIDE your crops AFTER the harvest" (May 28, 1942, *EPS* 153). This was the difference, he insisted, between "*Usura* and *partaggio*." The usury system forces natural values and production—for example, a given quantity of wheat—to measure up to prior monetary debts. The Physiocratic Pound thought that it ought to be the *source* of value. The institution of interest divides the "fruits of labor and nature" (April 6, 1942, RS 83) *before* the harvest. If the harvest is bad, the interest must still be paid in money or the farmer must forfeit real property. As we have seen, foreclosure is the destruction of real values to prop up artificial percentages on paper. An honest money system should derive its values from what is yielded when nature and labor work together. The role of debtor and creditor ought to be reversed. Monetary values ought to reflect the volume of production, rather than be assigned by creditors, who artificially inflate costs by adding bank charges to real values. Pound follows J. A. Hobson, Lenin, and Douglas in asserting that if this is not done, imperialism and global conflict are inevitable. Sounding a great deal like Crèvecoeur, he argues that *Usura* is "a corrosive charge that finally undermines ANY nation. Undermines it at home, drives it into unsound foreign relations, drives it OUT of land gone to waste (needlessly left to rot, to erode) drives it into indecent incursions into less civilized countries, or smaller or weaker countries. Always eating away at the life inside the nation" (May 28, 1942, RS 153).

If Pound is right, then when the Populists campaigned for a government sympathetic to farmers and other producers, they were, in effect, campaigning for a different system of values, which they called "democratic." The usury system is antidemocratic because it benefits the powerful few at the expense of the vulnerable many by controlling the measure of value (money itself) and therefore its signification in prices.

If quantity theory is the basis for a science of money, then the political question of who controls the supply of money can never be disassociated from political goals, as these necessarily reflect social values. The amount of available money is clearly contingent upon any judgment of what amount is "correct," which automatically becomes a problem of prices and ultimately of value. Once seen as the arbiter of value, few thoughtful people can argue that the Federal Reserve is a nonpolitical institution.

Still, the Federal Reserve Act of 1913 seemed to settle the problem of political control over the money supply. If its passage laid to rest the money question as a popular political issue, concern about banks continued. The deeper issue, some thought, was not the problem of a private monopoly over money but, rather, the monopoly over credit, and this remained hidden from public oversight, since the loan policy of private banks remained outside governmental control, even as their lending rate reflected the rate established by the Federal Reserve Board. Without a democracy of credit, the old Populist demand that the "money of this country should be kept as much as possible in the hands of the people" remained a utopic dream (Unger 1964 40). The founding of the Federal Reserve was an unwieldy compromise, credit itself was still effectively a monopoly of the banks.

The Art in Finance: Charles Ferguson, the *New Age*, and Arthur Kitson

Shortly after the founding of the Federal Reserve, Charles Ferguson, an ardent Wilsonian and financial visionary, published two books about the power of banks as centers of "social credit."[7] *The Great News* (1915) and *Revolution Absolute* (1918) reveal a grasp of credit and the potential power of finance that anticipates the power of international banking and monetary funds to shape and contain the coming world.

In spite of the war then raging in Europe, and because he was convinced that the war reflected irresolvable contradictions between an emerging business system and a superannuated political system that perverted the functions of both, Ferguson believed that "in the long run it will be clearly seen that the international business system—in spite of its cruelties and in spite of the tragic miscarriages of this last terrible year—is, on the whole, a serious effort of Western civilization to escape from provincialism into a spacious kingdom of the free spirit." And he continued, "the business system has been forced into self-contradiction and brought disaster to the world, because it has not yet been treated with moral seriousness" (Ferguson 1915 3, 4).[8] The only institution capable of resolving such contradictions was the bank. Ferguson saw banks as the new world power, superseding nations. He argued:

> *The bank as credit-centre is the most subtle and powerful organ of social control that has yet appeared within the universal field of politics.* A way has been found whereby a single central organ can determine the general direction of enterprise and administer the artistic and scientific abilities of a community. It can dispose not only of actual values but also of potential values. It can command time-distance as railroads and telegraphs command space-distance. The bulk of its transactions are actuarial and prophetic. It reaches forward and handles the stuff of the future. [Ferguson's emphasis, 1915 163]

Ferguson's understanding of the vatic power of finance infuses the financial system with the poetic and the paranoid in ways that are typically Jeffersonian. Jefferson saw, Ferguson argued, that "the development of credit, contractualism and corporate finance was compelling the whole fabric of wealth to break loose from nature and become a kind of prodigious work of art" (29).[9] Importantly, Ferguson understood credit power as a form of imaginative power (156–60). Ferguson worried that the patent artificiality of a modern economy based on financial values rather than actual production tended to confuse industry with commerce. The first is concerned primarily with humankind's relationship to nature and is essentially a progressive operation; the second is concerned with our relationship to other people. Commercial competition works against industry, even destroys it by causing destructive wars. Accepting, as he does, much of Hobson's analysis in *Imperialism*, Ferguson envisions a proto-Douglasite solution in his call for "Public Service Banks," and "credit-administration" as the solution to modern problems of government (276–78).

Financial credit has no basis in things in existence. Rather it is founded on things that exist in the imagination. In this sense, Ferguson was right, credit is very much like art; it is engaged in the creation of tangible values from invisible desires.[10] He saw that the "financial revolution" succeeded in defining wealth primarily in what we might now call "textual" terms. It was based, not so much on production or "goods in the shop" as on control over the possibility of production and the ultimate distribution of goods. And this control was invested in pieces of paper that—Federal Reserve or no Federal Reserve—remained under the control of the creditor class.

Ferguson's ideas found ears most immediately in England, where the war effort was bringing the existing financial arrangements into question. A. R. Orage's eclectic weekly, *New Age*, "An Independent Socialist Review of Politics, Literature, and Art," proved to be an influential vehicle for criticism of the British financial establishment (Redman 18).[11] Orage, as Leon Surette has shown, was already "the crossroads for the two dominant radical ideological postures of pre-war Britain" (Surette 1983 437). The *New Age* represented a kind of "middle ground" between the ideals of Fabian Democratic Socialism and the Ruskinian critique of modernity best represented by the conservatism of Hilaire Belloc and G. K. Chesterton (Surette 1983).

Orage's magazine opened its pages to Major C. H. Douglas (1879–1952), the founder of Social Credit, as well as to antibank writers like Arthur Kitson, author of the antibullionist work *The Scientific Solution of the Money Question* (1894). As Flory has noticed, this book led to his friendship with William Jennings Bryan (Flory 1989 40). Kitson even worked for Bryan in the campaign of 1896, thus linking American Populism to English monetary reform movements.[12] By his own account, Kitson's work helped inspire Douglas, and as early as 1921, Kitson pronounced himself a Douglasite (Kitson 12).

Douglas's works, *Social Credit* (1918), *Economic Democracy* (1919), and *Credit Power and Democracy* (1920) (the last book with an extensive commentary by Orage), which became the basis of a worldwide Social Credit movement, were serialized in the *New Age*. Douglas was an "attentive" reader of Charles Ferguson (Munson 185) and he was well aware of the American Populist critique of capitalism; the revised edition of *Social Credit* (1933) would feature the peroration of Bryan's "Cross of Gold" Speech.[13]

Ezra Pound wrote for Orage's paper for ten years, between 1911 and 1921 (Redman 17). His "Homage to Sextus Propertius," one of his greatest poems, appeared in the same issue with Douglas's *Economic Democracy* (Kenner 302). Like Orage, Pound was converted to Social Credit by Douglas's powerful claims for a practical simple solution to the "money question."

There can be little doubt that Pound's experience at the *New Age* reaffirmed the centrality of the populistic political issues he had grown up with. I agree with Tim Redman that "during his decade-long association with Orage and *The New Age* Pound received . . . a complete political and economic education, including doctrine, rhetoric and attitudes that will show up, time and again, in his political and economic writings of the thirties and forties" (50). If *The New Age* was Pound's Oxford and Cambridge, and if, as Surette argues, Pound's encounter with Douglas was his "conversion experience" (Surette 1983 451), the "money question" propounded by the American populists had fully prepared him to absorb what he found there.

By the early 1930s, inspired by the Great Depression, William Carlos Williams was also lecturing on Social Credit.[14] Mike Weaver, in what is almost the only discussion of Williams's Social Credit views, reports that Williams became interested in Douglas's movement not, as is generally believed, primarily because of Pound, but rather through Gorham Munson, the literary critic and founder of the Social Credit review *New Democracy* (1933–1936) (Weaver 103–4).[15] As Weaver also points out, James Laughlin, later Pound's and Williams's publisher, wrote for *New Democracy* and his publishing house, *New Directions,* "was born within the pages of *New Democracy* and so named by Munson" (104).

The manifesto of the American Social Credit Movement is frankly Jeffersonian, standing for "Democracy, that form of society in which government and communal organization exist for the benefit of the individuals composing the community" and "for the Bill of Rights" (authored by Jefferson) (quoted in Weaver 105). Distancing itself from Major Douglas's well-known anti-Semitic leanings, the ASCM explicitly "abominated" anti-Semitism. It was also "unalterably opposed to totalitarianism and collectivism, social systems in which the individual exists only for the group. No Fascism. No Communism" (Weaver 105). Douglas's system was to be "a third resolvent force" that would destroy the violently oppositional character of contemporary Left/Right politics. It promised Jeffersonian answers to twentieth-century economic and social problems. Jeffersonian ideology, then, underlies Social Credit as Pound and Williams understood it.

What Was Social Credit?

Like other economic reformers, including Karl Marx, C. H. Douglas was obsessed with the moral problem of poverty amid plenty. The series of questions that opens *The Monopoly of Credit* (1931) approaches the economic question much as Henry George had in *Progress and Poverty* (1879). They are the same that drove the American Populists to their political insurrection, questions many were asking themselves in the depression year of 1931. Finally, they form the "Ariadne's thread" binding together Pound's *Cantos:*

> How is it possible for a world which is suffering from over-production to be in economic distress? Where does money come from? Why should we economise when we are making too many goods? How can an unemployment problem, together with a manufacturing and agricultural organization which cannot obtain orders, exist side by side with a poverty problem? Must we balance our budget? Why should we

be asked to have confidence in our money system if it works properly? [Douglas 1931, no page number]

These questions, as Gorham Munson points out, are consumerist. Douglas is concerned primarily with the just distribution of goods—not profits. "A consumers' policy," Munson claims, "is automatically bound to be democratic, classless, socially just, since in the nature of things it must be a policy for everybody" (Munson 192).

> The latent psychological strength of a consumers' policy can hardly be underestimated. The consumers' will is the will-to-plenty. It is a life-or-death matter to the consumer to acquire the necessaries of existence, but modern man is completely unsatisfied with a brute subsistence. His urgency to get goods and services extending into the categories of comforts, amenities, and luxuries is acute. In present circumstances almost everyone is striving for a higher standard of living, and this creates an unremitting pressure against the ceiling of artificial scarcity. A rising standard of living is precisely the aim of a consumers' policy, and is the test for economic democracy whenever it shall be instituted. [Munson 192]

As Douglas saw them, the major problems for consumers were twofold. First, there was a paradox of overproduction in an economic system that determined value in terms of scarcity. This led to the odd problem of certain useful goods not being worth the cost of production. Second, the technological imperative within industry to make production more efficient also reduced the need for labor. Notions of efficiency based on the unexamined premises of cost accounting, that is, on financial, not social, values, meant that unemployment was as much a product of capitalism as the goods produced. One of the unresolved contradictions of contemporary consumer capitalism remains the fact that unemployed people without income cannot consume goods very readily. Yet reduced demand means reduced profits unless more workers are laid off to reduce costs, further reducing demand; this is what economists call "under-consumption"—a phenomenon long denied, as it contradicted Say's Law of Markets, "the rock-bed foundation of classical economics. Say's Law states that 'the whole of the costs of production must necessarily be spent in the aggregate, directly, or indirectly, on purchasing the product' " (Surette 1979 83). Underconsumption suggests that productive power is not, as once held by orthodox economists, automatically matched by purchasing power, prices are not "an emanation from the production of real commodities or services" (Douglas 1931 23). Instead, the increase of productive power made available by improving machinery steadily reduces the base of wage earners, thereby reducing aggregate purchasing power. The capitalistic ideal of business efficiency is belied by the social inefficiency it creates. "Cost-cutting" by reducing labor costs really means shifting the burden of costs elsewhere; laid-off workers are put on the public dole. In effect, the public pays them not to work in order to maintain private profits.

In the face of these contradictions, Douglas promoted "economic democracy." Its principal enemy, he tried to show, was "the credit monopoly." Douglas called finance "the nerve system of distribution" and observed that "Finance, i.e., money, is the starting point of every action which requires either the cooperation of the community or the use of its assets" (1931 2). The problem, of course, is that finance is not under any sort of democratic control, yet it acts like an "Invisible Government" (1933 66). By controlling credit, the Invisible Government of Finance determines not only what is produced but also who is able to buy it. In Douglas's analysis, it turns out that purchasing power—the ability of consumers to pay for goods—was forever inadequate to pay for everything produced. Prices are not the reflection of the total costs of production, as generally claimed, but are arbitrarily created when banks loan money at interest to producers, who, in turn, distribute it to their employees and shareholders in the form of wages, salaries, and dividends. Under such a system, purchasing power can never keep up with production. The costs of such a credit economy, especially the costs of servicing debts, which are paid off by the people through taxes and bank charges, must sap consumer purchasing power.

In theory, the primary goal of industry is to produce goods, but the purpose of capitalism is to make money. Industrial efficiency therefore demands that the most goods be produced with the least possible cost and sold at the highest possible price. Douglas noted that the cost of labor is the easiest of all costs to control, yet these "costs," once deposited with the labor force in the form of salaries and wages, are its purchasing power. The logic that leads to the investment in labor-saving machinery to reduce labor costs consequently results in a larger and larger mass of unemployed workers, thereby reducing aggregate purchasing power. In response, prices fall, reducing profits, leading to layoffs in an endless spiral of industrial depression. The logic of industrial capitalism demands unemployment, while social justice and an efficient market demand jobs. The unemployed, of course, barely subsisting on "the dole" or other forms of charitable relief, are not only unfairly stigmatized by a moral code that equates work anachronistically with virtue but are also denied the means to relieve the economy of its glut of goods. In short, industrial efficiency is at odds with social efficiency; the result is industrial crisis.

What Douglas discerned through his experience as an aircraft manufacturer during World War I and in the economic dislocation that followed was a condensed and intensified version of the drama of industry, which some economic historians call "capital accumulation and disaccumulation."[16] The enormous expansion of industry made necessary by the war effort, financed by government credits, produced real economic prosperity. Douglas noticed that "war is a consumer whose necessities are so imperative they become superior to all questions of legal and financial restriction" (1933 134). Under wartime conditions, "the bounds which are placed upon production are defined by intrinsic forces and not by the artifical limitations" of customary financial procedure: "finance has to follow production instead of, as is the normal case, production having to follow finance" (135). Of fundamental importance to Douglas was his realization that "immediately [as] production is expanded at anything like its possible rate, the idea that the financial costs of that expansion can be recovered in prices is seen in its full absurdity" (135–36). Wartime industrial expansion recreated in compressed form the accumulationist phase of capital typical of most of the nineteenth century, when classical economics came of age. The failure to understand the contingent nature of classical economy, Douglas argued, led to the incoherent attempt to extract war reparations from Germany in such a way as to damage the home industries of both Britain and France (1933 156–59).[17] This "classical" attempt to restore the financial status quo ante was crowned by the disastrous return to the gold standard by Britain in 1925, in order to restore a prewar basis of credit that was now irrelevant.

Douglas is an economist poised between an older regime of capital accumulation, the great expanding industrial world of steam and steel of the nineteenth century, and the new age of consumer capitalism, driven by disaccumulative modes. Douglas was only one of the first thinkers to see that consumption must become the "fulcrum of economic growth" (Livingston 1994 5) and that the older canons of value, which stressed saving and endless toil as the foundational virtues both economic and personal, were not only bound to fail but must be overcome to avoid the collapse of capitalism—or "civilization" itself.

Capitalist disaccumulation: the term is meant to imply the reverse of Marx's "general law of accumulation" formulated in part 7 of the first volume of *Capital*. As Martin Sklar writes, capital accumulation is fundamentally the "expansion of goods-production capacity" (1992 156), that is, it "denotes a certain relationship among people in the production process, involving the ratio between labor time represented by those exercising labor-power, and the social labor-time embodied in the means of production—or between living labor or past, 'dead' labor" (154–55). Douglas teaches precisely this point. "Past 'dead' labor" is properly what Douglas calls "the cultural inheritance," the value of which should belong as birthright to all "members of the living community." It forms the basis of "social credit" and should be distributed in the form of dividends (1933 189, 190). As Sklar describes it, capital accumulation proceeds inevitably to a state of disaccumulation: the relationship between labor-time expended by living workers and the social-labor time embodied in the means of production "is one of capital accumulation so long as an increased production and operation of means of production require an increased employment of living human labor-power measured in hours of socially necessary labor" (1992 155). In other words, capital accumulation requires that most labor be used to build tools, machines, and factories and their components (the means of production) rather than manufacturing goods to be sold directly to the consumer. Insofar as this accumulation takes place—and it occurred throughout the nineteenth century in Western Europe, Britain, the United States, and Japan—it withdraws funds from the consumer sector, incidentally underwriting industry and thrift, two of the virtues underpinning the republican sense of self.

There is, then, in its accumulative phase, a division of the economy into two unequal sectors, the capital goods sector, or "Department I," and "Department II," the consumer goods sector (see Livingston 1994 8). As industrial development proceeds from accumulation to disaccumulative modes, through "the on-going net release of labor-power, measured in aggregate labor time, from goods production . . . , it means that less and less labor-power is required for the production of the goods necessary for sustaining and reproducing physical and social life. The people are increasingly freed to apply their labor, or life-time, to other pursuits and fields of endeavour" (Sklar 1992 157). More brutally, under the anachronistic morality of the regime of capital accumulation, these people find themselves unemployed and unfairly stigmatized as idlers and parasites.

Developed during the phase of capital accumulation, classical economy has no cure for unemployment. It has been unable to describe the relationship of production to labor under conditions of capital disaccumulation, the phase, as I have indicated above, in which conditions of profitable production demand less and less labor. Blinded by Say's Law of Markets, which assumes that there is an automatic balance between purchasing power and production, and between wages and employment, orthodox economy could only "cure" unemployment by assuming that wages must be too high and could only suggest that wages be cut until labor became so cheap that it could no longer afford to remain idle. Because production was assumed to produce purchasing power equal to the value of goods produced, overproduction could paradoxically be blamed on lack of labor. The practical result was underconsumption; low wages prevented needy workers from purchasing the very goods they produced, while those same goods, unable to find a market at home, were shipped halfway round the world to find buyers.[18] Despite high unemployment at home, prices would remain as high as the foreign market would bear.

A crisis of increasing unemployment and high prices—the so-called high cost of living—had been chronic in England since the 1870s. J. A. Hobson's *Imperialism* (1902), Lenin's primary source for his own more famous critique, explored the frightening international ramifications, which suggested that world war was the inevitable result of the need to expand markets. In the 1920s, having barely survived the first of such wars, Englishmen were much concerned with the domestic aspect of the problem of overproduction and underemployment. Pound confronts the "orthodoxy" of the economic establishment with this problem in Canto 22 by recounting a conversation with Douglas ("C.H.") and John Maynard Keynes ("Mr. Bukos").[19]

And C.H. [Douglas] said the renowned Mr. Bukos [Keynes],
"What is the cause of the H. C. L. [high cost of living]?"
and Mr. Bukos,
The economist consulted of nations, said:
"Lack of labor."
And there were two million men out of work.
And C. H. shut up, he said
He would save his breath to cool his own porridge,
But I didn't and went on plaguing Mr. Bukos
Who said finally: "I am an orthodox
"Economist."
Jesu Christo!
Standu del paradiso terrestre
Pesando come si fesse compagna d'Adamo!
[22:101–2][20]

If the established economists were baffled—and remember that this Keynes was not yet the heretical Keynes of *The General Theory of Employment, Interest, and Money* of 1936, so was the differently orthodox Left. The British Labor Party responded to the depression with the doctrinaire call for full employment and the right to work.

Douglas felt that they were deluded. The Left labored under the assumption that the poor were poor because the rich were rich, that the problem was simply a fairer distribution of purchasing power and the "surplus value" sweated from workers to benefit the bourgeoisie. The Marxist position was based on what Douglas considered a false premise, namely that labor "creates all wealth; that Capital and Capitalism are one and the same thing, both being of the devil" (Douglas 1920 2). Douglas argued that wealth is the result of the cultural heritage, carried by the science, technology, and skills passed down from generation to generation. The industrial era began when men learned to tap into the solar energy trapped in coal, to release unforeseen amounts of energy. This energy ought to have "increased the credit power of the community" by "the increased capacity of the community to deliver goods and services" far beyond the cost of raising the coal (Douglas 1920 119). Goods ought to be cheaper as a result of the increased efficiency. Instead, because of the way costs are calculated, and because the basis of credit is faulty—inhering in money, not goods or technical improvements—the cost of coal is "passed along" into the goods derived from it, accruing "costs" at each moment it is exchanged. One ramification is that any strike by miners for higher wages is futile, because the higher costs represented by those wages will instantly mean higher prices for the goods the miners need to buy, thereby wiping out any gain in their standard of living.

Douglas's critique again confirms that industrial and financial capitalism have contradictory agendas. This contradiction between productive capacity and profits accounts for the familiar paradox of poverty amid plenty. Conceived as "effective demand," money can never be value itself but only its measure; it is the sign of wealth, not its actuality. But because capitalism is finally interested in making money, not goods, money has come to be mistaken for what it merely represents. It is a problem of accounting and more; it is a problem in the meaning of money itself.

As we have seen, Douglas did not believe that ownership per se but rather finance capital stood in conflict with production. The banks to which the factories were indebted effectively controlled them. In the spirit of Jefferson, Douglas concluded that finance has never had reservations about making money even at the expense of production. Finance is, therefore, parasitical in its essence. Producing nothing itself, it monopolizes the credit necessary for others to produce and skims profits—in the form of bank charges, which are simply arbitrary percentages—from every exchange.

Because they neglected the crucial role of finance, Douglas believed that the Left was treating a symptom as a cause. Even if full employment could somehow be enforced by a Labor government, or even a social revolution, it was not the answer to a just distribution of the fruits of labor because purchasing power could never keep pace with production. Douglas saw that money—that is, purchasing power—was always being drawn out of the system by bank charges on the one hand and taxes on the other. This money did not recirculate. It was used to cancel old debts, while new debts were required to put new money back into the system. Since interest and taxes are payable only in money, not in goods, the result was a structural economic anemia. On balance, there would always be more goods than money. The result was an industrial system racked by feverish bouts of production when credit was cheap and money was available. When this pushed up wages, thereby increasing costs, interest rates were raised, making money scarcer. Finally the lack of money (really credit) crippled purchasing power, leading to gluts of goods, business slumps, and massive unemployment.

In Marxist terms, the endemic economic dysfunction just described is the result of capital disaccumulation. It reflects the difficulties in making the transition from an economy driven by "the priority of Department I," the industrial goods sector (Livingston 1994 8), to Department II, the consumer goods sector. Under a regime of disaccumulation, in which consumer production begins to predominate, consumer demand must be mobilized to drive the economy. In the early stages of this shift, circa 1919, the year of Douglas's *Economic Democracy*, mechanisms to increase and stimulate consumer demand, specifically consumer credit, did not exist (Livingston 1994 11). On the contrary, what was clear to Douglas was the disastrous effect of taxation on the would-be consumer's ability to buy the goods he or she wanted, because money is "effective demand" (1933 131–32). As such, money itself became "the very keystone of the structure" of modern economics (132). Taxation, Douglas assumed, must exist to pay down the public debt. It was used to cancel debts incurred during the process of capital accumulation and investment. Directly or indirectly, taxation served as a levy, which crippled consumer purchasing power because it removed the medium of demand, money, from the economy.

Douglas described this structural contradiction in his "A plus B theorem." Since this formula would not only become the principal point of attack for critics of Douglas's economic panacea from both the Left and the Right, but also become part of Pound's *Cantos*, it is important to understand its implications and limitations. As Pound read the theorem virtually verbatim into Canto 38 we might begin there, with due allowance made for his interjected asperity.[21]

A factory
has also another aspect, which we call the financial aspect
It gives people the power to buy (wages, dividends
which are power to buy) but it is also the cause of prices
or values, financial, I mean financial values
It pays workers, and *for* material.
What it pays in wages and dividends
stays fluid, as power to buy, and this power is less,

per forza, damn blast your intellex, is less
than the total payments made by the factory
(as wages, dividends, AND payments for raw material
bank charges etcetera)
and all, that is the whole, that is the total
of these is added into the total of prices
caused by that factory, any damn factory
and there is and must be therefore a clog
and the power to purchase can never
(under the present system) catch up with
prices at large. [38:190]

Here we see the refutation of Say's Law and an analysis that agrees with Marx's two-sector model of capital accumulation. In his own description, Douglas divided the payments made by factories—what economists now call the "income stream"—into two groups. Group A consisted of all payments made to individuals (wages, salaries and dividends); Group B consisted of all payments made to other organizations (raw materials, bank charges, and other external costs). Group A describes Department II, the consumer sector, and Group B describes the income stream in Department I. The substance of this critique of "the present system" is based on the following formulation of the interrelationship and meaning of these two groups:

> Now *the rate of flow of purchasing power to individuals is represented by A, but since all payments go into prices, the rate of flow of prices cannot be less than A+B. The product of any factory may be considered as something which the public ought to be able to buy, although in many cases it is an intermediate product of no use to individuals but only to a subsequent manufacture; but since A will not purchase A+B, a proportion of the product at least equivalent to B must be distributed by a form of purchasing power which is not comprised in the descriptions grouped under A.* . . . this additional purchasing power is provided by loan-credit (bank overdrafts) or export credit. [Douglas's emphasis, 1920 21–22]

It is clear that "the external factor—credit" (23) stands between the product and the purchaser. Credit finances both the production of the means of production (Department I, which is comprised of goods that never reach the consumer) and the consumer goods and the wages created by production (A + B)—because they are both "produced by borrowed money; the money we buy them with goes to extinguish the debt; but it itself is derived from credits that have been borrowed from the banks, and consequently its value must reappear in selling prices somewhere, and be recovered again from the consumer if the banks are to be repaid their advances. *It is clear therefore, that one credit is only cancelled by the creation of another larger credit"* (24, my emphasis). Credit is not merely "a clog," that is, sabotage, in the system. It wields a truly despotic power over the distribution of purchasing power by continuously sucking value out of the system—and not just surplus value (profits) but real value. Under such a system, credit determines prices. Thus aggregate prices will always be higher on average than aggregate purchasing power: the consequence is poverty. Douglas concluded that private bank credit produced poverty as surely as it underwrote more "efficient" productive capacity.

Douglas saw that the remedy was to alter the basis of credit and thus to alter the nature and meaning of money. Money, he argued, should function only as a means of exchange, *not* as a measure of value. The "money problem" he wrote, *"is not a problem of value measurement. The proper function of a money system is to control and direct the production of goods and services.* As 'effective demand,' a money system is, or should be, an 'order' system, not a 'reward' system" (Douglas's emphasis, 1924 61–62). Money should be a servant of policy, not its maker; economically money should act as an effect, not a cause. Money ought to function much like a railway ticket (Douglas had once worked for a railroad), which "distributes transportation" (62). A bank should be like a railroad's ticket department, its "proper business" should be "to facilitate the distribution of the product in accordance with the desires of the public and to transmit the indications of those desires to those operating the industrial organization, to whom is committed the task of meeting them. They have no valid right to any voice in deciding either the qualifications of travellers, or the conditions under which they travel" (Douglas 1924 63).

Putting himself beyond the pale of respectable economists of his time by contradicting Say's Law, Douglas showed that "purchasing power is not, as might be gathered from the current discussion of the subject, an emanation from the production of real commodities or services much like the scent from a rose, but, on the contrary, is produced by an entirely distinct process, that is to say, the banking system" (Douglas 1931 23).

A reform of the banking system resulting in its democratization, was, therefore, the remedy for this great contradiction. Money was to be limited to the means of exchange. And money is

> any medium which has reached such a degree of acceptability that no matter what it is made of, and no matter why people want it, no one will refuse it in exchange for his product. So long as this definition holds good, it is obvious that the possession of money establishes an absolute lien on the services of others in direct proportion to the fraction of the whole stock controlled, and further that the whole stock of financial wealth inclusive of credit, in the world, should be sufficient to balance the aggregate book price of the world's material assets and prospective production. [Quoted in Mairet 14]

In short, money should be the sign of production, not of credit. A unit of money ought to be a share of the gross planetary product—its aggregate book price. This sort of money simply measures a certain quantity, or "fraction," of "material assets," the "price" of which is a function of its potential quantity. Such money is a ration ticket, demystified of its claims to be wealth (1933 132).[22] Such money could be considered the universal language of production. So conceived, money cannot be a measure of value in things, rather the *potential* production of things ("useful productive capacity") would determine the value of money. Note Douglas's equation of financial wealth with material assets and *prospective production*—not actual production. Douglas seems to mean that money equals real capital plus credit, assuming that credit is based on the social credit embodied in productive potential, *not* on bank debts.

Douglas's vision of prices is one of the most interesting and difficult to accept of his proposals. In his view, "credit-issue and price-making are the positive and negative aspects of the same thing," and to control either it is "necessary to transfer the credit-system entirely away from *currency,* on which it now rests, to *useful productive capacity.* The issue of credit instruments will then not result in an expansion of money for the same or a diminishing amount of goods, which is inflation, but in an expansion of goods for the same or a diminishing amount of money, which is deflation" (Douglas's emphasis, Mairet 94). This different notion of costing would encourage production "below cost," because the price of each unit of production would be a diminishing proportion of the whole. Wages, in turn, would become dividends, because they would be based on a percentage of total production. Wages (now dividends) would be created by increased production, rather than charged against it in the form of higher prices. Since in Pound's homely reformulation "money would be a certificate of work done" (*SP* 212),[23] there would be no struggle between capital and labor for control of "surplus value"—there could be none. Profits would be determined by the turnover of goods and market share.

Douglas's system is still capitalism, but it is capitalism without scarcity economics. This compelling vision of a modern economic engine is the utopian element in Douglas's work, based on what he considered to be modern industrial realities. The problem of production, he knew, was solved. Distribution was impeded by a currency that no longer spoke the language of modern production and modern consumer demand. It was encumbered by an outdated morality of getting and saving that rewarded labor as the only virtue and wrongly saw inevitable unemployment and necessary consumption as idleness and waste.

Douglas shrewdly saw that the "unemployment problem" was really an employment problem. "If the unemployment problem was solved tomorrow," he wrote, "and every individual capable of employment was employed and paid according to the existing canons of the financial system, the result could only be to precipitate an economic and financial catastrophe of the first magnitude" because of the resulting overproduction (1924 114–15). In fact, the only thing that prevented such a catastrophe was the systematic sabotage of production by workers desperate to keep working and finance eager to derive profit from artificial scarcity.

So the answer to the crisis in capitalism lay in the distribution of products and in the distribution of work, both of which are determined by the amount of money available. The solution was to make money more exchangeable, to put money to work as the agent of distribution.

"Let the credit out," as Williams says in *Paterson*. Released from its role as the measure of value, money could do what it does best, facilitate exchanges. This would require that money lose its commodity status. As credit has been wrongly tied up with the potential to make money, not to create wealth, the effect has been a kind of financial tautology: money must be made out of money. The truer basis of credit registered by the sign of money, Douglas argued, was actual things made by people and their machines and the capacity to produce such things as needed. This capacity could never belong to one person; it was always and at every moment the summation of industrial progress. Douglas confounded both the financial establishment and the Left by arguing that "all credit-values are derived from the community, regarded as a permanent institution; not merely from the present generation of workers 'by hand and brain' " (1920 38). This power was "Social Credit." All citizens, not just a particular class, had a right to a piece of it.

Under these strictures, money can never be confused with wealth, and it can never be confused with capital. Money remains only the sign of purchasing power, or effective demand. Capital, in fact, is decisively divorced from money and returned to a cultural basis; it becomes the communal assets of social and technical progress. To put the matter in linguistic terms, Douglas's money is reduced—but also freed—to be a system of signs that are intimately connected to referents. Under Social Credit, the world's "financial assets" could equal but not exceed the world's "material assets and prospective production." Voicing the demands of consumers, such money could call forth all produceable goods, rather than translating all values back into the abstract language of debt.

Money values based on the abundant capacities of production, not the purely negative values caused by artificial scarcity, would be like poetic language.[24] It would register what was possible. It would be an affirmative mode of expression, never an unwanted obligation. This latter aspect of Douglasite money in particular attracted the poets.

Sylvio Gesell: Natural Money and Natural Language

In the mid-1930s, Pound would take Douglas one step further through his interest in the *Schwundgeld*, or "shrinking money," proposed by the economist Sylvio Gesell (1852–1930).[25] Gesell was a German, a successful businessman and for a few days in 1919 the finance minister of the Lindhauer government of Bavaria (Carpenter 523). Pound read Gesell closely after discovering him in the work of Irving Fisher, the Yale economist (Carpenter 524). One volume of Gesell's principal work, *The Natural Economic Order* (1906), the "Land Part," remains in Pound's library at the Brunnenburg;[26] the portions on money are heavily marked.

Sylvio Gesell is a compelling figure and a vivid writer. He is forgotten largely because, while his work is in dialogue with Marx, Gesell admires Proudhon. Because of Marx's successful polemic against the great French economist who gave us the phrase "Property is theft," Proudhon is largely unread and his theories undervalued. Gesell reminds us that Proudhon was perhaps the first political economist to realize that what capitalists call overproduction is, if left unchecked, the death of capital (Gesell 6). Why? "As soon as capital ceases to yield the traditional interest, money strikes and brings work to a standstill. Money, therefore acts as a serum against the 'building plague' and the 'working fury.' It renders capital (houses, industrial plant, ships) immune from the menace of its own increase" (the phrases in single quotation marks come from Proudon; Gesell 7). For Gesell, who follows Adam Smith in this matter, surplus value is built on scarcity. Production, insofar as it reduces scarcity, reduces the surplus values derivable from each item produced. If surplus value cannot be converted into sufficient profits, then production ceases as the money to underwrite such production is invested elsewhere. Rather than being an agent of distribution, money tends to make itself scarce just when it is most needed.

> Proudhon asks: why are we short of houses, machinery and ships? And he also gave the correct answer: because money limits the building of them. Or to use his own words: "Because money is a sentinel posted at the entrance to the markets, with orders to let no one pass. Money, you imagine, is the key that opens the gates of the market (by which term is meant the exchange of products): that is not true—money is the bolt that bars them." [Gesell 7]

Pound penciled Proudhon's image of the sentinel, and for good reason; it provided him with an image of scarcity economics consistent with the Jeffersonian version of capitalism, which sees the availability of money as the arbiter and regulator of markets. Gesell also makes another distinction that confirmed Pound's thinking; he argues that Marx confuses capital with real wealth by assuming that money in and of itself is capital, and also by assuming that goods are the same as real wealth. They may be so but only if they can be used. But Gesell is not just confirming what to Pound were simple facts. He offers an ingenious way out of the problem. He follows Proudhon in realizing that surplus value must somehow be detached from money and reattached to the goods that the money is supposed to stand for. He argues:

> Goods not money are the real foundation of economic life. Goods and their compounds make up 99% of our wealth, money only 1%. Therefore let us treat goods as we treat foundations: that is, let us not tamper with them. We must accept goods as they appear on the market. We cannot alter them. If they rot, break, perish, let them do so; it is their nature. . . . we cannot save the newspaper in the hands of the newsvendor from being reduced, two hours later, to waste-paper, if it fails to find a purchaser. Moreover we must remember that money is a universal medium for saving; all the money which serves commerce as a medium of exchange comes to the savings banks and lies there until it can be enticed into circulation again by interest. And how can we ever raise goods again to the level of ready money (gold) in the eyes of the savers? How can we induce them, instead of saving money, to fill their chests or store-rooms with straw, books, bacon, oil, hides, guano, dynamite, porcelain, etc. And yet this is what Proudhon really aimed at in attempting to bring goods and money to a common level. Proudhon had overlooked the fact that money is not only a medium of exchange but also a medium of saving, and that money and potatoes, money and lime, money and cloth can never in any circumstances be looked upon as things of equal worth in the chests of the savers. A youth saving against old age will prefer a single gold coin to the contents of the largest warehouse. [Gesell 8]

Gesell continues, in a passage heavily marked by Pound:

> Let us, then, make an end to the privilege of money. Nobody, not even savers, speculators, or capitalists, must find money, as a commodity, preferable to the contents of the markets, shops and warehouses. If money is not to hold sway over goods, it must deteriorate as they do. Let it be attacked by moth and rust, let it sicken, let it run away; and when it comes to die let its possessor pay the cost of burial. Then, and not till then, shall we be able to say that money and goods are on an equal footing and perfect equivalence—as Proudhon aimed at making them. [Gesell 9]

Gesell's "shrinking money"—"vegetable money," as Lewis Hyde calls it—would actually decay over time by accruing "negative interest" as little stamps are affixed to each note, reducing its value by 1 percent month by month. Gesell proposes, in effect, a direct tax on money. The idea is to force savers to keep money in circulation so as to make one bill do the work of many; he wants to increase its "velocity," to use the jargon of the economists. Hoarded, such money would decay into worthlessness like so many onions under the sink. This is one way to avoid the monopoly of credit; let the time element inherent in credit literally adhere to the money itself. Instead of causing money to grow unnaturally through the institution of usury, this money decays organically in accordance with nature and things. "To the extent that it imitates the perishability of organic produce," Richard Sieburth writes, "stamp scrip fulfills Pound's longing for a truly 'natural' or 'motivated' system of signs" (154).

Pound's need to bring money and language together is evident throughout his prose, where the term "money" often sounds as if it should mean "language." This passage is obviously influenced by Gesell:

> Money is not a product of nature but the invention of man. And man has made it into a pernicious instrument through lack of foresight. The nations have forgotten the differences between animal, vegetable and mineral; or rather, finance has chosen to represent all three of the natural categories by a single means of exchange, and failed to take account of the consequences. Metal is durable, but it does not reproduce itself. If you sow gold you will not be able to reap a harvest many times greater than the gold you sowed. The vegetable leads a more or less autonomous existence, but its natural reproductiveness can be increased by cultivation. The animal gives to and takes from the vegetable world: manure in exchange for food.
>   Fascinated by the lustre of a metal, man made it into chains. Then he invented something against nature, a false representation in the mineral world of laws which apply only to animals and vegetables. [SP 316]

The problem with the kind of money we have is that it is not natural. It is like an inaccurate or false language, which is not true to its referents. Pound wants money to serve a mimetic function, to provide "a 'money picture' of extant goods" (SP 247). Taking Gesell's imagery of decay literally, Pound divides all goods into three classes, transient, durable, and permanent.[27] In the transient category are things like "fresh vegetables, fake art, battleships." Durables include roads, public works, "afforestation." The final "permanent" category is assigned to "scientific discoveries, works of art, classics" (SP 184–85). Pound added: "These latter can be put in a class by themselves, as they are always in use and never consumed; or they are, in jargon, "consumed" but not destroyed by consumption" (*SP* 185). Sieburth reminds us that this triad—the permanent, the durable, and the transient—is a structure that unifies *The Cantos* (Sieburth 1987 154). Pound, naturally, hoped his poem would fall in the permanent category. The bad poet, the bad economist, "the shyster," Pound complained, "is always trying to pass off class 1 for class 2 or 3" (*SP* 185). Somehow, money ought to be able to account for all three states of nature.

Yet, surely, to imagine separate forms of money for all classes of nature is to miss the point of money. The purpose of money is to provide a system of signification that allows a single system of value to apply to all classes of things and, increasingly, even states of being or consciousness. The structure of money and credit is grammatical, not lexical. The problem plunges us at once into semiotics and abstruse literary theory.

There is a moment in *Gulliver's Travels* (1726) when, in the course of visiting the Great Academy of Lagado, Gulliver visits three professors who are busy improving the language of their country. One energy-saving scheme was bent on "abolishing all words whatsoever" in the interest of health and saving wear and tear on the vocal apparatus. The idea has always struck me as being consistent with Pound's "representative money." One professor suggests:

> Since words are only names for *things*, it would be more convenient for all men to carry about with them such *things* as were necessary to express the particular business they are to discourse on. . . . many of the most learned and wise adhere to the new scheme of expressing themselves by *things*, which hath only this inconvenience attending it, that if a man's business be very great, and of various kinds, he must be obliged in proportion to carry a greater bundle of *things* upon his back, unless he can afford one or two strong servants to attend him. I have often seen two of those sages almost sinking under the weight of their packs, like pedlars among us; who when they met in the streets would lay down their loads, open their sacks and hold conversation for an hour together, then put up their implements, help each other to resume their burthens, and take their leave. [Swift's emphasis, 150–51]

Swift's Lagodan professors offer an extreme example of the problem Pound's money raises. Their supremely literal language is like no language at all; it is the linguistic analog of the premonetary barter economy that economists love to invoke in their histories of money—the same economy that Gesell and Pound want to restore by making money and things equivalent. The Ladogan professors "barter" with words. A true language, like a monetary system, uses signs to accomplish its transactions, and the Ladogan experience notwithstanding, it does so largely out of convenience. The truth is, no people, no matter how "primitive," conducts business on a regular basis via simple barter,[28] just as no language ever known shows any evidence of requiring grunts and gestures. All are always "complete and articulate" (Langer 103). Almost all of the time, we exchange signs of value (money or sometimes the promise to perform a certain amount of labor) for a thing.

Any money system is less complete than a language, since despite the best efforts of the capitalist, much in human experience remains unquantifiable. Capitalism has undoubtedly propelled money and monetary valuation relentlessly into the moral universe once the exclusive domain of priests, poets, and other guardians of morality, ethics, and language, so Pound's confusion about money is a complex nostalgia for an unfallen economic world, a world where things and their values maintain a mystical connection. Gesell's *Schwundgeld* attracted him because of its faithful mimesis of the real wealth of real things.

The problem here is the problem of time and value—credit—which Pound once brilliantly defined as "the future tense of money" (*SP* 278). Despite the strongly nounlike character of Pound's Gesellite vegetable money, prior to reading Gesell, Pound recognized that money generally behaves more like verbs than nouns. Echoing Douglas, Pound insists in *The ABC of Economics* (1933) that "*under the present system* there are never enough credit slips [e.g., cash] to deal with the product; to distribute the product; to purchase the product; to conjugate ANY of the necessary verbs of sane economics or a decent and agreeable life" (Pound's emphasis, *SP* 212). If credit signifies future values, cash values must signify present value, and debt ought to be money's past tense. In actuality, debt is the monetary way of expressing the value of the future—one reason why, for banks, debts are assets. In fact, outstanding debts are bought and sold every day by banks and governments, so we can say that future values are represented in the present by the prices of debts. The discount at which these debts are sold represents the difference between past expectations, present realities, and future hopes of collecting on the debt. If money signifies as a verb, rather than a noun, it tends to burden us with the dead expectations of the past, while foreclosing the future.

On reading Gesell, Pound recognized that the new form of money completed a full monetary language. The ascendancy of finance had made money *too* verblike; Gesell's *Schwundgeld* redressed the balance, returning to money its specificity and rootedness in things. Combining what he had learned from Douglas and Gesell, Pound foresaw a world in which money could speak with a Ladogan literalness without the inconvenience of bartering things. Money could have a kind of hieroglyphic actuality. It would behave as Ernest Fenollosa had once claimed Chinese ideograms behaved, as "vivid shorthand pictures of the operations of nature" (*CWC* 8).

Volitionist Economics and Pound's Fascism

"Volitionist economics" is Pound's synthesis of Jeffersonian, Physiocratic, Douglasite, Gesellite, and linguistic influences. "I remain a Jeffersonian republican" he says in his treatise *The ABC of Economics*, but he insists that "you must bring your Jefferson up to date. T.J. had already seen that agriculture would in great measure give way to manufacturing etc" (*SP* 213). Volitionism focuses on money; its solutions tend to be Gesellite, as its theory derives from Douglas: "No Douglasite can improve on Gesell's criteria for money. No Gesellite will get deeper than Douglas's fountain of values" (*SP* 246).

As its name suggests, Volitionist economics has something to do with the will. In fact, it is based on a fundamental optimism about human motivation. Pound's notion of the will is not Nietzsche's "will to power," which Pound explicitly scorns as the "vulgar" fantasy of a "hysterical teuto-pollak" (*JM* 99).[29] In Pound's moral universe, the will to power would seem to be far closer to the motivation of the enemies of a just system, who operate on greed and "squeeze" (87:586). The will motivating Pound's Volitionism is fundamentally different; it is "the will to order" (*JM* 99): "The science of economics will not get very far until it grants the existence of will as a component; i.e. will toward order, will toward 'justice' or fairness, desire for civilization, amenities included. The intensity of that will is definitely a component in any solution" (*SP* 210).

To Mussolini and others conversant with the European philosophical tradition, the will was a lever with which to unseat reason, the god of the Enlightenment. In Continental philosophy, the will indicates the irruption of the irrational and archaic, the expression of the anarchic and antisocial "instinctive life" (Nietzsche 1886 48). Whether it is the will of Schopenhauer or Nietzsche or the drives of Freud, this sort of will can never know fairness, justice, or order; it wants only to prevail, to overcome, to survive.[30]

What Pound calls the "will to order" is what everyone else would call reason.[31] But Pound, like anyone facing the morally crippling alienations of modernity, understood that reason alone was no longer its own adequate justification. Despite his overt linking of the will to Dante's *directio voluntatis*, he wants to endow reason with a motivation that is not identical with the Christian or post-Christian conscience. Hence his conscription of the will, the motive force of the Nietzschean counterenlightenment, under the sign of order. Hence too, his enlistment of Confucius, whose non-Western ethics have not been subjected to the desperate criticism of post-Enlightenment Western philosophy.

In *Jefferson and/or Mussolini* the Confucian adage, "renovate, day by day renew," which Pound had made the slogan of literary modernism in "make it new," becomes the translation and justification of Mussolini's "La rivoluzione continua" (*JM* 113). Pound's translation seems deeply mistaken in supposing that the ethical renewal of an agrarian society can be translated into the permanent "revolution rooted in the technique of industry"—to quote a chapter title from Wyndham Lewis's *The Art of Being Ruled* (1926), a book to which Pound's *Jefferson and/or Mussolini* seems to respond.

Nonetheless, it is just this paradoxical neo-Jeffersonian, Confucian will to order, rather than the will to power, that Pound rather surprisingly attributed to Mussolini (*JM* 99)—surprisingly because Mussolini made no secret of his admiration for Nietzsche. Mussolini speaks of the "will to power" often and in frankly Nietzschean terms (Mussolini 1935 7, 26, 30). Nonetheless, in considering what Pound meant by the will, we must accept Pound's sense of it if we are to get anywhere with Volitionist economics. For a Modernist who is also not a Socialist, Pound is remarkably anti-Nietzschean. He subscribes neither to Nietzsche's pessimistic critique of reason nor to his tragic hero cult.[32]

Nor did he seem to worry that continuous social renovation and the stable political order he envisioned might be incommensurate. One could say, with Emilio Gentile, that Pound never confronted the implications of the "Futurist" side of Fascism, that "dynamic feeling of modernity that was expressed in the ideal of 'continual revolution,' an ideal that impelled Fascism never to rest content with its accomplishments or even to guarantee its permanence in power with a prudent politics of conservation but to feel itself obliged, almost condemned, to obey the command of its original essence and to project itself into the future, towards new realities to be constructed" (Gentile 74–75).

Perhaps this tragic impulse was not so obvious in the early 1930s, when Pound was forming his view of Fascism, although Mussolini's glorification of struggle, war, and death ought to have made it clear. Despite Mussolini's rhetoric, it was possible before Ethiopia, before the Italian intervention in the Spanish Civil War, for Pound to imagine Italian Fascism as a program of internal economic, moral, cultural, and political renewal that would know when to stop. In *Jefferson and/or Mussolini*, Pound scoffs at the political naivete expressed in a pro-Bolshevik poem by Louis Aragon that exults in the fact that there are no brakes to the revolutionary engine (*JM* 24); Pound clearly believed that Mussolini would not repeat Soviet mistakes.

Pound looked to Fascism to promote his twentieth-century Jeffersonianism because the Fascists were the epitome of the party of action. Fascism solved a major difficulty as far as Pound was concerned, because it seemed to supply the political will necessary to instigate the economic reforms needed to renovate Western civilization. Pound found people stupefied, in a state of "abulia," when confronted by the mystifying complexity of modernity and, especially, economic discourse. He ruefully quoted Arthur Griffith's "You can't move 'em with a cold thing like economics" throughout *The Cantos* and his prose (*SP* 209).

To move people Pound needed the irrational, but in his own work this mostly consisted of turning up the volume and hectoring his audience, whereas the Fascists shrewdly marketed thenselves as a spiritual movement (Mussolini 1935 7–14). Pound didn't know how to move people with a cold thing like economics because he didn't understand the irrational mystique of the will to power—even his own. One could almost say that the whole tragedy of Pound's relationship with Fascism was precisely that he hadn't read his Nietzsche.[33]

Volitionist economics has two aspects. First, it brings an indictment of economic abuses that need to be questioned, abolished, or reformed and offers suggestions about improving the system. These are contained in the eight-point questionnaire that Pound was sending to correspondents, including Mussolini and President Roosevelt, in the 1930s. It read as follows:

VOLITIONIST ECONOMICS

WHICH of the following statements do you agree with?

1. It is an outrage that the state shd. run into debt to individuals by the act and in the creation of real wealth.
2. Several nations recognize the necessity of distributing purchasing power. They do actually distribute it. The question is whether as favour to corporations; as reward for not having a job; or impartially and per capita.
3. A country CAN have one currency for internal use, and another good both for home and foreign use.
4. If money is regarded as certificate of work done, taxes are no longer necessary.
5. It is possible to concentrate all taxation onto the actual paper money of a country (or onto one sort of its money).
6. You can issue valid paper money against any commodity UP TO the amount of that commodity that people WANT.
7. Some of the commonest failures of clarity among economists are due to using one word to signify two or more different concepts: such as DEMAND, meaning sometimes WANT and sometimes power to buy; authoritative meaning also responsible.
8. It is an outrage that the owner of one commodity can not exchange it with someone possessing another, without being impeded or taxed by a third party holding a monopoly over some third substance or controlling some convention, regardless of what it be called.

It is important to note that several of Pound's proposals have in fact come to pass. His belief "that a country CAN have one currency for internal use, and another good both for home and foreign use," for instance, anticipates monetary supplements like food stamps. His second point recognizes the necessity of the welfare state in a world where the problem of production has been solved. In that case, the state must distribute purchasing power. His specific recommendation, that purchasing power should be distributed on a per capita basis, as a dividend rather than a dole, was tried in Sweden and, for a time, in Alaska. On two points he declares his "outrage": on point 1, that the state run into debt to individuals by the act of creating real wealth; and on point 8, that people wanting to exchange commodities should not be impeded or taxed by some third party holding a monopoly on the medium of exchange. Several of his points, including this last, earned the hearty assent of John Dewey (Beinecke), but as they imply the end of finance capitalism, they have never been tried.

I hope it is no longer necessary to insist that Pound's proposals are serious; at any rate they are not the prescriptions of a quack. In considering his connection to Fascism we must understand that his initial interest in the movement was simply expedient. Pound thought that Mussolini was in a position to enact some of his economic proposals. An unfinished and as far as I know unpublished essay called "Notes on Douglas (C.H.)" (c. 1934, Beinecke Library) makes this belief very clear. The piece was written so that Pound could explain Douglas "to a young American marxist," possibly Louis Zukofsky.

"I admit that I am a Jeffersonian," Pound begins. "I [was] a Douglasite before there were any . . . , and I am strong for Mussolini." He notes that "Douglas is NOT for Mussolini," but that doesn't matter because "Douglasism is an *economic* theory, italian fascism is a political FACT. There is nothing in Douglas' economics that conflicts with political fascism" (Pound's emphasis). He adds, "Douglas is politically a democrat in his sense of the term which is certainly NOT Jefferson's sense of the term" (1).[34]

Pound sees Mussolini as having a "common aim" with Douglas and Marx, "to wipe out flagrant injustice, an injustice that flames still more violently in an epoch of coordinated machinery than it did in Marx'[s] day" (1). The injustice is that "the whole advantage, or almost the whole advantage of mechanical invention and of concentrated 'power' (electric etc.) has been exploited by a small group of bloodsuckers, often unconscious of the substance which arrived in the etherial [*sic*] form of bank notes on their office tables" (2). The solution is "Douglasism."[35] Douglasism in turn, is described a as a kind of communism of distribution (2).

Pound's critique of capitalism as expressed in his "Notes on Douglas" is purely Populist, certainly not Fascist. Pound was against militarism (which he saw as the work of arms contractors and bankers; see *JM* 72) and had little interest in youth cults, mass spectacles, or mystic Italian nationalism, which he seems to have accepted simply as the Italian way of doing things (*JM* 25–28, 50–51). What fundamentally interested Pound in Italian Fascism was the possibility it offered for what Emilio Gentile has called "the conquest of modernity" (Gentile 58). That is, Pound admired the attempt by Mussolini to overcome and control the impersonal economic forces unleashed by modernization. Italian Fascists and Pound's Volitionism share a background of "political modernism," which Gentile (following Marshall Berman) defines as "those political ideologies that arose in connection with modernization, ideologies that seek to render human beings capable of mastering the processes of modernization in order not to be overwhelmed by the 'vortex of modernity' " (Gentile 58). Volitionist economics is an attempt to formulate a practical program for those who have the will to master the forces of modernity—a will that Mussolini had in abundance.

In his essay, Pound next turns to the role of the State. He compares Mussolini's "l'idée statale" (which Pound glosses elsewhere as "the spirit of the people" [*JM* viii]) to the mot of that "pustulent frenchman," Louis XIV: "L['Jétat, c'est moi," and to the Bolshevik notion that "the state or the government belonged to the people" (3), which Pound doesn't believe (see *JM* 93), and, finally, to Jefferson's comment: "The best government is that which governs least" (3). Pound believes that "the prevalent incomprehension of fascism ... is due to muddle as to the meaning of 'state' " (2). The average American or English reader mistakes " 'state' to mean 'government' " (2). Mussolini's idea of the state is, to use his own language, "no mere mechanical device for defining the sphere within which the individual may duly exercise his supposed rights," nor a cult of personality, but "an inwardly accepted standard and role of conduct" (Mussolini 1935 13). Pound believes that Jefferson merely distrusted government because he had never come across any good governments: "The highest flight of Jefferson's imagination cd. not go beyond the idea of a government that ... abstained from being a positive and galling evil" (3).

Unlike traditional notions of the state, even Jefferson's, "the state for Mussolini includes every individual in the country" (2–3)—one reason why "totalitarian" is a positive word, not an epithet, to Pound. Under the sign of order, totalitarianism is simply the fulfillment of a totally inclusive organic politics.

The just state, Pound believed, would be run by men of good will— that is, men who possessed the will to order, like the men he felt had directed the American republic through the Civil War. In *Jefferson and/or Mussolini*, he envisions a strangely undemocratic, rather John Adams-like, version of Jeffersonian democracy in which an inner spiritual core of benign willing keeps the republic intact beneath the formalities of day-to-day politics.

> Jefferson thought the formal features of the American system would work . . . , but the condition of their working was that inside them there should be a *de facto* government composed of sincere men willing the national good. When the men of understanding are too lazy to impart the results of their understanding, and when the nucleus of the national mind hasn't the moral force to translate knowledge into action I don't believe it matters a damn what legal forms there are in a government. The nation will get the staggers. [*JM* 95]

Here, will is "moral force," the "directio voluntatis" of Dante. It is "formal"—almost Platonic and is pointed toward an invisible order that supersedes even legality itself—a remarkable judgment. You can see that Pound wants to free the state to act; "The best government," he wrote, "is that which translates the best thought most speedily into action" (91). What is best derives from moral force, which is, in Mussolini's case, the "will for the welfare of Italy": "not Italy as a bureaucracy, or Italy as a state machinery stuck on top of the people, but for Italy organic, composed of the last ploughman and the last girl in the olive yards." Unless you believe that Mussolini is working from a sincere concern for Italy, Pound argues, "you will have a great deal of trouble about the un-Jeffersonian details of his surfaces" (34).

For Pound, Mussolini's concern for the welfare of Italy was self-evident—like Jefferson's deep concern for the United States. Pound's faith makes the Fascist state benign: "The concept of a state actually doing good to private individuals is not Benito Mussolini's personal patent, he has done more to make it an actuality than any other character in our history" ("Notes" 3–4).

Coming to the point, Pound writes, "That Mussolini has worke[d]

ALWAYS in the domain of the possible, without dogmas, but with a will directed to good has nothing whatever to do with an economic mechanism which he cd. take up tomorrow, put into operation quicker than any other than wd. be possible out in any country save [I]taly and in no way jostle or in any way alter FASCISM. One might *almost* but not quite say: fascism is a means of getting something done. Douglasism is something to do" (Pound's emphasis, "Notes" 4).

Pound's belief that Mussolini is without "dogmas" is very instructive in taking the measure of Pound's early attraction to Il Duce. It seems clear that the man, not the party, interests Pound. And Pound is interested because he thinks that Mussolini might enact the economic reforms necessary to restore social justice. Pound thinks it a good thing that Douglasism won't disturb Fascism only because as a result Mussolini might be more likely to implement Social Credit reforms. Even such an unfriendly biographer as Humphrey Carpenter admits that "it was not totally unreasonable for Ezra to hope that the Fascist Government might listen to Douglas's economic views. Fascism had no economic policy of its own, and the Mussolini regime was not committed to an economic dogma" (Carpenter 491).[36]

As Surette and others have noticed, Pound's attraction to Fascism was primarily personal. In Pound's meeting with Mussolini in January 1933, he handed him a copy of *A Draft of XXX Cantos* and "a document that summed up what [Pound] believed to be the essence of Social Credit in eighteen [*sic*] paragraphs" (Carpenter 490–91).[37] Mussolini's reception was politely bland and noncommittal, as recorded at the opening of Canto 41: "Ma questo," / said the Boss, "e divertente" (41:202). Confronted by the earnest poet, Mussolini apparently also asked "Why do you want to/ '—perche si vuol mettere—'/ your ideas in order?" (87:583)—words Pound remembered in the DTC at Pisa. Pound apparently heard no Nietzschean ironies in the question and interpreted Mussolini's polite amusement as some intuitive grasp of his joint poetic and economic project.

In the early 1930s, at least, it is safe to say that Pound is not a Fascist in the Nietzschean sense of the term that we take for granted. He is "strong for Mussolini" because he sees the dictator as an energetic doer of good; like many American journalists of the period, he regarded Mussolini as a kind of Italian Teddy Roosevelt. But because of his misunderstanding of Mussolini's conception of the will, it seems clear that Pound "had little idea of Italian Government policy, and even less of what fascism meant" (Carpenter 491).

For Pound, Italian Fascism meant an opportunity to renovate civilization, to conquer modernity in the name of order. For him, Fascism is the synthesis of Jeffersonian and Confucian political economies adjusted to the industrial age. This synthesis is possible for Pound because all three social visions are predicated on an ideal of class collaboration rather than class struggle.

Confucianism, which one might characterize as a highly ethical and literate feudalism, stresses a hierarchy based on mutual obligation. As Pound translates it, "if each has his part that is due him, there is no pauper, there is harmony, there is no want among the inhabitants" (GK 19). The first concern of such a polity is social justice and the domestic economy: everyone gets a fair share.

In Pound's account, Jeffersonian democracy succeeded insofar as there was a harmonious understanding between the men who governed and the people. The governing clique becomes "the nucleus of the national mind" (JM 95)—another way of characterizing that sincere group of men, or perhaps a single hero, "willing the national good." To instill such goodness is the purpose of Confucian teaching and the reason Pound would later translate The Analects. The national good is closely bound up with good internal government (JM 112); good internal government, in turn, ends class struggle by eliminating the "special interests," oppressors who tend to use and corrupt governments to further their own selfish ends. These people obviously cannot be incorporated into the "national mind." They are "outsiders," economically, politically, and, in the extreme case, racially. The "national mind" manifesting the national will cannot afford ambivalence. To keep the national mind clear and undivided, there must be no class struggle, as one class, the workers, would then be left outside the state. There must be no irrational outbreaks from the revolutionary unconscious either, for the Fascist state is *consciously* revolutionary (Mussolini 1935 23). All classes must therefore be given an equal share in the state to ensure that no class is at a disadvantage. The Fascist idea that the state is the "supreme expression of national life" and "the synthesis of all the material and non-material values of the race" (Agresti 104) speaks to this need for moral renewal through class collaboration. A vertical trade union organization redirects the energies of economic struggle from a horizontal conflict between classes to the vertical integration of the "guild" (corporazione), uniting the energies of each industry in a common purpose. (One result is that class struggle is transformed into national struggle and internal tensions are invested in foreign policy rather than in domestic disputes.) In the words of Olivia Rossetti Agresti, a Fascist economist and a longtime friend of Pound:

> The recognition of the essential identity of interest differentiates the Fascists from Socialist trade unionism; it also explains the different goals and diverse methods of the two schools of economic thought. Socialist trade unionism works through the class struggle; Fascist syndicalism works through class collaboration and aims at organizing the guild state in which all of the facets of production—capital, scientific research, technical direction, manual and clerical labor—are recognized as essential each in their degree, the several interests being conciliated and subordinated to the general or national interest of which they are an integral part. The theory and practice of Fascist economics derives from a conception of the State, not as a mere policeman keeping order and seeing fair play, not as an instrument in the service of some party or class, not as a force dominating but apart from the people, but as the supreme expression of national life. "All within the State, nothing outside the State" is the formulation in which the leader of Fascism—Mussolini—expresses this conception. [Agresti 104–6]

Fundamental to the success of "l'idée statale" is a trustworthy state. Pound's trust in the state, justified by his personal faith in Mussolini and his basic misunderstanding of Mussolini's sense of the will, is antithetical to Jeffersonianism as commonly understood. If Jefferson stood for less government, that is to say, for less legislation to bind the liberties of the people through the extension of federal power, Mussolini stood for less government in a different sense; he meant less restraint on the State's ability to act but also a consequent decrease in the legal machinery that protects the people from the will of the State. When the will of the State is firmly identified with the will of the people, of course, there is no need for such protection.

Jeffersonianism and Fascism have radically contrasting notions of the line between public and private. The pith of Jeffersonianism is that life is really a private affair between man and his land; government is a necessary evil whose primary purpose is to safeguard his privacy and autonomy. The Fascist idea is that life is mostly a public business, the essence of which is the relation between the citizen and the State; the purpose of government is to enforce a heroic, self-sacrificing sense of public duty.

Confucianism offered Pound what was, in effect, a synthesis of these opposite theories of government by positing the public duty as the corollary of the private conscience. A sense of duty is learned not from the State but from the heart: "One looks into the heart and then acts" (*C* 27). The "will to order" that drives Pound's utopia proceeds from the Confucian heart. Pound hadn't counted on the anarchic, tragic heroism of the post-Enlightenment will to power, which interpreted a Nietzschean social "struggle" as the unlikely principle of universal order.

Conclusion

Pound was convinced that distributive systems comparable to the visionary money of Douglas and Gesell had once existed (for instance at Woergl and in the Monte dei Paschi bank) and could be restored. In this sense, Pound's epic is not a Utopia; it is a record of the suppressed true history of the world. When he handed his *Cantos* to Mussolini, he assumed that Il Duce understood this point. Pound used his syncretistic amalgam of Volitionist economics to energize the Physiocratic economics of Jefferson, Douglas, and Gesell and as a poetic principle to locate sound economics throughout history. Knowing what to look for, he can interpret ancient history in Volitionist terms.

4

FERTILITY RITES/FINANCIAL RITES
Pound, Williams, and the Political
Economy of Sex

In the tradition of Sir James Frazer, Carlo Ginzburg's researches into the archives of the Inquisition have shown that fertility cults existed in northern Italy and probably much of Europe at least as late as the seventeenth century.[1] In midwinter, during the "ember days," the shortest days of the year, good witches called *benandanti*, armed with stalks of fennel, battled—or imagined they battled—witches armed with switches of sorghum (Ginzburg 1983 24). "The battles between the benandanti and the witches were a clash, with an uncertain outcome, between abundance and famine, a real battle conducted according to a precise ritual," Ginzburg concludes (25). This was clearly some sort of fertility rite, possibly dimly connected to the Eleusinian mysteries, the half-forgotten echoes of which, Ezra Pound speculated, might have underlain the Provençal cult of courtly love (*SR* 90). Certainly, as Leon Surette has demonstrated, Pound's description of "the mythic basis of humanity" (*SR* 92) with which the Provençal troubadours were in touch sounds like a sublimated version of a fertility cult; it is a fertility cult of ideas.[2]

> The consciousness of some [people] seems to rest, or to have its center more properly, in what the Greek psychologists called the *phantastikon*. Their minds are, that is, circumvolved about them like soap-bubbles reflecting sundry patches of the macro-cosmos. And with certain others their consciousness is "germinal." Their thoughts are in them as the thought of the tree is in the seed, or in the grass, or the grain, or the blossom. And these minds are the more poetic, and they affect mind about them, and transmute it as the seed the earth. And this sort of mind is close on the vital universe. [*SR* 92–93]

111

Later, Pound would articulate the agrarian political economy implicit in this statement. In "Date Line" (1934) Pound noted: "By 1934 Frazer is sufficiently digested for us to know that opposing systems of European morality go back to the opposed temperaments of those who thought copulation was good for the crops and the opposed faction who thought it was bad for the crops (the scarcity economists of pre-history)" (*LE* 85). These passages suggest that Pound recognized primal mythic structures of economy embedded in our psychosexual nature. It seems that we are mentally organized either like bubbles or like seeds. Echoing Jefferson's invocation of the husbandman's "germ of virtue," some folks, according to Pound, are endowed with "germinal" consciousness, an inborn affinity with the processes of an abundant nature. The "scarcity economists of prehistory," on the other hand, are those likely to have an abstract, sharply limited sense of the "vital universe." It seems clear that Pound is giving an economic twist to the age-old argument for cultural priority between poets and philosophers. Pound's image of the bubble is not only the traditional image of financial speculation, where hollow artificial values are allowed to expand until they burst, but it suggests too how the bubble reflects rather than experiences. The bubble refers to, and satirizes, the master trope of metaphysics—that the mind is a mirror and the problem of knowledge is due to our "glassy essence"—(Rorty 1979 12, 17–61), by playing with the double meanings of speculation. A speculative mind is, above all, representational rather than imaginative or poetic; philosophy's task is to make sense of the representations. Since Plato, the undertaking has proceeded through reductive analysis, which turns the plenitude of experience into a few powerful abstract concepts. In effect, from the poets' point of view, the philosopher exchanges the fertility of the metaphor, which promises imaginative abundance, for the antiseptic sterility of the syllogism, which reduces experience to essences. This is obviously one way the mind/body problem can be played out—and the binaries proliferate, but they are all implicit in Pound's primal economy: philosophy is interested in unity, poetry in multiplicity; philosophy is pedantic, poetry is eloquent; philosophy is analytical, poetry is organic, philosophy is abstract, poetry concrete; and so forth.

There is a powerful economic connection here. As Marc Shell has shown, the origins of Western philosophy are intimately linked to the invention of money itself (Shell 1978 11–62), and the language of philosophy is saturated with the technical language of money and money-making. Not only is logic the money of mind, as Marx, following Hobbes, remarked, but many key terms, like "hypothesis" and "dialectic" (and, as we have seen, "speculation"), are hopelessly entangled with the rituals of economic transactions, with hypothecation and with making change, for example (1978, 45–48).

From the poetic viewpoint, represented here by Pound but shared by Williams and others, the intimate connection of philosophy to money has an important sexual dimension, because sexuality itself, inasmuch as it has to do with reproduction, is an economic issue. More precisely, sex is part of the economy of nature—the economy prior to economy, so to speak. Money, however, and especially moneymaking, like Western metaphysics, is explicitly, unabashedly, contrary to the pre-economy of nature because it is homosexual, that is, it works through "the economy of the same," it reproduces without recourse to the Other. Well before Luce Irigaray had this insight, which forms the foundation of her devastating attack on metaphysics,[3] myth-minded heterosexists like Pound and Robert Graves had already perceived that "Platonic love" was, in Graves's words, "intellectual homosexuality," it was the "male intellect trying to make itself spiritually self-sufficient" (Graves 11–12). The consequence was the continuous ejection of the female and the female principle from discourse—the invention of "the feminine," with all of the ideological baggage that goes with it. A second consequence was the promotion of abstract value as the model of all value, the denigration of the particular for the universal, and the denial of difference for what Irigaray sees as the conceptual sterility and solipsism of the "economy of the same." The ongoing confusion between money and wealth is simply one obvious part of the collateral damage from this philosophical and historical disaster.

The dialectical opposition in Ezra Pound's work, which Leon Surette has codified as "Amor" and "Usura," is, then, part of the struggle between poetry and philosophy, seen as the struggle between fertility and usury. In the language of political economy, it is the struggle between natural abundance and artificial scarcity. In American Jeffersonian terms it is a struggle between an agrarian political economy in harmony with nature and a financial one based on profits derived from the active creation of scarcity, especially the rationing of money by bankers who control value and the distribution of wealth.

A main theme of *The Cantos* is the struggle for recognition of a poetic, germinal consciousness, embodied in male figures like Sigismondo Malatesta, Confucius, Dante, Mussolini, and various artists. These male figures are accompanied by a variety of female ones, some historical, some mythic, who are to be read (sometimes simultaneously) as incarnations of Aphroditean beauty, like Eleanor of Aquitaine and Helen or a more dangerous figure, Circe. All are, however, mobilized against Usura, that is, the sin of usury raised to the level of pervasive evil, a malevolent and hyperactive false consciousness, a sterile, sexually disabling, and perverse destroyer, which suppresses the natural abundance and fertility of the earth and the germinal imagination, the true source of wealth and poetry.

Pound's notion of germinal consciousness explains, in part, the extraordinary affirmative power of Pound's agrarian economics and his overfierce animus against Usura. Critics like Surette, Sieburth, and Oderman[4] who have studied Pound's attitudes toward sex and love have shown how Pound's notion of fertility committed him to a heterosexist and productivist sexual politics.[5] I choose these terms without prejudice to try to suggest the economic bearing of sexuality for Pound. In his agrarian scheme there can be no significant difference between production and reproduction. His brief against homosexuality and the historical tropic links between homosexuality and usury, which date from Aristotle, will be discussed later in the chapter. Germinal consciousness is confirmed through coition, which Pound considered potentially capable in itself of producing visionary states (compare Oderman). The important line from Pound's rendering of Cavalcanti's "Donna mi prega" in Canto 36 is, Surette stresses, the untranslated "Sacrum, sacrum, inluminatio coitu" (36:180) (Surette 1979 57f.). Pound seems to have believed in a phallic ordering principle that G. R. S. Mead, in a lecture that Pound apparently heard, called the "Great Power" or "Universal Mind" and a female principle, "Great Thought" that produced everything.[6] Surette adds that "conceiving the two great principles of the Universe, Mind (potentiality) and Thought (incarnation) as male and female" ought to have appealed to the author of the 'Postcript' to [Rémy de Gourmont's] *Natural Philosophy of Love"* (1993 61).

Pound's vision requires a politics of sex that extends to his sense of an ideal republic. Necessarily, his utopia must be agrarian in ideology, if not in actual fact, in order to preserve the sacred link between creation and procreation, production, and reproduction. Pound's belief in the persistence of fertility cults through the Middle Ages is updated in *The Cantos* as Pound shows that fertility cults are, equally, economic programs. So the following is economics:

> By prong have I entered these hills:
> That the grass grow from my body,
> That I hear the roots speaking together,
> The air is new on my leaf,
> The forked boughs shake with the wind [47:238]

Note the colon: the sexual act causes the grass, which is the source of agricultural and ultimately, in Pound's view, cultural abundance. As noted earlier, the climax of *The Pisan Cantos* is the "marriage" between the freeholder and his land celebrated by Crèvecoeur and American agrarians, which becomes, in Pound, the "connubiam terrae," an aspect of a "cthonic mysterium" (82:540), a symbolic sexual union with the earth.

In Canto 39 Pound tropes Odysseus's adventures on Circe's island into an Eleusinian celebration, and Circe becomes a fertility goddess. There, "in her house of smooth stone" where "girls talked . . . of fucking," Odysseus finds Circe

> Venter venustus, cunni cultrix, of the velvet marge
> ver novum, canorum, ver novum [39:193]

> Belly beautiful, cunny tender, of the velvet marge
> New spring, singing, new spring
> [Terrell's trans. 160 12–13n]

Spring means both the season and source. The Tennysonian euphemism "velvet marge," alongside the Catullus-like honesty of the Latin, suggests that we need to reread nineteenth-century poetry to find the deeper, franker truths that its rhetoric skirts and eroticizes. The passage I quote is surrounded by Homer's Greek and the Latin of

Ovid and Catullus. The classical sources of spring are to be the source of a modern rebirth of the imagination and thus of art, because they are in touch with the imagination's sexual sources.

Later in the canto we seem to see the Eleusinian ritual itself in a vision of "fifty and forty together"—apparently couples coupling—"To the beat of the measure,"

Unceasing the measure
Flank by flank on the headland
    with the Goddess' eyes to seaward
By Circeo, by Terracina, with the stone eyes
    white toward the sea
With one measure, unceasing:
    "Fac deum!" [Make god!] "Est factus." [He is made.]
Ver Novum!
    ver novum
Thus made the spring . . . [39:195]

The spring being made here is also a renaissance of the arts, faithful to the primordial, pre-economic "measure." This act of synchronized sex is a ritual that will lead to germinal consciousness and measures of poetic—but also economic—value based on natural processes.

Williams was quick to note a political and economic subtext behind this celebration in a review of Pound's *Eleven New Cantos* (1935).

Suddenly in Canto XXXIX, there is disclosed an unfamiliar magnificence of fornication—the official sin of constituted stupidity. That sex will be accomplished in sin, is the blind behind which venality has worked to undo the world. Kids may go masturbating into asylums but profits must be preserved. But, if the poet has always seen through the absurdity, today he sees more clearly than formerly. Love versus usury, the living hell-stink of today. [*SE* 168]

Swept up in the mood produced by Pound's poems, Williams continues to excoriate "the buggery of professional thought," which dwarfs the "mind of man." Williams agrees with Pound that "the mind thrives on fornication which bespeaks an escape of the spirit to its own lordly domains" (*SE* 168).

If the issue really is, as Williams and Pound claim, "love versus usury," then it is up to the poets to promote love and expose usury. When Pound speaks of "love" as a regenerative force in the world, he does not mean the quietism implied by romantic love. To Pound

"Love" means something like "in tune with nature" or "righteous living." His interest in the Eleusinian sexual mysteries, Confucian ethics, and the Fascist experiment in Italy are all of a piece in this regard. So is his interest in the Monte dei Paschi. One of the most unexpected things about *The Cantos* is finding that a bank is actually one of its heroes.

The Monte dei Paschi: Institutional Fertility Cult

The historical struggle between abundance and scarcity, amor and usura, is the central drama of *The Cantos*. In *The Fifth Decad of Cantos* (1937), the champions in this struggle are banks. Pound divided banks into two groups, "good banks" and "hell banks," on the basis of the opposed principles of natural fertility and usury. The good bank of *The Cantos* is the Monte dei Paschi of Siena.

The Fifth Decad of Cantos opens with three cantos composed from the records of the Monte and devoted to the founding of the bank and the fortunes of Siena through the end of the Napoleonic period. Throughout this book, the Monte and the principle of fertility are contrasted with the destructive mendacity of the Bank of England, war profiteers, and their academic sycophants. The most famous of all *The Cantos*, the great chant against usura, Canto 45, immediately follows the group devoted to the Monte, 42–44. Canto 46, filled with references to the founding of the Bank of England (46:233) and the populistic heresy that the Rothschilds caused the American Civil War (46:232–33), continues to make the case against usury. The fertility myth canto, number 47, with its repeated "begin thy plowing" (47:237), follows as a kind of counterpoint, recelebrating Eleusinian fertility rites.

Number 48 picks up where number 46 left off. We are given images of Verdun; corpses are being jammed into the earth so that the Kaiser may walk on level ground. It is alleged that the work of Browning and van Buren is likewise buried; images of bad government, peculation, and watered stock follow (48:240–42). Pound deftly puns on the economic term "net," as in net profit, assuming the voice of a leisure-class woman who has bought "net gloves / made like fishnet" (48:242) and contrasting them to the "spread threads" that Polynesian navigators, in touch with the vital universe, string across their outrigger canoes to navigate across the ocean. Canto 49 is the sublime "Seven Lakes Canto," a set piece of Chinoiserie and Confucian order. It's the first hint of the heavy Confucian barrage that will follow in the next group of cantos (*Cantos 52–71* [1940]). Finally, Canto 51 begins with a reprise of the chant against usura and ends at the Congress of Vienna, with "Geryon twin with Usura" (51:251) triumphant, catching the unwary in his netlike "eel-fisher's basket" (51:252).

For the careful reader of *The Fifth Decad*, the parallels to the period of the Great War and the Versailles Treaty ("the bankers' peace," as Gorham Munson called it) should have been evident amid the increasing international tension and air of crisis that proved to be the prologue to World War II. The lesson of *The Fifth Decad* can be summed up in another Munson phrase: "War is economic peace, peace is economic war" (Munson 222).[7] But *The Fifth Decad* also shows that there have been and are alternatives to Usura. The drama of these cantos hangs on Pound's belief that viable alternatives to the dominant economic system are constantly being proposed and squashed by the forces of financial evil as it tries to maintain its precarious hegemony. The alternative to the "Bankers' Peace," which seems to be the result of Pound's historicizing in *The Fifth Decad*, is provided by Pound himself in the opening of the next cluster of cantos, *Cantos 52–71*, which appeared in 1940. Referring back to the *Fifth Decad*, Pound writes:

> And I have told you how things were under Duke
> > Leopold in Siena
> And the true basis of credit, that is
> > the abundance of nature
> with the whole folk behind it [52:257]

When Pound became aware of it, the Monte dei Paschi, literally "Mount of the pastures," had been functioning in Siena, Italy, for nearly three hundred years. Pound noted in 1935 that "you could open an account there tomorrow" (*SP* 240). You still can. The Monte dei Paschi is the oldest continuously operating bank in the world, older than the Bank of England.[8] Pound's principles led him to recognize the Jeffersonian and even Eleusinian implications of the Monte dei Paschi when he came upon the massive compilation of its documents in Narciso Mengozzi's *Il Monte dei Paschi di Siene e le Aziende in Esso Ri-*

unite (9 vols., Siena, 1891–1925).[9] It was natural for him to oppose this "good bank" to that familiar Populist target the Bank of England.

Still, why would Pound give over a significant portion of his life's work to the documents surrounding the founding of an obscure bank in seventeenth-century Siena? Pound's Agrarian ideology led him to believe that true wealth, and therefore true credit, existed in the fertility of nature. Pound translated the details of the Sienese bank's founding into his *Cantos* in hopes that it would find modern imitators.

As its name suggests, the Monte dei Paschi was based on the revenue from the *paschi*, or pastures, near Siena. Specifically, it derived its revenue from the grazing rights to these lands and the profits derived from the natural increase of the sheep that reproduced there. "The lesson is the very basis of solid banking," Pound wrote. "The CREDIT rests *in ultimate* on the ABUNDANCE OF NATURE, on the growing grass which can nourish the living sheep" (Pound's emphasis, *SP* 240).[10] The Monte was not a warehouse. It stored no grain, but it did promote agriculture, which had been the basis of wealth in the Siena region from time immemorial. Importantly, this bank is based on the principle of natural fertility, not the "perversion" of compound interest (Kenner 427). These are Physiocratic principles solidly in the Jeffersonian tradition.

Even in the preindustrial seventeenth century, the Monte dei Paschi was distinguished from the Monti di Pietà [Mounts of Pity], which operated in Siena and throughout Italy. These were really glorified pawnshops that "lent only on pledges / that is on stuff actually hocked" (42:210), and they were licensed to charge a ruinous interest, "taking from 20 to 50 percent on petty loans" (Nelson 19). These Monti had a sordid history. Originally run by Jews who had been invited to come to Italy in the hopes of stimulating trade, they were taken over by Christian friars amid a revival of the worst kind of anti-Semitism. Mouthing hypocrisies, "the Observantine preachers regurgitated the oft-discredited charges of ritual murder, incited mobs to attacks on Jewish life and property, and harangued the people and their magistrates to destroy the Jews, and establish Christian pawnshops, the *monti di pietà*" (Nelson 19). Then they took over, sophistically justifying the usury they had condemned as a reflection of real costs (Nelson 22).[11]

In 1622 Siena was trying to recover from a military defeat by

Florence. Something more equitable than the Monti di Pietà was called for to revive the credit of the city, which "had no income" (42:211). Pound translated part of the proposal for the new bank:

> . . . wd be we believe useful
> and beneficient that there be place to lend licitly
> MONEY to receive licitly money
> at moderate and legitimate interest [42:210]

Such lending and receiving could not be done at the Monti di Pietà. What was needed was:

> A mount, a bank, a fund a bottom an
> Institution of credit
> a place to send cheques in and out of
> and not yet a banco di giro [a bank for the transfer of credits]
> [42:209]

The first line above spells out the meanings of "monte." Its associations suggest an institution that is literally a part of nature. Pound exploits the richness of the word throughout *The Cantos* where the ancient association of mountains with holiness recurs.[12] Elsewhere in these cantos Pound will translate the Italian word for interest, *frutto*, as "fruit" to stress the naturalness of the Monte dei Paschi. Thus we read that "who puts his coin in [the Monte] in it shall hold his luoghi [place] / bearing 5% fruitage per annum" (43:221).[13] The fruit analogy is aided by the verb "to bear." Pound would argue, following some canonists, that the relatively low interest of 5 percent is not usurious but correlates with nature:[14] "The practices of rent or interest arise out of the natural disposition of grain and animals to multiply" (*SP* 226). Finally, the *banco di giro* is, through the etymological connection to "gyre" and the sense of circulation, a kind of financial vortex. It reminds us that Pound's favorite image of a scene of artistic renaissance is an image of circulation, very much an image of an active artistic economy. A good bank may finance a vortex and in that sense may be one. Significantly, I think, the "good bank" as vortex is the opposite of the familiar Populist image of the "financial Octopus." Rather than gathering everything to itself, the banco di giro, the gyre bank, distributes and underwrites.

The Monte dei Paschi demonstrates its moral health by stipulating that the magistrate in charge

give his chief care that the specie
be lent to whomso can best USE IT
(id est, più utilmente)
to the good of their houses, to benefit of their business
as of weaving, the wool trade, the silk trade
And that (7thly) the overabundance every five years shall
                          the Bailey
distribute to workers of the contrade (the wards) holding in
reserve a prudent proportion as against unforeseen losses
though there shd. be NO such losses
and 9th that the borrowers can pay up before the end of
                          their
term whenso it be to their interest [42:209–10]

The values that Pound wants to promote are evident in his translation. First, he highlights use value. Usury, like finance capitalism generally, promotes exchange values at the expense of use values. By their very nature, exchange values inhere not in things but in the money that one can get for things. Second, Pound hints at the Aristotelian distinction between "economy," household management, and chresmatistics, moneymaking, when he points immediately to the use of these loans for "the good" of houses. These loans are not for speculation in real estate; they are to benefit the businesses trading and manufacturing real goods, like wool and silk—not for creating merely paper values. Third, "interest" is assigned to the borrower, not the bank. The Monte is a bank working in the debtor's interest.

Finally, Pound notes the extraordinary charitable aspect of the Monte dei Paschi. It disburses its surplus back to the people. In 1989, the Monte earned profits of $222.2 million. Of this sum, 25 percent, over $55 million, was "assigned to donations and public works" (Green 64). A recent report notes:

The bank, in fact, was not, nor is it now, a bank out to make a profit for its shareholders. It has no shareholders, except, in a sense, [Siena] and its people. It prides itself not only on being the guardian of Siena's economic well-being but also on its support for city museums and such institutions as the University of Siena and the municipal hospital. Each year half of Il Monte's profits may be turned over to charity, welfare and public works for the benefit of the local economy; the autostrada itself was paid for by the bank to provide Siena's modern lifeline to the rest of Italy (Green 600).

This idea of returning bank profits directly to the people (as opposed to businesses) is consistent with the Social Credit theory that governments can be their own bankers and actually return dividends to the people. The extent to which the Monte dei Paschi can operate in this fashion proved to Pound that Douglas was correct.

Why does the Monte dei Paschi seem impossible? The extent to which we feel that it must not be so, that there must be a catch, is the degree to which we have absorbed financial orthodoxy. Pound argued that the orthodox financial system has actively prevented the dissemination of information about banks based on such principles as the venerable institution of Siena.

Usura as Perversion

Ezra Pound had spent "seventeen years on the [usury] case" (46:233) by "a.d.1935" (46:234) when he was composing Canto 46; "a.d." in this case may well mean "after Douglas," whom Pound had met in 1918 at the *New Age.* Like other American Populists, Pound dated the beginnings of modern monetary evil to the founding of the Bank of England in 1694. As we know, the American financial community descends directly from it, via Hamilton's Bank of the United States, which worked on the same usurious principles. William Paterson,[15] the founder of the Bank of England, described its workings by saying "the bank

> . . . *hath benefit of interest on all*
> *the moneys which it, the bank creates out of nothing*
> [46:233, Pound's emphasis]

Pound has this quotation underlined in the text—italics aren't strong enough. This, you might say, is the heart of darkness inside usura. The diabolical power of this parody of procreation is, for Pound, the satanic double of the poetic imagination.

To Pound, the principles on which banks of discount are founded are perverse. Outstanding loans are counted as "assets"; money deposited is a "liability." Bank "profits" are not really surplus value but a form of legal graft that simply adds costs to goods by inflating prices. Like the Populists, Pound doesn't buy the argument that interest is the cost of risking capital. Interest may have some justification in the private lender, lending private funds, but banks lend public money for private gain. Instead of offering the service of distributing money for the public convenience, banks make a business of creating debts. This is *contra naturam.*

Usury is like a disease. We have seen how Crèvecoeur speaks of healthy farms "cankered" with debt; his image is explicitly of venereal disease. John Taylor of Caroline, the Jeffersonian ideologue, saw the English financial system as "a painted courtezan, who corrupts and plunders her admirers"; he cannot imagine that "the United States will gain an addition of present or future happiness, by divorcing the healthy and chaste country girl whom they first espoused . . . to marry a second-hand town lady, so diseased and ulcerated, that the English people are heartily willing to part with her" (quoted in Schlesinger 23). Whitman uses similar imagery in his wild diatribe "The 18th Presidency of the United States," printed for the 1856 election. Among an amazing number of epithets, the "nominating dictators" who control American politics are characterized as "blind men, deaf men, pimpled men, scarred inside with the vile disorder [e.g., by gonorrhea], gaudy outside with gold chains made from the people's money and harlot's money twisted together" (Whitman 1313–14). "Azure hath a canker by Usura," says Pound (45:230). Williams would compare the usury issue to cancer in *Paterson* (*P* 182–83).[16] Varying his imagery slightly, Pound calls it a "a beast with a hundred legs" (15:64). Like all parasitical growths, however, usury has a weird and perverse lifelikeness, because banks operate through the principle of unnatural increase, that is, compound interest, a problem that has worried moralists since Aristotle because such growth was presumed to be hostile to life. There is a long literary tradition associating usury and "unnatural" sexuality. Aristotle makes Usury the "most hated" form of wealth getting because it "makes gain out of money itself, and not from the natural object of it. For money was intended to be used in exchange, but not to increase as interest. And this term interest, which means the birth of money from money, is applied to the breeding of money because the offspring resembles the parent. Whereof of all modes of getting wealth this is the most unnatural" (*Politics* 1:10, quoted in Lewis Hyde 112). Williams, in his review of Canto 39, contrasts the glories of heterosexual love, "fornication," against the "buggery" of professional thought" (*SE* 168). Fornication is liberating, "an escape of the spirit to its own lordly domains," the intellectual buggery of professional profiteers, whether academics, usurers, or businessmen, means that "the world is narrowed, penned up, herded to be hog-driven to a very real slaughter, pending only the cue to start it at its own throat again—to enrich— whom?" (168)—a horrific image of the political economy of anal sex that uncannily predicts the totalitarian holocausts and World War II. Pound, of course, was steeped in the medieval polemic against usury:

> Usura slayeth the child in the womb
> It stayeth the young man's courting
> It hath brought palsey to bed,lyeth
> between the young bride and her bridegroom
>   CONTRA NATURAM
>   [45:230]

The "unnatural" procreation of money is one reason why Dante (and Pound) consign the Usurers to the same circle of Hell as the Sodomites and goes a long way to explain a persistent rhetorical association between usurers and "unnatural" sex. "By great wisdom sodomy and usury were seen coupled together," Pound wrote. "If there comes ever a rebirth or a resurrection of Christian Church, one and Catholic, a recognition of divinity as *La somma sapienza e il primo amore* it will come with a recognition and the abjuration of the great sin *contra naturam*, of the prime sin against natural abundance" (*SP* 235).[17] The other linkage between sodomy and usury is the persistent association in Western literature between gold and excrement.[18] Thus Pound is consistent in his choice of adjectives when he speaks of the "buggering bank" in a summation of his views on the banks in Canto 77 (Kenner 426n).

Usury, then, is literally contrary to nature. It has a diabolical oppositeness. Pound exploits the imaginative possibilities of this idea quite early in *The Cantos*, first in the "Tale of the Honest Sailor" told in Canto 12 and then in the so-called Hell Cantos, Cantos 14 and 15.

The "Tale of the Honest Sailor" is derived from a story of John Quinn's. In the Canto, it is told by "*Jim X . . .* / in a bankers' meeting" (12:55). "Bored by their hard luck stories . . . ,"

> Bored with their proprieties,
>   as they sat, the ranked presbyterians,
> Directors, dealers through holding companies,
> Deacons in churches, owning slum properties,
> *Alias* usurers in excelsis,

the quintessential essence of usurers,
The purveyors of employment, whining over their twenty p.c.
and the hard times,
And the bust-up of Brazilian securities
(S.A. securities),
And the general uncertainty of all investment
Save investment in new bank buildings,
productive of bank buildings,
And not likely to ease distribution . . . [12:55]

The linkage between usury and explicitly Christian religious hypocrisy is part of the muckraking heritage of the American reform period.[19] The story of "The Honest Sailor" is an especially appropriate one for a bankers' meeting because it is a story of "unnatural increase" about a sailor, "a heavy drinker, / A hell of a cuss, a rowster, a boozer," and, finally, a father who thinks he's a mother, because in his final spree before reforming he was buggered by "a rich merchant in Stambouli." The poor fellow is brought to a hospital and is operated on. A child taken from a prostitute in the next ward is exhibited as though it had been taken out of him. Believing the child to be his son, the sailor reforms and launches a successful career based on the familiar economic pieties of a hundred years ago: save and get ahead. The story proceeds like those Horatio Alger tales so full of Carnegie-like Presbyterian uplift—until the final scandalous moment when the dying sailor confesses to his beloved son that he isn't the youth's father but his mother. At this moment in the poem, Pound's tone, style, and moral become medieval, and the tale becomes like one of Chaucer's bawdy fabliaux. A more honest diction, from a more honest time, a time prior to usura, surfaces in the tale of the Honest Sailor to speak truths silenced by the complacent, post-Victorian veneer of the godly-usurers, " 'I am not your fader but your moder,' quod he, / 'Your fader was a rich merchant in Stambouli' " (12:57).

This is a fabliau of finance, of a world where everything is "perverse" or is going in the wrong direction. Under the regime of finance, creation itself is backward. The success narrative of the thrifty saver who

. . . saved up his pay money
and kept on savin' his pay money,
And bought a share in the ship,
and finally had half shares,

Then a ship,
        and in time a whole line of steamers;
And educated the kid [12:56]

in the best capitalist style turns out to have founded his whole enterprise on the unsuccessfully sublimated guilty knowledge of his self-
prostitution. His "son" is the unintended consequence of a business
transaction. The story is based on the blind faith of the sailor and the
clever manipulations of the hypocritical doctors who got him to believe that he could have a son. The doctors' ploy allowed the "Honest"
sailor to imagine that his homosexual relations with the merchant
were truly procreative and not merely a sexual relation.[20] These "doctors," (like Williams's doctors in *Paterson* [*P* 182]) are figures for professional economists, who insist on making natural a system of
wealth that is inherently artificial, even perverse. In light of the Presbyterian audience for Quinn's jocularity, we should read this as a story
about Original Sin. The purpose of this story in *The Cantos* is to suggest that usury is the Original Sin of capital. The "Tale of the Honest
Sailor" is a kind of creation myth for finance capitalism. If usury is
buggery, a system that creates unnatural wealth "unnaturally," then it
follows that the civilization founded on this unnatural, perverse rock
is itself perverse, a Hell on earth. The rotten theology of such a Hell,
preached by "Deacons in churches, owning slum properties" (12:55) is
the ideology that justifies this mass (in both senses) of corruption that
is modern life.

Similarly, in Cantos 14 and 15, the Hell Cantos, Pound plays on the
reversal of values that makes the financial worldview possible. Thus
the "politicians" (Lloyd George and the Presbyterian president Woodrow Wilson) are shown amid

The stench of wet coal
[Georg]e and [Wilso]n, their wrists bound to
their ankles,
Standing bare bum,
Faces smeared on their rumps,
        wide eye on flat buttock,
Bush hanging for beard,
        Addressing crowds through their arse-holes. [14:61]

War "profiteers" are seen "drinking blood sweetened with sh——t"
(14:61). As in a banking system, where debts are "assets" and sums of

money available to savers are "liabilities," there is a reversal of natural human circulation. The usurers—in their manifold forms as politicians, profiteers, and so forth—speak through their assholes and dine on excrement.[21] In the usury/buggery world, things go in where they should come out and the natural circulation that sustains nature and life is reversed.

The financial system is a vortex in reverse, a system of negative energy with a vested interest in getting things backward. Wealth is called money; profit is wrongly considered abundance. (In reality, profits are the dividends of scarcity, because in a financial system, scarcity determines value.) Such a system is at war both with procreation and with poetry, which are based in nature and abundance. Desire, which finance perverts into a devouring cupidity, is, in nature, selfless—it wants to give; it is prolific.

Williams explores these parallel economies in a number of poems. In "Late for Summer Weather" (1935), he describes a poor couple, obviously unemployed, "Fat Lost Ambling / nowhere." He watches as "they kick

> their way through
> heaps of
> fallen maple leaves
>
> still green—
> crisp as dollar bills
> Nothing to do. Hot cha! [CP1 384]

The salacious "Hot Cha!" hints that the pair are on their way to do something sexual togther, maybe to roll around on those crisp green leaves that are like dollar bills. With "nothing to do" and nowhere to go, they have the opportunity to notice and the time to satisfy their desires. For the moment they share in the wealth of nature, as though they were rich in money. Emotionally, literally, they are living in Indian Summer—on borrowed time—and they know it; for this reason they are tardy, late for summer weather. Soon the warmth will be gone and leaves that are crisp with promise will become, again, just dead leaves. Williams is not indulging in a romanticization of the plight of these lucky unfortunates. He has effectively deeroticized them in his description of his "dirty sweater" and her "Grey flapping pants / red skirt and / broken down black pumps" in earlier stanzas (CP1 384).

Instead, he is noticing that, outside the money economy, another, more primal, economy still functions. The couple *and* the maple tree that produces and sheds its leaves so freely, are part of it.

Williams has other poems like this one in which the opposition between the erotic and the monetary provides a loose dialectical tension on which the poem rides. The brief, erotically charged "The Girl (with big breasts)" (1937) is one example:

THE GIRL

with big breasts
under a blue sweater

bareheaded—
crossing the street

reading a newspaper
stops, turns

and looks down
as though

she had seen a dime
on the pavement. [*CP1* 444]

Like "Late for Summer Weather," this poem balances two forms of attention. The poet's attention is arrested by the girl's figure and the promise of sexual abundance and fertility signaled by her large breasts. She is represented as a kind of fertility goddess; yet her attention is caught by the "dime" she seems to see on the street. The purpose of the poem is to contrast two systems of desire, one based on natural abundance—"big breasts"—the other on tokens of a simulated reality, "dimes."

"A Woman in Front of a Bank," published in *The Clouds* (1948) in the midst of *Paterson,* clearly establishes the antithesis I want to illustrate between sexuality and finance. Because it also finds a way to comment on poetic form, this important poem should be read as a meditation on the impact of financial structures on the imagination:

The bank is a matter of columns,
like . convention,
unlike invention; but the pediments
sit there in the sun

to convince the doubting of
investments "solid
as rock"—upon which the world
stands, the world of finance,

the only world: Just there,
talking with another woman while
rocking a baby carriage
back and forth stands a woman in

a pink cotton dress, bare legged
and headed whose legs
are two columns to hold up
her face, like Lenin's (her loosely

arranged hair profusely blond) or
Darwin's and there you
have it:
a woman in front of a bank. [*CP2* 126–27]

This poem is much less ambitious but, perhaps, deeper than Pound's
grandiose contrasts of "good" and "hell banks." Like Pound's Monte
dei Paschi, the woman represents an economy based on the principle
of natural (and human) fertility—on "invention" (a privileged word in
Williams's work) rather than "convention." The woman rocking her
baby in the carriage talking to another woman is presented as the antithesis of the bank. She is, in fact, a fertility goddess, the true "good
bank," whose "legs / are two columns to hold up / her face." Yet she
is human too, capable of human speech as opposed to the bank's conventional clichés and the advertising slogans ("solid as a rock") that
limit the bank to its narrow, mistaken, economic "world of finance, /
the only world."

The bank's world is, first, "a matter of columns" and pediments,
cultural conventions manifested in the persistence of classical archi-
tecture. Perhaps because the original banks of the classical period were
temples, where money changers set up their benches (from which we
have inherited the word "bank"), the convention of building banks to
look like temples has continued well into our century. For very good
reasons, the banks want to establish an image of permanence; they live
off the perception that they are safe, conventional, and not subject to
fits of speculation or panic, that they are, in effect, "classics"—timeless, rock solid, ahistorical institutions.

Moreover, the columns that hold up the bank's classical pediment and give it its classical facade are also the bookkeeper's columns of accounts: debits and credits. These, we know, must "balance." Balance implies harmony. The institution of interest, however—what antibank agitators call usury—requires that the books shall never balance; they will always tilt, and tilt decisively, in favor of the bank. The usury that banks charge on loans is their profit; thus the profits of banks depend, as Douglas pointed out, on the simple fact that debts will never be wholly repaid. "With usura," Pound famously wrote, "no man shall have a house of good stone" (45:229). Usura guarantees banks the profits to build grandiose marble temples to their own mastery. Williams's poem shrewdly takes the measure of such classicism and records that the banks are only a facade, a stage set. The world, after all, does not "stand on finance." Finance stands on the world.

But the columns in the poem also represent the "conventions" of poetry. In this context they must represent a corrupt tradition, for the suggestion is that the temple of poetry has been turned into a countinghouse. Williams looked for a poetic unit that could abandon "old-time rigidities" within a line that could somehow be "a well-conceived form within which modification may exist" (SL 136)—like a woman, perhaps, whose form changes in pregnancy.

The existence of the woman in the poem—indeed the existence of females as such—is a challenge to the artificial claims of the money economy represented by the bank. The woman's heroic—even Lenin-like—revolutionary and procreative power, symbolized by her child, relegates the bank to the background.

Through the juxtaposition of the woman and the bank, Williams reminds us that the bank operates through the principle of unnatural increase, that is, compound interest. The Monte dei Paschi bank is based on the fertility of nature, not on compound interest. It does take interest, but it is calibrated to natural increase and so may be said to bear at least a passing resemblance to real costs. Most important, the credit it distributes is based on real values—on sheep in the fields. It is not created "ex nihil" by the stroke of a pen—or computer key—in a diabolical parody of poetic power. The woman in front of the bank represents the same principle of natural fertility that has sustained the Monte dei Paschi. Her procreative power reduces the bank to what it really is, a pretentious facade hiding a set of conventions that denies life. She reminds us that debt is the enemy of fertility, foreclosing dreams, children, a fertile future. Williams's message, which is so much like Pound's, is significantly more democratic—or at least more demotic. It not only conveys but *is* a democratic response to the tyranny of plutocracy.

In the real, historical world, there is no clear division between sexuality and finance. "Usura" permeates all relations, including sexual relations—it "lyeth / between young bride and her bridegroom"—and as a result sex becomes "unnatural." Williams shares the antibuggery cant of Pound and pursues the connection between homosexuality (this time between women) and money in *Paterson*. The ideological function of this pairing is, I believe, similar to Pound's and offers further evidence of the way the poets' mutual bias against financial practice has far-reaching implications in their views concerning sexuality and the mythic structures of economy.

"Unnatural" sex and money also surfaces in *Paterson*, book 4, part 1, "The Run to the Sea." Book 4 is, in fact, the most explicitly concerned with economic issues of all the books of *Paterson*. In book 4 we find a Social Credit money tract pasted into the poem, followed by pages on money and credit (*P* 180–85). It must mean something, then, that the book begins with "An Idyl," an odd, mock-pastoral featuring the adventures of the virgin (but not virginal) Phyllis, from Ramapo, New Jersey, who becomes the masseuse for a rich lesbian poetess. Simultaneously, Phyllis is carrying on a sexual but unconsummated affair with the poet Paterson. If this situation weren't complicated enough, Phyllis also has a fiancé and is extremely—the poem suggests unnaturally—close to her drunken father, a man of fallen estate, to whom she writes her semiliterate letters: "I won't wrestle with you all night on the bed any more because you got the D.T.'s. I can't take it, your [sic] too strong for me" (*P* 150).

As the object of all desire in the poem, Phyllis has some sort of symbolic role to play. Judging from her letters and her hardheaded realism, she may represent the American language. Her "virginity" is stressed, and part 3 of book 4 begins with an interjected reminder seemingly spoken by the poet's wife, Flossie Williams: "Haven't you forgotten your virgin purpose, the language?" (*P* 186). Phyllis is this virgin purpose. She elicits poems from both Paterson and the Poetess as they attempt, only semisuccessfully, to seduce her. Despite her naked petting with Paterson, and her trip to Anticosti, Quebec, in the Poetess's yacht, Phyllis remains a virgin, and that, apparently, is the point of this section.

If Phyllis is the language, then Paterson *and* Corydon, the Poetess, are aspects of Williams. In *Paterson* "the poet is the suppressed androgyne, a male seeking reunion with his lost female counterpart," Joseph Riddel has argued (160–61). The observation fits well with the beginnings of *Paterson*, where Paterson, "a man like a city," is posed against "a woman like a flower" (*P* 7). The language, symbolized by the Paterson Falls, is what comes between them and joins them together.

The Phyllis and Corydon section complicates the picture, however. Corydon approaches the language (Phyllis) from a sophisticated perspective—sophisticated, that is, in the bad sense. Corydon "represents 'the great world' against the more or less primitive world of the provincial city," Williams told Marianne Moore. "She is informed, no sluggard, uses her talents as she can. There has to be that world against which the other [represented by Phyllis] tests herself" (*SL* 304). Corydon's worldly sophistication is made to represent Eliot's betrayal of American poetry—as we'll see in a moment.[22] But like Eliot's influence on American poetry, Corydon does have a seductive power over Phyllis. She flatters Phyllis and confuses her by complaining that she "has hands like a man" (*P* 149), but later she exclaims over Phyllis's "Wonderful / hands! I completely forget myself. / Some hands are silver, some gold and some, / a very few, like yours, diamonds. . . . " Then, ominously, she adds, "(If only I / could keep you!) You like it here?" (*P* 151). Corydon's hierarchies suggests that her tastes, in sex, in metaphor, are funded by canons of value that bring together the class system and codes of wealth. She wonders if she can buy Phyllis for more than a few hours at a time. Corydon's values have a certain effect on Phyllis as the section continues; she becomes more androgynous. In one scene she wears her father's shirt to a rendevous with Paterson (*P* 155). In the end she rides atop him and, apparently, Phyllis's assumption of power is part of what makes him seem to lose interest in her.

Paterson suspects he has approached her wrongly. He ought to have used force, he thinks, and we are to believe that Phyllis really wanted to be ravished. At the same time, however, he does speak her language—their lines run together. In the end, the poet seems to reject her:

Why do you torment yourself? I can't
think unless you're naked. I wouldn't blame

you if you beat me up, punched me,
anything at all . I wouldn't do

you that much honor. What! what did you say?
I said I wouldn't do you that much

honor . So that's all?
I'm afraid so. Something I shall always

desire, you've seen to that. Talk to me.
This is not the time for it. Why did you let

me come? Who knows why *did* you? I like
coming here, I need you. I know that .

hoping I'd take it from you, lacking
your consent. I've lost out haven't I?

You have. Pull down my slip .
He lay upon his back upon the couch.

She came, half-dressed, and straddled him
My thighs are sore from riding .

Oh let me breathe!   [*P* 168]

The problem for Paterson is that Phyllis, though a virgin, is, to his mind, quite corrupt, and anyway, if Phyllis is the American language, how is he to reject her? This part of the poem is really about his poetic frustrations. She's a flirt—"No. I'm good at saying that"—Phyllis says as Paterson strips her naked (*P* 154). She goes to him "Just to talk," she tells Corydon (*P* 153). Of course, what else can language do?

The corruption of Phyllis is connected to the "Big City." Williams told Edith Heal: "With the approach to the city [in *Paterson*], international character began to enter the river and pervert it; sexual perversions, such things that every metropolis when you get to know it houses. Certain human elements can't take the gaff, have to become perverts to satisfy certain longings. When human beings herd together, have to face each other, they are very likely to go crooked" (*IWWP* 79). Phyllis is a nurse. She writes her father that she's "having a fine time in the Big City as a Professional Woman ahem!" (*P* 150; we are supposed to register a double entendre here), where she makes big money massaging Corydon, who is recovering from some sort of accident. Corydon serenades her with poems, and their international character is stressed. Some are supposed to be in the manner of Yeats (*P* 166). The principal tone is confected from the manner of Eliot's *Four Quartets*, especially "The Dry Salvages," and *The Waste Land*, section 4, "Death by Water." Corydon herself is portrayed as a rich reactionary, out of touch with American reality. She stumbles over the name of Phyllis's hometown, Ramapo, a native American name she mistakes for "Rach-a-mo"—"What sort of life can you lead / in that horrid place," she wonders (*P* 150). When Phyllis tells her she trained as a nurse in Paterson, to Corydon the name of the city recalls Nicholas Murray Butler, who personifies the rich social reactionary.[23] It is revealing that Corydon associates Paterson with Butler, which is completely consistent with her remark that "they used to have silk mills there . / until the unions ruined them" (*P* 151).

Like her name, Corydon's poetry reflects her international sensibilities. She weakly pastoralizes the three rocks at the end of Welfare Island into sheep:

> the three rocks tapering off into the water .
> are all that's left of the elemental, the primitive
> in this environment. I call them my sheep . [*P* 152]

Phyllis's comment in a letter to her father is biting: "If they're sheep I'm the Queen of England. They're white all right but it's from the gulls that crap them up all day long" (*P* 160). Phyllis is right, of course. If she were the Queen of England, the rocks would be sheep; Corydon writes like the Queen of England and thinks like a Queen. She can recognize the "elemental" and the "primitive" but can never acknowledge them.

These three rocks are intended to remind us of "The Dry Salvages," three rocks off Cape Anne that give the title to the third of Eliot's *Four Quartets* (1944). In an introductory note to that poem Eliot tendentiously explains that the name "dry salvages" "presumably" is derived from "les trois sauvages" (Eliot 1962 130). Eliot's etymologizing may explain Corydon's overwrought attribution of the primitive and elemental to the rocks in the East River.

The Poetess's poem "Corydon, a pastoral" (*P* 160) is, however, good enough satire. Williams does not descend quite to parody in presenting her verses. Because they serve as a critique of Eliot, Williams employs dramatic irony. He allows the Poetess to write better than she knows. One section begins with a helicopter searching for a body in the river. It

> searches the hellgate current for some corpse,
> lest the gulls feed on it
> and its identity and its sex, *as* its hopes, and its
> despairs and its moles and its marks and
> its teeth and its nails no longer be decipherable
> and so lost .
>   therefore present
>   forever present .
> The gulls, vortices of despair, circle and give
> voice to their wild responses until the thing
> is gone . then ravening, having scattered
> to survive, close again upon the focus,
> the bare stones, three harbor stones, except
> for that . useless
>   unprofaned . . . [*P* 160–61]

"It Stinks!" (*P* 161) Phyllis says. This may have been Williams's reaction to *The Four Quartets*—we know it was his reaction to *The Waste Land*. The weighty references to time: "therefore present / forever present" are supposed to mimic the stately opening of "Burnt Norton" (1941).

> Time present and time past
> Are both perhaps present in time future
> And time future contained in time past, [Eliot 1962 117]

which, remains "a perpetual possibility / only in a world of speculation" (Eliot 1962 117). This "speculation," Williams turns into "financial speculation" in the final stanzas of Corydon's poem within a poem. In this section, he is already chiming the allusion to "Burnt Norton" with the passage from *The Waste Land* about

> Phlebas the Phoenecian, a fortnight dead,
> Forgot the cry of gulls, and the deep sea swell
> And the profit and loss.
>   A current under sea
> Picked his bones in whispers. As he rose and fell
> He passed the stages of his age and youth
> Entering the whirlpool. [Eliot 1962 46]

In Corydon's unwitting satire, poor Phlebas is made into an uniden-
tified, unidentifiable corpse of indeterminate sex (like Eliot's Tiresias)
for "gulls" who, like gullible critics, circle in "vortices of despair"—
possibly a jab at the pretensions and failures of the London Vortex—to
feed on Eliot's submerged meanings. Phyllis reports that Corydon
thinks the corpse must be that of "a Hindu Princess," a thrust at
Eliot's Sanskrit hocus-pocus "Datta, Dayadhvam. Damyata" at the end
of his poem (Eliot 1962 50).

Eliot's themes of the drowned figure, his pontifications about time,
and the financial images of profit and loss (they are financial because
they are connected to the up and down of the sea swell) all mark this
moment in Corydon's verses. They are fulfilled in her poetic description of a hellish Manhattan, a city where sexual connection has become financial speculation in the pseudoerotics of the ups and downs
of the market.

>   While in the tall
> buildings (sliding up and down) is where
> the money's made
>   up and down
>   directed missiles
> in the greased shafts of the tall buildings .
> They stand torpid in cages, in violent motion
> unmoved
>   but alert!
>   predatory minds, un-
> affected
>   UNINCONVENIENCED
>   unsexed, up
> and down (without wing motion) This is how
> the money's made . . . [P 164–65]

Lest we miss the intimations of sexual dysfunction, Williams has
Corydon expand on the "canned fish" in the elevator "Packed woman
to / woman (or man to woman what's the difference?)" (P 165). They
are "pressed together / talking excitedly . of the next sandwich" (P
165) as they read about the drowned student in the river. This is the
passage Williams seems to have had in mind when he explained to
Heal that "when human beings herd together, have to face each other,
they are very likely to go crooked" (IWWP 79). These people are de-

sexed, unhealthy "gone / to fat or gristle"; they are "adipose," scle-rotic, "expressionless." They are diseased, because they take part in a desiccated mockery of creation and procreation.

Williams doesn't shrink from the far-reaching political implica-tions of these urbanites' unhealthy practices. The elevator becomes, momentarily, a missile—a package of destructive energy as Eliot's chant from "The Hollow Men" (1925), "This is the way the world ends" (Eliot 1962 59), is troped into "this is the way the money's made." Finance here, as in Pound, funds the military/industrial com-plex. With nuclear apocalypse in the background, the chant and the echoes of Eliot turn the physically torpid, "unsexed" but predatory dealings of the moneymakers into a perverse mockery of the pure rites of Eleusis. Instead of Pound's vision of the natural up-and-down mo-tion of couples coupling to some natural, mystical "measure" that in-spired Williams in his review, we have the "sliding up and down" of phallic (missilelike) elevators in the greased shafts of the buildings. Their ups and downs mimic the fluctuations of the market that pre-sent the opportunities from which financial traders skim their profits.

These are the rites of the perverse fertility cult of modernity. The sterile fruits of these rituals fund Corydon and explain her homosexu-ality and her loneliness ("Oh I could cry! / cry on your young shoulder for what I know / I feel so alone" [P 165]). What Corydon knows is that, somehow, her reliance on the operations of finance capitalism to fund her leisure, her yacht, and her dalliance with Phyllis have also resulted in her lesbianism. Williams, judging from his comments to Heal, regards lesbianism as a form of illness. In fact, Williams's ideo-logical need for a "Natural economy" based on the natural model of procreative production makes it necessary for him to regard homo-sexuality as a disease. This was, of course, also the informed judgment of psychoanalysis in 1951, when this poem was written.

But the ideological roots of Williams's brief against homosexuality go deeper—just as they do in Pound. Williams's attack is founded on economic principles inherited from sources deep in the embattled poetic tradition. What is remarkable is how the Jeffersonian tradition allowed the poets to recognize the integral economic aspects in the "poetic" apprehension of reality. Those aspects were, of course, fore-grounded by the crisis in capitalism called the Great Depression. That crisis made the control of economic discourse, and therefore the reassertion of the ancient poetic position about sexuality, fertility, and abundance, an important weapon in the defense of poetry and, more broadly, in the poets' attempts to resolve the economic crisis and create a just world.

5

POESIS VERSUS PRODUCTION
The Economic Defense of Poetry
in the Age of Corporate Capitalism

It is curious that one should be asked to rewrite Sidney's *Defense of Poesy* in the year of grace 1913. During the intervening centuries, and before them, other centres of civilization had decided that good art was a blessing and that bad art was criminal, and they had spent some time and thought in trying to find means whereby to distinguish the true art from the sham. But in England now, in the age of Gosse as in the age of Gosson we are asked if the arts are moral. We are asked to define the relation of the arts to economics, we are asked what position the arts hold in the ideal republic. And it is obviously the opinion of many people less objectionable than the Sidney Webbs that the arts had better not exist at all.

—Ezra Pound, "The Serious Artist"

W HAT *is* the "relation of the arts to economics" in the twentieth century? And what is the status of the poet in the age of Corporate Capitalism, a period saturated by the discourse of political economy and the authority of economists, where the "serious artist" is tolerated as a dreamer or (if he or she is a painter) as a potential investment opportunity?[1] The problem is compounded by the moral polemic of the Left and its puritanical ideology of use, sacrifice, and struggle. For more than a century now, poets have been asked to justify themselves in economic terms. The economic crisis that began in England in 1925 with the abortive attempt to reimpose the gold standard and became the Great Depression brought with it a keen awareness of the power of the economic. As a result, economic theory began to surface explicitly and consistently in poetry. An economic morality of modernism in

139

poetry, evident in its jagged edges, severe diction, impatience with formal restraint, and contempt for "rhetoric," can be read as the manifestations of a new kind of economic awareness.

The irruption of frankly economic discourse into a number of poems by important poets during the 1930s constitutes a defense of poetry. This defense is carried out by an appeal to the discourse of political economy—specifically economics proper—*not*, primarily, by an appeal to Literature or (Eliot to the contrary) to Culture. This defense recognizes that the idea of production, meaning both the mass production of commodities and the new social relations of production, distribution, and consumption that must accompany this process, has become the key conception through which Western civilization in the twentieth century defines itself. The modern defense of poesy questions the relationship between production and poesis. To those of the Marxist persuasion, like Louis Zukofsky, poesis must be a subcategory of production, so-called cultural production. For poets of the Left, poetry is a symptom; one of many relations of production determined by the dominant mode of production—in this case corporate capitalism. Others—Pound, Williams, Stevens, and Frost—argue more or less directly in poems that production is a subset of poesis. To these writers, poesis—poetic making—subsumes production, because only poetry can make sense of our productions. Only poetry is in touch with the mythic economic basis of humanity. Only poetry can make what we produce meaningful. While this claim suggests a return to a kind of Orphic poet as a maker who can literally sing the world into existence, these poets do not merely appeal to "culture," as though it were a transhistorical entity to which only poets and artists have access. Instead, their poetry proposes in more or less comprehensive ways means by which the products of the corporate industrial economy, from the mass-produced commodities themselves to the new social classes that corporate means of production create, can be put in their proper place. In short, their poetry attempts to teach its readers how to understand themselves and their relation to modernity. Of course, none of these poets agrees precisely on what such a relationship should be; poetry is not a political party. In their various ways, however, the poems and statements by certain contemporary critics under review in this chapter do, I think, offer a kind of rough consensus. They take the challenge put to poets—that poetry must somehow be socially "useful"—

very seriously. They are determined to prove that poetry matters. In Williams's words, in the late great "Asphodel, That Greeny Flower" (1955):

> It is difficult
> to get the news from poems
>   yet men die miserably every day
>   for lack
>   of what is found there. [CP2 318]

The period under consideration here is the 1930s. The reason is obvious; the Great Depression made a close examination of the relationship between the economic system and the political system a necessity. The political and economic crisis forced artists, like others, to search for solutions to what appeared to be the irresolvable structural problems of modern capitalism. These are the problems dealt with earlier in this study; specifically, the fatal link between overproduction and underemployment, imperialism, and war; more generally, it means the problematic relationship between production and reproduction, the economy of nature and human economies. These issues raised political questions about what and who industrial capitalism is for, as well as deeper issues concerning the relationship between modes and relations of production and "civilization" or "culture." Dealing with these problems meant confronting the *meanings* of production. Here the poets felt that they had something to contribute. Yet as they made their argument, they were careful to participate in the discourse of economics to an unprecedented degree. Williams would argue in a late talk that, since "money talks, . . . the poet, the modern poet [,] has admitted new subject matter to his dreams—that is, the serious poet has admitted the whole armamentarium of the industrial age into his poems—" (SE 282). As we shall see, it is not only as theme but often in the form of the poem itself that we find the "armamentarium of the industrial age" made manifest—but for now, I want to pursue Williams's statement to show how the industrial age and economic discourse surfaced in the poetry and criticism of the 1930s.

The Great Depression brought the poetic interest in economics to a head. The extraordinary political stress on poets in the 1930s was a reflection of economic conditions and the forceful rhetoric of utopic cures for the economic crisis. In the United States after the stock market crash of 1929, economic determinism seemed more than ever the key to the vicissitudes of modernity. The crash, Edmund Wilson notes, made him turn to *Das Kapital* (Wilson 495). Kenneth Burke, at the same time, for the same reasons, found himself taking "avid notes on corporate devices whereby business enterprisers had contrived to build up empires by purely financial manipulations" (Burke 1931 214).[2] The sudden interest that these two men took in political economy was shared by many, many others. To date, only Pound's economics has received anything like sufficient attention from literary critics, and they sought mostly to explain, or to explain away, the scandal of Pound's Fascism.[3] Pound, however, is just one of many poets who struggled in poems to reconcile the implications of their sudden belief in economic determinism with the ancient priority of the poetic imagination. For Social Credit Populists like Pound and Williams, the undertaking involved the reformation of the currency; for Louis Zukofsky during his Marxist phase in the 1930s, the revolution;[4] for Frost and Stevens, economic verse satire. In each case, we find an explicit economic message forming a "meter-making argument" (Emerson 450) in the poems themselves. This new sort of poetry was designed for immediate intervention in the social struggle for economic justice. Thus Williams wrote:

> Certainly there is no mystery to the fact
> that COSTS SPIRAL ACCORDING TO A REBUS—known
> or unknown, plotted or automatic. The fact
> of poverty is not a matter of argument. Language
> is not a vague province. There is a poetry
> of the movements of cost, known or unknown . [*P* 109]

Here Williams finds poetry in the fluctuation of prices, or monetary measure, then makes poetry out of his realization. The unexpected parallel of prices to his own metrical obsession with the "variable foot" certainly serves to broaden the potential scope of poetry and the poet. This connection puts the preceding section of *Paterson*, the "Beautiful Thing" episode (for the costs of her poverty, the marring of her beauty are the sources of Williams's meditation here), into an economic context and thus into a different zone of consciousness from the "merely" poetic or imaginary. Williams is claiming that the poetry of the "movements of costs" is able to signify and specify costs that are otherwise hidden behind the abstract veil of prices through its "not vague" but exact language. For him, good poetry is sound economics.

Elsewhere I have written on Louis Zukofsky's belief that good economics could be sound poetry. His allusions to Marx at the beginning of "Song 27" of his *Twenty-nine Songs* (1934), are designed to make his readers read *Capital*, especially "The Metamorphosis of Commodities," in the same way that they read Ovid (Marsh 1997; Zukofsky 1991 58). I see his method as a sort of poetic labor theory of value because it forces us to labor for meanings not explained in the poems themselves. We have already seen how, in 1934, the same year as Zukofsky's "Song 27," Pound wrote C. H. Douglas's "A+B Theorem," the heart of Douglasite economics, into Canto 38, a poem devoted to an exposé of what we now call the "military-industrial complex" (38:190). Like Zukofsky's spare citations of Marx's chapter (but not verse) in "Song 27," Pound's purpose cannot be "poetic" in any standard sense. He simply reproduces Douglas's prose chopped into verse form and spices it with occasional interjections, using much the same "documentary" method he had perfected in the Malatesta Cantos (Rainey). Clearly, for both writers any "poetry" involved is in the ideas of the economists to which they refer. Word music is here subordinated to ideas that may, perhaps, be seen as musical in the grander sense. Marx and Douglas are seen as composers of the formerly incoherent data of capitalism. In quite contradictory ways, of course, their ideas seem to bring order and to promise harmony in the corporate/industrial cosmos.

Pound's move, especially, seems an odd way to make an argument for the priority of poesis, imaginative making, over commodity production.[5] Without the explicit appeal to the discourse of economics, however, the poets' position runs the risk of committing them to an anachronistic political economy, for, economically speaking, poesis is an artisanal mode of production, the poet is figured as a "craftsman," as in Eliot's dedication to Pound in *The Waste Land:* "Il miglior fabbro." Seen in this light, the traditional defense of poetry threatens to become an attack on modern life, because it suggests that modernity itself is the worship of the false god of mass commodity production. In the 1930s, Pound, Williams, Stevens, and Zukofsky attempted to reach beyond this rather simplistic and self-defeating formula to revise the Modernist poem as a form of social labor.[6] Pound's reemphasis on Douglas's interest in the factory, for example, indicates poetry's renewed concern with the action of production, with the massive social phenomena of the modern, industrialized economy, phenomena supposedly beyond the pale of poetry.[7]

This chapter is about the economic morality of Modernism, a subject broached earlier in the austere republican aesthetic of Pound and Williams. Here I undertake a brief survey of the responses of other poets and thinkers, moving roughly from right to left across the political spectrum.

Production, the corporation, labor; today these massive social phenomena still remain virtually inarticulate. They gesture clumsily, sometimes with fists full of money, as though their movements could be understood in terms of profit and loss, gains and setbacks. Economists have assumed that money can be made to speak for these vast social formations. Reduced to numbers, their argument goes, modern life can be understood as a great pattern.

Economists are our modern court poets, consulted by presidents and premiers, who take alarm or solace from their elaborate visions and predictions. Despite their "science," the "predictions" of the economists and their corollary social judgments are only differently informed, not qualitatively superior, to those of poets. What makes economists like poets is their intense vision of an imaginary universe, growing, cycling, developing, and shrinking—to use a few common economic tropes. In the corporate capitalist age of political economy, Milton Friedman, not John Milton, justifies the ways of God to man.

Unlike Milton, however, twentieth-century economists (with the exception of the Marxists) have been unwilling to justify the economy on a moral basis. Their convenient appeal to "science" allows them to beg the question. In the economists' moral failure, the poets find their opening. The poet's urge to make the "system" accountable—morally, politically, personally—is, finally, the need of the poet for living speech in the midst of speechless, inarticulate modernity. This urge compels the modern poet, in Perry Meisel's words, to "act out the loss of something primary [he] wishes to regain" (Meisel 1). For the American poet this "primary" something, spread out on the field of history, was the lost Jeffersonian republic.

By the 1930s, however, the republic was an anachronism. The dominant critique of capitalism was dogmatically Marxist. Before any affirmative response to the problem of poesis and production could be reached, it was necessary to understand and, as it were, to turn in, or trope, the powerful criticism leveled against poesis by the Left. In the red glare of modern scientific Marxism, Jeffersonian self-sufficiency, even in Populism, its updated form, was interpreted as reactionary and regressive. The Left "social movement" of the 1930s was progressive in a far different spirit from the populistic anticapitalism that informed the poetry of Pound and Williams, largely because the role of the individual was conceived differently. The old Jeffersonian self-reliant individualism that underlay, via Whitman, much of the poetic heritage claimed by American poets was seen (rightly perhaps) as a danger to the class-consciousness necessary for effecting social reform.

The new consciousness of the Left was formulated in terms that accommodated Marxian historical materialism. The contradictions within capitalism were accepted by the Left as integral to the system, which was supposed to be inevitably on its way to a political catastrophe as the result of its own internal contradictions. The triumph of Socialism was a question merely of time.

Harold Rosenberg reported to *Poetry*[8] on the First American Writers Conference (held in New York City in April 1935) that all the speeches of the Congress were directed to the question: "What exactly is the role of the writer in the social movement, and what was his best method of performance?" (Rosenberg 225). The assumption that the writer's role is unavoidably social, and that his or her performance must be judged in social terms, was considered fundamental.

The underlying question of the place of art within a social movement brings us to the question of the use of poetry in the political struggle. In the 1930s, stresses in the political fabric made it difficult to tell the difference between Fascism and corporate capitalism. Williams, in a public speech advocating Social Credit remedies to the economic crisis, was probably speaking for many when he complained:

> For the situation today two cures are proposed: one, to drive out the whole concept of liberalism, the open hand, and set up a Dictatorship of Labor, the clenched fist, in its stead; and the other, to strengthen the grip of the existent dictatorship by the banks driving out what original liberalism yet remains to us and, by thus officially recognizing Credit Monopoly with its familiar trends, place Fascism definitely in control. ["Revolutions Revalued," *RI* 100]

Williams proposed the artist as the vanguard of some middle alternative, because the artist is a "strong" individual and "the individual genius is the basis of all social excellence whether as inventor, organizer or governor" (*RI* 104). Williams was afraid that the artist would be seduced or coopted into propaganda, "to fight a battle at which he is a tyro while neglecting a fight in which he is an expert" (*RI* 105).

In spite of Williams's reservations, however, the Left was setting the agenda; even poets across the political spectrum addressed the issue of the role of the artist. The question that had originally exercised the Modernist poets was "What was poetry?" The new questions were: what is poetry for and who is it for?

Although T. S. Eliot disavowed "any connection with politics" (13), his Norton lectures delivered at Harvard during 1931–1932, published under the telling title *The Use of Poetry and the Use of Criticism* (1933), take up the question of the proper "use of poetry" and the question of its social utility, via the familiar Eliotic appeals to "culture" and "civilization." Poetry is to be the bulwark against the "barbarism" (15) of what looms implicitly as the godless industrial proletariat.

Eliot's introductory lecture was given November 4, 1932, the day after Franklin Delano Roosevelt's election. For a nonpolitical lecture, Eliot's rereading of Charles Eliot Norton's gloomy prognostications concerning Western civilization and the prophecy of imminent social disintegration, though written in 1869, suggest an anti-Roosevelt agenda. Why did Eliot choose these grumblings of President Norton's?

> The future is very dark in Europe, and to me it looks as if we were entering upon a period quite new in history—one in which the questions on which the parties will divide, and from which outbreak after outbreak of passion and violence will arise, will no longer be political but immediately social. . . . Whether our period of economic enterprise, unlimited competition, and unrestrained individualism, is the highest stage of human progress is to me very doubtful; and sometimes, when I see the existing conditions of European (to say nothing of American) social order, bad as they are for the mass alike of upper and lower classes, I wonder whether our civilization can maintain itself against the forces which are banding together for the destruction of many of the institutions in which it is embodied. [Eliot's ellipses, 1933 14]

Eliot implies that poetry has as its mission the rescue of civilization, because "the poetry of a people takes its life from the people's speech and in turn gives life to it; and represents its highest point of consciousness, its greatest power and its most delicate sensibility" (15). This interesting trope of circulation and exchange is derived from subliminal economic assumptions; it is ideological in its notion that the masses are the producers of a speech that must be articulated by an elite group of speakers that can inject it with a "higher" consciousness, power, and sensibility. I do not say that Eliot is wrong. Rather my point is that his idea ("program" is too strong a word) of circulation does not rescue poetry or the people's speech from the vulgarity of modern commercial life. Eliot's seemingly high Tory imagery is not significantly different from that of modern consumer capitalism, which uses another articulate elite, this time the advertising and propaganda "industry," to shape the inarticulate wishes of the people into desirable objects that it can sell back to them.

Absent Christianity or other forms of religious belief, corporate consumer capitalism is, for all intents and purposes, what we mean by civilization. It is not what Eliot thinks he means, of course, because he assumes "higher" means spiritual, but his invocation of literature as a civilizing force locates a problem of industrial societies—they are constantly trying to "civilize" their own civilizations. "The forces banding together to destroy its institutions" are not aliens but its own disenfranchised masses *and* the productive forces that have created them. Eliot plants his curses on both houses and wishes, like President Norton, for the cloistered hardships of piety, power, and sensibility within the imaginary unity of the preindustrial, agrarian, God-fearing Middle Ages.

In the openly reactionary *I'll Take My Stand* (1930), the Fugitive poet and critic Donald Davidson confronts the notion of the extinction of the artist by industrial society (47). He proposes to restore the harmonious relation between artist and society through the overthrow of the industrial state and the reestablishment of an agrarian republic of virtue (50–51). "Agrarian restoration" (51) is tellingly linked to the dismantling of the corporation and the reestablishment of a Jeffersonian moral personality.

Davidson dismisses the Arnoldian (and Eliotic) idea that "we can win men to beauty by simply loving the beautiful and preaching its merits as they are revealed to us in an admirable body of tradition" as well as through any attempt to "civilize from the top down" (51). "Our whole powerful economic system rests on mass motives—the motives of society's lowest common denominator," Davidson argues; the only option for the artist is "to remake life itself" (51). Thus "he will ally himself with programs of agrarian restoration," for "only in an agrarian society does there remain much hope of a balanced life, where the arts are not luxuries to be purchased but belong as a matter of course in the routine of his living" (51–52). This plan is more up-to-date than Eliot's in that it grounds society and the arts in political economy rather than in spiritual revelation. The problem is that the agrarian and republican political economy that Davidson has in mind has been steadily disappearing from the very moment that Jefferson himself identified it in the late eighteenth century.

This identical hope for a republican restoration, under the sign of Jefferson and Confucius, lies behind much of Pound's *Cantos*. Like Davidson, Pound recognized that resistance to industrialism is "desperate counsel" (50), but unlike Davidson, Pound saw that a retreat to the rural hinterland would do no good. Rather, industrialism itself must be civilized, its contradictions reconciled, its principal signifying medium, money, rationalized as the bearer of total cultural values. "Totalitarian" is a positive term in Pound's vocabulary because it expresses the same wish he shared with Davidson that arts could "belong as a matter of course in the routine of living." The artists' interest in economic questions was therefore vital to the creation and reception of good art. Pound saw that there is no essential difference between literary and cultural criticism, because the pressing aesthetic question of the day was also a social one with enormous political and economic implications: what is art for?

Nearer the Left, Kenneth Burke's[9] first book, *Counter-Statement* (1931), offers a chapter, "The Status of Art," that addresses the "criterion of usefulness" (1931 63) posed by the development of technology and its cult of use and efficiency. Later, he offers a "program" that explicitly addresses the relation between the political economy and the artist. Burke's visionary program, with its recognition that only subsidized unemployment and a radical transvaluation of the values of toil in favor of the arts of leisure can save capitalism from its own tendency toward overproduction, strikingly echoes the vision, if not the precise mechanism, behind the Douglasite Social Credit movement that entranced Pound and Williams (Burke 1931 107–22).

Burke takes the measure of what he calls an "'anti-industrial' aesthetic" (115), noting that "politically, agrarian conservatism is the equivalent of anti-industrialist radicalism" (117). The farmer is the true conservative, therefore a radical in terms of an industrialized economy tied to ceaseless technical innovation and change. For the artist to ally himself with the farmer involves a contradiction, however, because, "morally, the artist, as innovator, will experiment to formulate the cultural counterpart to industrialism (manifesting, for instance, a tendency toward the irreligiosity of the city); and this cultural counterpart will involve the destruction of values—such as the cluster of emphases stimulating commercial ambition—which are now shared by agrarian and industrialist elements alike" (118). Here Burke puts his finger on a crucial problem. Modernism is a product of the modern metropolis, and its slogans—"Make it new" and so forth—are consistent with the flux of modern life. Modernism's alliance with agrarian ideology is only a temporary convergence of interests. No modern artist can go back to the agrarian world without sacrificing his modernity. The only way out is not back but forward. Burke's articulation of this problem in his chapter called "Program" is notably at ease with economic language:

> We advocate the anti-industrialist progam not as mere demogogic vandalism, but as the facing of a necessity, which necessity is: technological unemployment must be made technological leisure; leisure—we must learn from capitalism itself—must be subsidized from excess profits; the appropriation of excess profits, in whatever form this process takes, constitutes the "dole"; and if the dole is to be accepted without demoralization, we must so alter the current "philosophy" of ambition, work, earnings, economic glory, that the recipients of the dole can receive it, not as paupers, but as slave-owners (slave owners, living off the labor of the automata . . .). [Burke 1931 116–17]

Burke's plan allows for an "anti-industrialist aesthetic" that accepts the reality of an industrial economy. Burke understood that "technological efficiency," which is in one sense the aesthetic of industrial capitalism, necessitates a kind of psychological "inefficiency" to counteract the repressive stresses loaded on the pyche by efficient regimentation (120–21). The artists' role will be "subversive" (119) and will provide the inefficiency necessary for social and personal health. Not that Burke wants a merely "therapeutic" role for the artist; rather, he wants to put the machine in its place as the slave, not the master, of humanity. The role of the artist is to complete the tranformation of unemployment to leisure, from leisure to a kind of ongoing insurgency "against the cultural code behind our contemporary economic ambitiousness" (121).

Burke's notion of the artistic struggle is quite different from that proposed by the Left. Burke understood that the artist cannot easily be a political advocate because the artist is not often a morally consistent animal. The moral health of art is contained in its "immorality." Art's "usefulness" in the human struggle against the machine was to put usefulness in its place as a merely contingent value, not a transcendent one.[10] Burke's program takes us far beyond the Left (and most everyone else) where the doctrine of use is an article of faith and the artist is pictured as a cultural evangelist.

An exchange more typical of its time and place is found in the pages of *Poetry* in the summer of 1934. Harriet Monroe's essay "Art and Propaganda"[11] allows that "all art of all the ages is propaganda" (210). But Monroe adds: "If all art is propaganda, a heroic effort to convert the world, its force comes from the artist's spirit and not from his will—that is, it is a force elusive, intangible and free, not to be directed or confined. Thus the deliberate propagandist rarely achieves art, and the artist, though possessed by a cause, can rarely become a successful propagandist" (211). Despite what appears at first glance to be a concession to the Left's effort to politicize poetry openly, Monroe's piece became an attack on Stanley Burnshaw, then poetry editor at the *New Masses*. In a reply to *Poetry*,[12] Burnshaw notes a good deal of confusion in Monroe's position, but his own position is far from clear. "Marxist criticism," he claimed. "finds bad art to be bad propaganda, good art good propaganda and every creator of a good work of art successful both as artist and propagandist" (352). This circular statement begs the larger question of Marxist determinations of social value, of what was "good." It certainly was out of touch with Soviet—if not Marxist—realities. To Burnshaw, "good" means "allied with the proletariat," and he claims:

> The poet allied with the proletariat may write about any theme that interests him. Being a normal rounded human being, he will not be excited exclusively by strikers and Stalin, although these are excellent themes. He will see the implications of the class struggle in number-

less events and objects ignored by bourgeois poets. Not every one of his poems, obviously, will explicitly call for revolution, but the totality of his work will be a weapon fighting on the side of the revolutionary proletariat (353).[13]

Statements like these caused Burke to notice how "the theory of economic causation seemed to rest on the assumption that there is only one possible aesthetic response to a given situation and that this situation is solely an economic one" (Burke 1931 80). That is to say, "possible" is made to equal "correct," just as, in Burnshaw's formulation, "good" "useful" poetry becomes quite literally inconceivable except in alliance with the proletariat.

The moral difficulty is that the Left's criterion of "use" in art is a short step from the "expedient" in politics. The total politics justified by Marx's searching analysis of political consciousness under capitalism determined the all-encompassing shape of the "struggle" that became the operative word in the politics of both Left and Right in the 1930s.[14] The politics of struggle (which among other things suggested to Hitler the title *Mein Kampf*), married to the urge to be of use, turned to overstatement and evil. Auden's refrain in "Spain" (1937), "Today the struggle," led almost inevitably to the lines that later caused the older poet grief in this too expedient political poem: "Today the deliberate increase in the chances of death, / The conscious acceptance of guilt in the necessary murder" (1979 54). Such ideas undoubtedly found echoes in the corrupt consciences of those that Auden's poem logically implies, that is, "necessary murderers." If his were, so to speak, "good murderers," they were morally indistinguishable from "bad" murderers like the men running Dachau, which Auden, "In Time of War," properly, usefully, condemned in 1938, a year after "Spain."[15] Auden's "correct" condemnation of Dachau is, however, not some sort of compensation for the convenient morality of "Spain"—although Auden later repudiated the poem. My point is simply that "useful" poetry of this kind can claim no exemption in the "rightness" or "wrongness" of its politics; there can be no nonpolitical appeal to History.[16]

The doctrine of use also led, as Auden accurately observed, to "the expending of powers / On the flat ephemeral pamphlet and the boring meeting" (1979 54) or even to silence. One thinks of all the poems that George Oppen did not write in the thirty years after *Discrete Series*

(1934) because he assumed that they would interfere with his pursuit of his deeply felt Communist ideals. Those aborted poems are a loss for which there can be no adequate compensation. Ezra Pound's urgent pamphleteering and eventual surrender to hatred and bigotry deformed the epic *Cantos* because he wrote some of them like political tracts. The biggest problem with these parts of *The Cantos* is precisely that they were written to be of immediate polemical use. The local uses to which Pound hoped to put his poem make some of it useless— or nearly useless—as literature. It is reduced in those moments to a historical document.

In the politics of struggle in the 1930s, Communism and Fascism were Scylla and Charybdis for poets, who were repeatedly asked in questionnaires, and pressured by both Left and Right, to endorse various political programs—including economic ones. The poet was continuously being asked, and was therefore presumably asking himself, "Do you intend your poetry to be useful to yourself or to others?"[17] The purportedly useful ideals behind Communism, no less than Fascism, were great destroyers of poets in the 1930s, not only literally within the Soviet Union, but also by convincing poetic spirits that poetry was, in and of itself, bourgeois or reactionary. Mike Weaver, in his study of Williams, remarks on the "intellectual terrorism" of the period, when advice, cajolery, and threats of nonpublication were used to bring writers into political line (Weaver 100). If poetry is to conform to the "useful" with its unspoken modifier, "socially," then the poem is confined to a social, that is, a political, position. The poem becomes a moral commentary on life, and loses its privileged status as something closer to life itself. The poet ceases to "write primarily" as Emerson had it in "The Poet," and writes "secondarily" (Emerson 449). The poem is no longer what Williams called "the embodiment of knowledge" but only a part of what he tried to distinguish it from: the "inhuman" "misconceptions" of Science or Philosophy (*EK* 83).[18] "Useful" poetry loses its primary function and falls from art to criticism. Instruction is privileged over delight. The poem's field, narrowed from being itself, becomes persuasion and is contingent and mortal. In short, the poem moves from "art" to "propaganda." As Burke puts it, the poet and poem are caught between the issues of information and the idea of form.[19] Under these conditions, poetry is no longer a foundational language; instead, poetry fulfills a program imposed upon it by history, or, rather, by a "useful" theory of history. Such poetry is indeed a "production," *already made* by historical forces—not true *poesis*, or making.

The problem of the useful poem is like the Modernist architectural adage that "form follows function." The assumption is that we know for once and for all what *all* the functions of a space or house are, and that we can know exactly what is useful and what is not. The politicized notion of useful poem depends on a faith in efficiency and rationality that is central to modernity.

It was extremely difficult for poets to accept the utilitarian claims made on the poem without irony. A brief look at three poets' responses to the economic moralizing of the Left shows how economic concerns and left-wing pressure served as a goad to force poets to produce poems that acknowledged the economic debate and, as a result, became part of it. Robert Frost's "Build Soil," Wallace Stevens's "The Man with the Blue Guitar," and an important review by Williams of George Oppen's *Discrete Series*, show how irony and satire became an important defensive weapon for poets in their resistance to the political correctness of the day.

In "Build Soil: A Political Pastoral" a poem published in *A Further Range* (1936) but presented as the Phi Beta Kappa poem at Columbia University on May 31, 1932, Robert Frost staged the economic question quite explicitly. "Build Soil" is a Virgilian ecologue, a dialogue between modern "shepherds" Tityrus and Meliboeus, who talk about up-to-date issues like Socialism, dictatorship, property, and the market. "Make a late start to market" Tityrus concludes, after echoing Jefferson's doubts about the morality of commerce in *Notes from Virginia:*

> I'm perplexed myself
> To find the good in commerce. Why should I
> Have to sell you my apples and buy yours?

Commerce, Tityrus, concedes, may be "like any bandying / Of words or toys, it ministers to health" (321). But if "to market it is our destiny to go,"

> There is still more we never bring or should bring;
> More that should be kept back—the soil for instance,
> In my opinion—though we both know poets

Who fall all over each other to bring soil
And even subsoil and hardpan to market. [321]

Beyond Frost's double entendre, this "soil" is intimately connected to
the poetic imagination, anchored in his sense of self. This, in turn, is
literally indistiguishable from property, or the farm / homestead.

Build soil. Turn the farm in upon itself
Until it can contain itself no more,
But, sweating-full, drips oil and wine a little.
I will go to my run-out social mind
And be as unsocial with it as I can.
The thought I have, and my first impulse is
To take to market—I will turn it under.
The thought from that thought—I will turn it under.
And so on to the limit of my nature. [323]

Tityrus's "nature"—that is, his selfhood—is his "farm." And the farm
is defined and maintains its integrity by means of the conscious rejection of the market and the social relations dependent on markets. From
the perspective of the Left, this is a denial of History itself.

When "Build Soil" finally appeared in *The Further Range* (1936), it
"enraged the Left," Stanley Burnshaw recalls, which had been hoping
against hope that Frost would turn his gifts to its purposes (Burnshaw
42).[20] Frost was "turning in" at the moment when it seemed imperative for everyone to turn out. By denying the power of the market and
market forces, Frost is denying the stage theory of capitalist development, which the Left believed would lead inexorably to Socialism.
Moreover, Frost is deliberately posing the issue as one of poesis against
production. This seemingly reactionary moment in Frost is one reason why critics as distinguished as R. P. Blackmur and Newton Arvin
dismiss Frost as "minor."[21] In his important study of Frost, Richard
Poirier quotes from a review by leftist critic Granville Hicks of *West-
Running Brook* (1928) a passage that, in Poirier's view, provides whatever flimsy basis their might be for contemporary feelings about
Frost's irrelevance: "[Frost] has created the ordered world in which
he lives by the exclusion of many, many chaotic elements in the real
world. Perhaps it is a fact that explains why Frost is, even at his best,
a very perfect minor poet, not the major poet America is looking for"
(quoted in Poirier 1979 240). The tone of this review illustrates very

well the frankly political pressures being brought to bear on poetry and poets, and this pressure only intensified in the 1930s. Frost is irrelevant because in his poems he is not engaging in political economic discourse *in the right way.*

Despite its classical antecedents, "Build Soil," at least, was intensely relevant as a defense of poesy in the age of corporate capitalism. It represents one version of the question that was energizing poets across the political spectrum. Frost's recuperation of a sophisticated classical genre suggests, of course, that he is intensely concerned with the historical status of the American republic, which, like Rome in Virgil's time, was already an Empire in fact, if not in name. Frost's purpose is to force production, social labor, the market, and History to acknowledge the poet. It is the pastoral, yeoman self that Frost poses against "the market," which wants to determine all politically significant social relations in modern life. In his "political pastoral" Frost is invoking a tradition that he considers more central to any conceivable democracy or republic than commodity production. The effect is to ironize production and to twit the Left with its own materialism. Pastoral has always been political, as Frost seems to have understood better than his critics. The importance of Frost's revision of Virgil lies not in what appears to be a solipsistic poetic quietism but rather in the "turning," or, as Poirier insists, "troping," motion that the poem both preaches and enacts.

Production "turns out" commodities. Troping turns in, or turns over, language. If, as we suspect, things are for all intents and purposes thoughts, then it is clear that troping, as the form of imaginative production, as poesis, must have priority over all other forms of production. "Build Soil" argues that the value of thoughts cannot be determined in the market, they can only be judged by their ability to make further thoughts, and thus to build the soil of self, which provides the lone vantage from which all thoughts can be put in their "proper" place.

In his study of Frost, Poirier sheds light on how the recuperation of poesis could work for poets by linking two passages in Emerson (for Poirier the founder of American writing) and Bergson, the philosopher of High Modernism. Poirier has been discussing Frost's "West-Running Brook" with its curious "backward motion":

> see how the brook
> In that white wave runs counter to itself.
> It is from that in water we were from
> Long, long before we were from any creature.
> Here we, in our impatience of the steps
> Get back to the beginning of beginnings,
> The stream of everything that runs away [Frost 259]

Poirier highlights this Bergsonian countervalence at work in the stream of life Frost had portrayed in "West-Running Brook":

> It is this backward motion toward the source
> Against the stream, that most we see ourselves in,
> The tribute of the current to the source [Frost 260]

Poirier links these lines to the following passage from Emerson's essay "Nature" (not *Nature*): "The direction is forever onward, but the artist still goes back for materials and begins again with the first elements on the most advanced stage" (1977 266). The artist here is "Nature," not History (Emerson 547), which prevents Emerson from sounding to us like Engels, but both History and Nature must, finally, be signs for our own tendency to trope the past. Poirier next connects Emerson's metaphor to something from Bergson: "our consciousness is continually drawn the opposite way. . . . This retrospective vision . . . must detach itself from the *already made* and attach itself to the *being-made*," which Poirier equates to "Emerson's 'advanced stage' of 'first elements' " (1977 267). This imaginative journey there and back again describes exactly the work of the poets of the 1930s, the work of counterstatement. We recognize in this troping gesture Frost's "turning in" to build the soil of self that he spoke of in "Build Soil." Significantly, this same countervailing motion recurs in a very similar Bergsonian life stream when Williams describes the waters of the Passaic taking the cataract in book 1 of *Paterson* (1946):

> All lightness lost, weight regained in
> the repulse, a fury of escape driving them to rebound
> upon those coming after—
> nevertheless keeping to the stream, they
> retake their course, the air full
> of the tumult and of spray
> connotative of the equal air, coeval,
> filling the void [*P* 8]

Then later in book 3 (1949), Williams again tropes this theme in the description of the burning Paterson Library:

> the waterfall of the
> flames, a cataract reversed, shooting
> upward (what difference does it make?) [*P* 121]

What difference? In this section about the great fire that destroyed Paterson, Williams's archetypal corporate city, the difference is precisely in the assertion, achieved by reaching back to "first elements,"—fire, poesis—that a recovery of the countervailing sources of poetry, and thus a natural economy, can purge the corporation and reestablish the preeminence of poetry itself.

Wallace Stevens, who worked in a corporate environment with Hartford Mutual Life Insurance, seems most fully to have absorbed the imaginative possibilities inherent in the corporate liberal position, which allowed him, among other things, the luxury of appearing "nonpolitical" while giving him a firm position from which to engage, criticize, and meditate on the alternatives on the both the Left and the Right without subscribing to particular programs. His outlook is worth exploring, for if less overtly economic than that of Pound or Zukofsky, it is, despite appearances, more political. Stevens's poems address the issue that underlies the struggle of the poet to make sense of political economy, the issue of selfhood.

In a letter to Ronald Latimer concerning "Mr. Burnshaw and the Statue," a poem that explicitly engaged the Left by invoking the *New Masses* critic, Stevens allied himself with a middle economic position:

> I believe in what Mr. Filene calls "up-to-date capitalism." I don't believe in Communism: I do believe in up-to-date capitalism. It is an extraordinary experience for myself to deal with a thing like Communism; it is like dealing with the Democratic platform, or with the provisions of the Frazier-Lemke bill [a New Deal bill concerning the refinancing of farm mortgages]. Nevertheless, one has to live and think in the actual world. [Quoted in Longenbach 145–46][22]

The "up-to-date" capitalism that Stevens associated with Edward Filene, owner of the Boston department store, depends on the redistribution of wealth from the top down and has much in common with Franklin Delano Roosevelt's New Deal.[23] It recognizes the potential for social disequilibrium within capitalism as surplus value rises to the top in the form of corporate profits but finds no useful or profitable outlet in investment. Briefly, the corporate reconstruction of capitalism in the early twentieth century broke the link between investment and capitalization. If profits are not to be dissipated in financial speculation, as happened in the great bubble and Crash of the late 1920s, they must finance the link between production and consumption in the form of wages or a public dole.[24] Filene, the inventor of the famous Boston "bargain basement," sought ways in his own business to recirculate that wealth back to the people.

The abundance of economic structures and metaphors in Stevens's poems prompted Frank Lentricchia to speak of his "capitalism of mind" (Lentricchia 1988 227). Stevens's meditations on Socialism, in "Mr. Burnshaw and the Statue" (a section of "Owl's Clover," 1936), in *The Man with the Blue Guitar* (1937), and on Lenin in "Description Without Place" (1945) make him a trenchant critic of the problem that the Left posed for the poet and poetry. His imaginative "capitalism" is not just some reflexive "collaboration" with the economic structures from which, as a insurance lawyer, he undoubtedly benefited but a considered response to the imaginative opportunities he recognized in capitalist financial structures and the intractable problem, for the poet, of a social self. Unlike Frost and Zukofsky, Stevens rejoiced in the poetic possibilities offered by the "metamorphosis of commodities" and saw the Communist millennium as

> A time in which the poets' politics
> Will rule the poets' world. Yet that will be
> A world impossible for poets, who
> Complain and prophesy, in their complaints
> And are never of the world in which they live [1989 80]

This from "Mr. Burnshaw and the Statue." In "The Man with the Blue Guitar," Stevens raises the question of the individual, living by the rhythm of his own "tom-tom" heartbeat, who lacks, in the Communist formulation, any individual or personal political relevance.

> Tom-tom, c'est moi. The blue guitar
> And I are one. The orchestra
>
> Fills the high hall with shuffling men
> High as the hall. The Whirling noise

Of a multitude dwindles, all said,
To his breath that lies awake at night.

I know that timid breathing. Where
Do I begin and end? And where,

As I strum the thing, do I pick up
That which momentously declares

Itself not to be I and yet
Must be [1982 171]

Social labor is not the basis for poetic production, "The Man with the Blue Guitar" claims; nor, when all is said and done, is the self simply social. For the poet/guitarist's blues implicitly resist the collective Red orchestra, with its vaguely proletarian "shuffling men." In solitude the individual ironically "dwindles" to the self's breath, or spirit. The problem that Socialism has set the self both instigates and informs this meditation on the relationship between the poet and the poem, symbolized by the guitar, that the poet can "pick up" and that "momentously declares" itself in the sounds the poet elicits through it. Since the sounds the poet produces are products of instrument and poet at once, the question is: where does the artist begin and end? In confronting the Left, any answer to that question commits the poet to a further confrontation with the question of where political economy begins and ends: Where in the self is the border between public and private?

Stevens's question lies near the heart of the ontological problem of "the corporation"—one reason why, as we shall see, the representation of the corporation in poetry becomes a central problem in the Modernist epic.

Williams's ironic response to the utilitarian economy of the Left is reflected in his review of George Oppen's *Discrete Series* (1934), called "The New Poetical Economy." Coincidentally, this review appears in the same issue of *Poetry*[25] as Harriet Monroe's remarks on art and propaganda that exercised Stanley Burnshaw. Williams worried that "people are beginning to forget that poems are constructions" and might instead judge them according to their party affiliations, on whether they were Communist or Fascist. He was impressed by Oppen's poems because the words are plain words; the metric is taken from speech; the colors, images, moods, are not suburban, not peasant-restricted to serve as a pertinent example. *A Discrete Series.* This the work of a "stinking" intellectual if you please. That is, you should use the man as you would use any other mechanic—to serve a purpose for which training, his head, his general abilities fit him, to build with—that others may build after him. [1985 58]

Williams understands that the enemies of the poem are intellectuals, not mechanics. But intellectuals, being often "suburban"—that is, out of touch—tend to sentimentalize the working classes into peasant masses; they forget the technical aspect of poems as they forget that mechanics are the masters of rigorous techniques. For Williams, the "good poem" is grounded in technique; it is not what poems say but how they say it. A poem's "importance lies in what the poem *is*," he emphasized. A poem is first "a technical matter, as with all facts, compelling the recognition of a mechanical structure." This recognition can result in "a direct liberation of the intelligence" (55) far more significant than instilling correct moral behavior.

It is the acceptable fact of a poem as a mechanism that is the proof of its meaning and this is as technical a matter as in the case of any other machine. Without the poem being a workable mechanism in its own right, a mechanism which arises from, while as the same time it constitutes the meaning of, the poem as a whole, it will remain ineffective. And what it says regarding the use or worth of that particular piece of "propaganda" which it is detailing will never be convincing. [56]

If the poetic mechanism of the poem, and not content, is the poetry, then it makes sense to pare the poem down to its most essential components—plain words, the movement of speech. Interestingly, the result is a "machine." The implications are double: (1) that machines are acts of the imagination and therefore like poems and (2) the unintended consequence that the mind that thinks machines may also be like a machine and may generate (or imagine) societies that are also giant machines:

An imaginable new social order would require a skeleton of severe discipline for its realization and maintenance. Thus by a sharp restriction to essentials, the seriousness of a new order is brought to realization. Poetry might turn this condition to its own ends. Only by being an object sharply defined and without redundancy will its form project whatever meaning is required of it. It could well be, at the same time, first and last a poem facing as it must the dialectical necessities of its day. [57]

I quote this review at length because it rehearses more fully things that Williams said elsewhere.[26] This essay importantly shows how his ideas about the form and function of poetry are used to resist the leftist version of poetry and the fetish of use. Against their severe and rigorous economic morality, Williams's gesture toward the "dialectical necessities of the day" is loaded with irony. He does not mean the poem to face the class struggle that is the Struggle of History; he means it to face up to whatever political window dressing, or propaganda, is current.

Mulling over the situation of poetry fourteen years later in a talk delivered in 1948, Williams reflected that "a bad sign to me is always a religious or social tinge beginning to creep into a poet's work. You can put it down as a general rule that when a poet, in the broadest sense, begins to devote himself to the *subject matter* of his poems, *genre*, he has come to an end of his poetic means" (Williams's emphasis, *SE* 288). There is an important ambivalence here. Speaking after the Second World War, after the Great Depression, but in the midst of writing *Paterson*, a poem more than slightly tinged with social, political, and economic "subject matter," Williams seems to be arguing that the poem may address social and even religious questions as long as they are not what the poem is about.[27] Does *Paterson* do so? Is the Social Credit "Advertisement" in book 4 (*P* 180) placed there in the playful spirit of something in a New Historicist essay? Or does it, in *every* sense, matter? Because Williams has included a piece of Social Credit propaganda in it, can we say that *Paterson* is a "Social Credit poem"?[28] The answer, I think, is both yes and no. The Social Credit flyer is supported by a meditation on credit in the pages immediately following. "What is credit?" the poet asks, and "What is money?" (*P* 183)—basic Social Credit questions. Williams's answers, however, are not strictly Social Credit answers. They are not inconsistent with Social Credit aims, but they don't depend on the institutionalization of Social Credit either. Credit is "the Parthenon"; money is "the gold entrusted to Phideas for the / statue of Pallas Athena, that he 'put aside' / for private purposes" (*P* 183). Finally, Williams answers Pound's response to Williams's revision of Pound's "Usura" canto (Canto 45), early in book 2 (*P* 50). There Williams had affirmed "invention" as the implicit antidote to "usura," and now, in book 4, he prints Pound's acquiescence:

> IN
>   venshun
> O.KAY
>   in venshun [*P* 184]

And Williams sums up

> Credit makes solid
> is related directly to the effort,
> work: value created and received,
> "the radiant gist" against all that
> scants our lives [*P* 185]

So credit is invention made solid by work. This appears to be a restatement of the labor theory of poetic value. It returns the basis of value to poesis. It does not, however, invest value in any specific political economic remedy, like Social Credit. That which is made and endures, like the Parthenon, like *Paterson* itself, is the basis of credit. The subject matter of Williams's poem, then, is not Social Credit or any other political program but the invention and effort, that is, poesis, or making, which is his struggle to create the poem.[29]

If *Paterson* offers making as the basis of credit and thus of the epic's value, then how can Williams admonish himself (using the voice of his wife) at the beginning of the next section, book 4, section 3, by asking: "Haven't you forgotten your virgin purpose, / the language?" The answer is equivocal. "What language? 'The past is for those who / lived in the past,' is all she told me" (*P* 186). It appears that there is no "virgin language" and thus no "pure" poetry. Poetry is shaped by its resistance to "all that scants our lives." It is not just a saying but a response. The poet, living in the present, confronting modernity, must take the language as he finds it; impure, politicized, no virgin at all, resistant maybe (like Phyllis in *Paterson*) but also like the wise old whore, the Whitman-like "grandmother" who since his poetic breakthrough in "The Wanderer" (1914) had been Williams's muse.

The defense of a conception of poesis under which the discourse of political economy could be properly placed drove poets of very different political persuasions in the 1930s. Given the existing critiques of capitalism and the moral profundity of the Socialist position, it seems that even for non-Socialists like Williams and Pound, poesis had to be recuperated in terms of social labor and the discourse of economics if it was to be progressive or "useful"—if, that is, poets were to avoid the reactionary stigma of the poet/artisan equation. In their poems of the 1930s, when the Great Depression demanded the reexamination of the premises of capitalism and thus of modernity itself, poets had no choice but to undertake a defense of poesy in terms of political economy: poesis versus production.

6

DEWEY, WILLIAMS, AND
THE PRAGMATIC POEM

FROM OUR CURRENT vantage point we can now see that the poetic leap
into the arena of economics was a belated part of a much larger debate
about corporate capitalism with roots in the late nineteenth century.
What Martin J. Sklar has usefully labeled the "corporate reconstruction" of American capitalism was already in the works by 1890 when
"the last great depression of competitive capitalism" (1988 43) galva-
nized all sectors of American society, creating "a revulsion against the
unregulated market" (53). A new formulation of capitalism was, in
Sklar's periodization, complete by 1916. Gradually superseding the
old "competitive" model, a "corporate liberal" consensus was by that
time hammered out and the political, legal, and economic framework
in place that allowed for regulation of the economy sufficient to keep
it relatively stable and to mitigate, if not prevent, the worst contradictions and excesses inherent in capitalism.

Since unrestricted markets and truly unimpeded "free" enterprise
have been discredited, corporate liberalism was (and remains) the
American alternative to either of two viable political economic solutions to the problems caused by an industrialized economy. The first
is state capitalism, variations of which marked the European nations
through the end of the Second World War. ("Fascism" is the term that
describes the more militantly nationalistic version of state capitalism.) But state capitalism also describes the political economies of
France and (to a lesser degree) England during the first half of the century. The second alternative to corporate liberalism is, of course, Socialism, which after 1917 produced its own version of the corporate
state in the new Soviet Union (Sklar 1988 36–37).

As we have seen, the poetic response to corporate capitalism followed these broad trends. The ascendancy of leftist Socialist ideology

in literature is well documented. Pound and Williams, through their work for Social Credit, believed in a form of state capitalism: the critique of capitalism that they share finds its roots in a Populistic version of Jeffersonianism that understood the necessity for government intervention in the market. Pound's eventual turn to the Italian version of state capitalism, Mussolini's Fascism, and Williams's more indigenously American belief in economic democracy derive from the same ideological source. We can understand the import of the two political choices these poets made by seeing how the two men dealt with the defining phenomenon of corporate capitalism, the corporation itself.

The Corporation and Moral Personality

Since 1886 the private corporation has legally been a "natural entity" with the same status before the law as a person (Sklar 1988 49). As Kenneth Burke points out in his brief history of capitalism, *Attitudes Towards History* (1937), however, the slipperiness of the purely legal "personhood" ascribed to corporations makes them morally obtuse:

> Men had been members of a religious corporation, a civic corporation, and a vocational corporation. They now had a chance to become members of a financial corporation, that emerged from the proliferation of partnerships until many members were included (significantly they were called "brothers")—and you finally arrived at the "joint-stock company." All that was needed was for earnest-minded judges to endow these strange creatures with a legal "personality" and their future was assured.
>
> Nay more: they were endowed with personality on some counts, and on other counts they were not (for sometimes they could flourish better as persons, as when they required the "freedom" of persons,—but at other times they could flourish better as non-persons, as when you tried to imprison them; or again, as persons, if they were venturing abroad, they might be called home when there was danger, their governments refusing to guaranty their safety if they insisted on tarrying, but as non-persons they could remain there calling on their governments to protect them). [Burke 1937 155]

Burke's satire reminds us that corporate relations had always existed— that what was truly different about the twentieth century was the ubiquity of corporate modes of production and its peculiar legal personhood, not the notion of the "corporate," or even "corporate selves," per se. The problems that corporate modes of production present to the self are manifold. Where does the individual fit in? How can he or she make contact with the often intangible corporate modes that determine so much of our experience? The flickering now-you-see-me, now-you-don't quality of the industrial corporation makes it altogether different from the medieval Church, say, in ways that make it morally suspect; it has no consistency.

John Dewey argued very cogently that "corporate personality" has no reality except in a purely legal sense. The corporation is a "right and duty bearing unit," and so is a "natural person"—there the resemblance ends. One of Dewey's purposes in his essay "Corporate Personality" (1931) was to "show that the question has been enormously complicated by the employment of a wrong logical method, and by the introduction of irrelevant conceptions, imported from legal discussions (and often into legal practice) from uncritical popular beliefs; from psychology and from a metaphysics ultimately derived from theology" (Dewey 1931 152). Using the pragmatic method, Dewey addressed the problem of corporate personality from its effects, not some "essence" derived from the philosophical habits of Greek philosophy (148). Dewey concluded that the problem of modernity is the problem, finally, of modern subjectivity. The subject now seems less a simple individual person and more and more a "right and duty bearing unit" (149). Such a unit could even include, in certain limited ways, corporate bodies, even industrial corporations.

In dealing with the populistic, Jeffersonian approach to the corporation, however, it is precisely the "irrelevant conceptions" of "uncritical popular belief" exemplified in the passage from Burke and the poetry of Pound and Williams that we must face. For Williams, the "special interests" are equivalent to the corporations. These are taken to be immensely powerful citizens, capable of interests (that is, desires and aversions) that can make their presence felt in the political process in ways that undoubtedly threaten to subordinate actual people (*SE* 152–53). The basis of popular feeling against the corporation should sound familiar; the corporations are thought to benefit the few at the expense of the many. The corporate form, as we can see from Burke's characterization, is interpreted as a legal dodge to avoid responsibility for one's actions.

Prior to the ascendancy of the corporation, full citizenship and the moral personality it implies had generally been defined, in the United States, in terms of a clear set of property relations. Citizens were property owners, although not all property owners—not women, for example—were full citizens. Thus the self has a history; it is historical. The deep linkage between private property and a private conscience able to act in public life when called upon to do so, with all of the inherent contradictions this capacity implies, lies at the heart of the American democratic experiment, as we have seen earlier in the writings of Crèvecoeur, Jefferson, and that French Jeffersonian Destutt de Tracy.

In particular, Destutt de Tracy's clear exposition explains how American Republican ideology derives personality from property. Together, property and personality are taken to be equivalent to the self. I take the following passage as typical of what I call the "Jeffersonian" moral personality:

> If we had not the idea of *personality*, and that of *property*, that is to say the consciousness of our *self*, we should certainly never have either *wants* or *means*; for to whom would appertain this *suffering* and this *power*[?] We should not exist for ourselves; but as soon as we recognize ourselves as possessors of our existence, and of its modes, we are necessarily by this alone a compound of weakness and of strength, of wants and means, of suffering and power, of passion and action, and consequently of rights and duties. [Destutt de Tracy's emphasis, 53–54]

In the twentieth century, the corporate liberal compromise, which created a regulated market through a redefinition of the individual, jeopardized this powerful ideological connection between property, personality, responsibility, and selfhood. If property is the basis of liberty, as Destutt de Tracy, Jefferson, and even Hegel, among others, have claimed, the freeholder is the archetype of the citizen (Livingston 1994 221–22). In the transition to a market economy from feudalism, it was the existence of the yeoman figure who justified this radical transformation in human affairs. Later, the progress of industry and finance would put the yeoman and his historically contingent moral personality, his republican self, in jeopardy.

The problem with defining the modern self on the basis of property is, as James Livingston points out, "that the resources denominated as property cannot function as the groundwork of the moral personality in any meaningful sense if large corporate bureaucracies, not individuals, can establish control over these resources" (222). In fact, by the end of the nineteenth century, the basis for the moral personality had collapsed along with the older forms of proprietary competitive capitalism. The "corporate reconstruction of American capitalism" in the period 1890–1920 required a complementary reconstruction of the moral personality.

The intense ideological struggle that this moral reconstruction entailed has not yet been fully resolved. In the United States, the corporate liberal solution has proved durable at the level of capitalism, but the reconstruction of the moral personality is still to be worked out, as Livingston's work shows. In his rendition, each individual person's difficult accommodation of the assertion of the corporation has resolved itself into two choices; one being pragmatism's immersion of the self in historical time, the other the Populist/High Modernist recolonization of an ahistorical "natural" order of being, an "extra-temporal space in which the figure of the freeholder, the yeoman, and the citizen-soldier once moved freely and meant more than business." During the period of transition, 1890–1920, "Pragmatism as William James sketched it was one version, or effect, of the first choice . . . ; Populism was one version, or effect, of the second voice; high literary modernism was another, although it was not convened until poets cast themselves in the role once reserved for the Gothic freeholder" (Livingston 1994 223). Clearly, the role of "gothic," or republican, freeholder appealed to many poets, but because they were poets, they often played it as a role and did not necessarily live as such freeholders themselves. In his "treasonous" but unmistakably American radio speeches, for example, Ezra Pound would make frequent appeals for Americans to "return to age old common sense concerning the homestead" (May 28, 1942, EPS 152), thereby tapping into the old republican ideal of the "American Farmer" who stands at the center of "the agrarian myth." But Pound wasn't exactly speaking from personal experience; he'd been living in a rented apartment in Rapallo, Italy, for twenty years. In fact, he never ever owned any "real property." Pound appealed to an ahistorical agrarian "common sense"—actually ideology—because it has functioned as the most consistent and compelling moral center of resistance to capitalist development in the United States since before our revolution. Moreover, the self-reliant "homesteader" figure may be a beleaguered remnant of earlier social relations, but he is also the basis for the individualism that underlies the Romantic conception of the "artist" as an integrated producer.[1]

In this chapter I will use Williams, not Pound, as a test for Livingston's hypothesis concerning the role of Pragmatism and the moral personality.[2] If, as he suggests, Pragmatism offered one means by which the moral personality could be reconstructed and reconciled to the forced redefinition of property and the self by the onset of corporate capitalist modes and relations of production, then we may be able to find it in the work of Williams. Let me say at once that I think we do find it, although, as we might expect, Williams expresses it in terms rather different from those used by Livingston or, for the most part, by the Pragmatists themselves.

The question before us is where, or on what, in the corporate age, a person may base the moral personality, the self. For Williams, the choice was Pragmatism—he needed to immerse himself in history to find himself in the present moment, in the world of what William James called "pure experience." From "The Wanderer" of 1914 to *Paterson* in the 1940s and 1950s, his poetry is about this immersion.

Pragmatism as a moral choice entails, however, the problem of moral relativism. Pragmatism, Livingston writes, "seems scandalous because, from the standpoint of the received tradition, it entails strictly situational ethics. Pragmatists cannot imagine a disembodied self, an Archimedean point undefiled by earthly relations of place, time and cause; so they cannot imagine an extra-situational or unconditional moral imperative. According to their critics, moral relativism—pure subjectivity—must follow" (1994 223). This critique will be especially important for our understanding of Williams because the critics of Pragmatism sound like poetic formalists. Again Livingston:

> The critics argue that genuine morality consists of claims (or rules) about what ought to be done which can be generalized beyond any given situation, beyond what is done in that particular historical circumstance. The personality they presuppose as the agent of genuinely moral claims must then lack a temporal dimension; indeed that moral personality must occupy, or amount to, an extra-temporal space. The

cartographers who draw this inner space by intricate inference—these are mainly philosophers—will call it thought, mind, or consciousness. Most other academics and intellectuals will call it something else (reason, art, law, culture, personality, human nature, etc.), but will nonetheless use the map because they assume it represents real and significant boundaries between thoughts and things. They will also assume that to dispense with the map, as pragmatists propose, is to adopt the anti-metaphysical mechanics of positivism or utilitarianism, and accordingly to preclude any radical criticism of the world as it exists. [1994 223]

The last point is the rub, for we already know that Williams's poetry is sharply critical of the Hamiltonian ascendancy of cash values in the United States, and as we can see in his work, he was attracted to the moral claims of Jeffersonianism. But the power of Williams's poetics is his awareness of the inadequacy of the Jeffersonian position, of the yeoman self, under the regime of corporate modernity. As a poet, he further recognizes that it can be resolved only at the level of form. That is, he believes that the reconstruction of the self is equivalent to the reconstruction of the poem. Likewise, finding a new poetic form implies the discovery of new possibilities for the self.

Livingston has observed that "the argument between pragmatists and their critics will tend, therefore, to sound like a quarrel between positivists and romantics, especially since the critics themselves believe that modern subjectivity contains or exhausts the possibilities of genuine selfhood" (1994 223). We find essentially this quarrel going on inside Williams's poetry and prose from 1914 onward. It is a quarrel about what Williams would call "the embodiment of knowledge"; it is about his struggle to assign the moral personality a place in temporal space, in history and in the body. Throughout, he struggles to become a poet in the Pragmatic mode.

Williams follows both William James and Dewey in arguing that any "Archimedean point" outside "the world of pure experience" (James 1977 170) cannot exist. In the essay "Does Consciousness Exist?" (1904), James had, as Livingston reminds us, effectively demolished the philosophical and ("neo-Kantian") fantasy called "consciousness" (1994 269–73).[3] John Dewey, almost alone among American philosophers, was immediately alive to the implications of James's essay (1994 258),[4] which were, in effect, "that consciousness did not exist outside its embodiment" (259).

The issue of the embodiment of consciousness is more or less what Williams is grappling with in his baffled, persistent series of philosophical essays of 1928–1929 posthumously collected under the title *The Embodiment of Knowledge* (1973). To propose an embodiment of knowledge is to challenge or revise the value of any "body of knowledge" that is distinct from its expression; that is to say, any knowledge that is conveyed by words but claims to be different from the words themselves. Ordinarily, a fund of knowledge, such as moral rules, scientific "laws," or historical "facts," is supposed to exist in the absence of any expression of its existence; it's just out there, inhuman information that can be lost and rediscovered. Williams's "essays," which read more like a series of beginnings to a work that never materializes, are concerned with the knowledge claims of art, specifically "poetry," or "writing," in relation to "Science" and "Philosophy," or, to return to Livingston's terms, they try to negotiate a place for the poem in relation to Positivism and Romanticism:

> Poetry must be defined not by its superficial features but by its character as an effect related to science and the other categories. As knowledge in a certain form. Poems must be—and this partakes of technique—considered as documents of men. Thus, without seeking a pungent example for the moment—new words must be based—or their criticism—on an increase of knowledge, and will be accepted or rejected solely on that score. But it is their bodies as poems, as with men, that is their destiny, differing from all writing which has not writing itself as its substance. [*EK* 74]

We can see that Williams is trying to establish poetry as a legitimate body of knowledge against Science and the "other categories" of knowledge that he labels "Philosophy." Williams assumes (not quite accurately, in my view) that Science and Philosophy use words to carry meanings—even Truths—but the words they use are not themselves the meanings. As he argued in his 1934 review of Oppen's *Discrete Series*, poetry is a superior form because its meaning *is* the words. "Prose," he will write in *The Wedge*, "may carry a load of ill-defined matter like a ship. But poetry is the machine which drives it, pruned to a perfect economy" (*CP2* 54). On the basis of ideas like this one, we can now see that Livingston's analogy (that the "argument between pragmatists and their critics will sound like a quarrel between positivists and romantics") is precisely what we find *inside* Williams's poetry—

especially *Paterson,* the most dialogic of his poems. Williams, in other words, is groping within himself for something like the Pragmatic resolution of the Romantic/Positivist argument. This struggle is rehearsed in many of Williams's prose essays as well as in a recurrent mental dialogue with the writings of John Dewey.

By Williams's definition, this is a historical struggle—"poems are documents of men"—taking place in the arena of experience, where poems, like men, can be recognized as bodies. We are dealing here with a corporeal—if not immediately corporate—situation; the affair of poetry, the business of writing, the realm of experience, has to do with bodies of knowledge. The site of the contest is some sort of body, the immediate problem is then to find out what a body is, where it is, and what forms it takes.

But what a body is is not as easy a matter to settle as it sounds, especially in the age of corporate capitalism, where increasingly bodies have invisible existences. The problem of the "corporate personality" complicated Williams's quest more or less directly.

The importance to Williams of Dewey's approach to the corporation, and thus to modernity itself, lies in Dewey's continuing effort to historicize philosophy, which, in effect, allowed him to historicize the self. This is the whole thrust of *Reconstruction in Philosophy* (1920), and it is emphasized at the outset of *Philosophy and Civilization* (1931): "Those of us who assert in the abstract definition of philosophy that it deals with eternal truth or reality untouched by local time and place, are forced to admit that philosophy as a concrete existence is historical, having temporal passage and diversity of local habitations" (Dewey 1931 4).[5]

Williams, I will show, came to the same realization about poetry through writing "The Wanderer" in 1914. The lesson of that poem is that there is no eternal poetry, no realm of poesy, and thus, of course, no "Archimedean," transhistorical realm of culture untouched by local time or place. As "The Wanderer" shows, it is not some mythical river that provides the site of poetic self-realization but the filthy Passaic.

The twentieth-century world that Williams confronted when composing "The Wanderer" was increasingly defined by "new social units," including corporations. Dewey concluded in his *Reconstruction in Philosophy* (1920) that these are "groupings for promoting the diversity of goods that men share" (204). These associations correspond to neither individual nor national boundaries. Rather, trade unions, professional associations, churches, and business corporations are the determining social units of modern life (Dewey 1920 204–13). And Dewey emphasizes in *Individualism Old and New* (1930) that "the influence business corporations exercise in determining present industrial and economic activities is both a cause and a symbol of the tendency to combination in all phases of life." He continues, "Associations tightly or loosely organized more and more define the opportunities, the choices and the actions of individuals. The need of the present is to apprehend the fact that, for better or worse, we are living in a corporate age" (1939 407).[6]

If moral opportunities, choices, and actions are defined, and to a greater or lesser degree determined, by associations, what then is the relation between public and private? Between self and world? These are the same questions that Stevens would pose later in "The Man with the Blue Guitar." They take on a real urgency for any poet but especially for the poet who, like Williams prior to the breakthrough represented by "The Wanderer," had founded his ideas about art and self-expression in terms of Romanticism.

Any disturbance of the relationship between self and world automatically redetermines the Romantic artistic ideal of "self-expression." Williams confronts Romantic idealism in "The Wanderer" when he decides that the poet's subject is not himself but his relation to his historical milieu.[7] The problem that Williams sets himself in that poem, and again in *Paterson*, is the question not simply of how he feels about Modernity but of how he shall be a mirror to it. It is a problem of representation. The problem is thus set in Pragmatic terms. Williams is asking, in "The Wanderer," not what the essence of modernity is but—opening up the potentially pragmatic issue—what modernity's consequences are for the artist and the mimetic project (Dewey 1931 148).

"The Wanderer": An Influence Drama

The trajectory of Williams's response to the problem of modernity lies between the primal question "How shall I be a mirror to this modernity?" (*CP1* 28), which we find Williams asking in his first major poem, "The Wanderer" (1914), and the formulation of a method—"no ideas but in things"—which captures the dilemma of modern subjectivity and becomes the sign under which he composed the epic *Paterson* (1946–1958). "Poetry," he wrote a correspondent, "an art, is what answer I have" (*SL* 238). The method of *Paterson* is the long Pragmatic answer to Williams's own primal modern question.

"The Wanderer" is what Harold Bloom would want to call Williams's first "strong poem"; it announces the beginning of Williams as a true poet. By reading the poem in Bloom's fashion we can see that "modernity" is a historical problem that demands a poetic answer. For Williams "modernity" itself is a problem of influence that is resolved by the poet's acceptance of history.

"The Wanderer" perfectly fulfills a kind of influence drama that Bloom calls the "Scene of Instruction." He has argued that "poetry is not an art passed on by *imitation*, but by *instruction*. There can be no instruction without a scene of instruction, a primal fixation upon a precursor (however composite, however idealized) and such a fixation is also a primal repression" (Bloom 1976 105). Bloom has invented six cabalistic "revisionary ratios" (Bloom 1973) to define the different types of defensive positions and reactions that new poets take in relation to their precursors, and together these make up a Scene of Instruction, which is "a six phased scene that strong poems must will to overcome by repressing their own freedom into the patterns of revisionary interpretation" (Bloom 1976 27).

This is what Bloom means by the Scene of Instruction. Briefly,

> a Primal Scene of Instruction [is] a model for the unavoidable imposition of influence. The Scene—really a complete play, or process—has six stages, through which the ephebe emerges: election (seizure by the precursor's power); covenant (a basic agreement of poetic vision between precursor and ephebe); the choice of rival inspiration (e.g. Wordsworth's Nature vs. Milton's Muse); the self-presentation of the ephebe as a new incarnation of the "Poetical Character"; the ephebe's interpretation of the precursor; and the ephebe's revision of the precursor. Each of these stages then becomes a level of interpretation in the reading of the ephebe's poem. [Bloom 1976 27][8]

The seven part "Wanderer" in fact, conforms to Bloom's schema almost exactly. The influences that Williams (and his poem) needs to overcome and that are subject to revisionary interpretation are Keats and Whitman, who appear in the poem through allusions to the Hyperion poems and "Crossing Brooklyn Ferry"; "The Wanderer" is a kind of awkward hybrid of both. Opening on the Hudson Ferry to Manhattan, "The Wanderer" has the the dramatic form of "The Fall of Hyperion," that is, it is structured around a series of tests that the poet must pass or he will die as a poet.

All of the stages that Bloom mentions occur in Williams's poem and in the same order. First, the poet describes an encounter with a mysterious "old queen" (*CP1* 28)[9] who becomes a kind of Whitmanesque power, subjecting him to ordeals of vision in ways derived from the way Keats's Moneta tests the ephebe in "The Fall of Hyperion." A Bloomian covenant begins in "Clarity," the poem's second section, when the ephebe exclaims: "I know this day I have at last seen her, / In whom age in age is united— / Indifferent, out of sequence, marvelously!" (28). The ephebe's willingness to worship the "marvelous" old queen leads to a series of tests in the form of confrontations with modernity, first on crowded Broadway and next on "the deserted streets of Paterson" (30) where the 1913 Silk Strike is in progress. These visions educate the ephebe, allowing him to become a modern poet. In making him so, Williams chooses Whitman as a rival inspiration superior to Keats. The scene is complicated and, perhaps, finally incomplete because the crisis of revision and reinterpretation results only in the final transumption of the Keats influence. The Whitman influence abides, to provoke Williams throughout his career. Williams's full "interpretation" of *that* strong precursor will only be completed in *Paterson*—one reason we need to look at "The Wanderer" before turning to the larger poem.

If we take Williams's question, "How shall I be a mirror to this modernity?" as a question that all poets of his generation should have been asking themselves, and if we assume that Williams wanted "The Wanderer" to stand as a kind of answer to the question, then the solution, paradoxically, seems to have involved going back to the past, in this case, to recuperate Whitman's "Crossing Brooklyn Ferry" as a new modern mirror.

Like other American male poets—Hart Crane, for example—Williams sought in Whitman an answer to the inadequacies of the English Romantic tradition that was proving irrelevant to the demands that twentieth-century America was making on the poetic imagination.

"The Wanderer," set on the Hudson River ferry, is quite consciously in dialogue with Whitman's poem of the East River crossing. But choosing Whitman as precursor meant rejecting another past represented by the English Romantic poets, specifically Keats. The drama of the poem is in the ephebe's struggle to mediate these competing influences and to realize, as the Scene of his Instruction unfolds, that he must overcome the Keats influence in favor of Whitman's. To put the question in very much broader terms, we could say that the drama of "The Wanderer" is Williams's struggle to choose America over England. In saying this, we say that Williams is embarked on a quest for his own American identity.

In his *Autobiography*, Williams recalls his principal early work, prior to "The Wanderer," as a vast romance, featuring "the aimless wandering . . . of the young prince . . . He went on, homeward or seeking a home that was his own, all this through a 'foreign' country whose language was barbarous." The poem was "poetically descriptive of nature, trees for the most part, 'forests' strange forests—wandering at random, without guide alone" (*A* 60). Williams's irony lets us know that what appeared to be a foreign country to his young poet-self was, simply, America. The barbarous language was his own American English. Thirty-five years after writing it, Williams clearly interprets "The Wanderer" as his liberation from this "aimless" wandering. The poem frees the young poet from his pose as a foreigner in his own land and from the fruitless task of trying to rewrite Keats rewriting Spenser in *Endymion*. In light of Williams's own reflections, the title of his first important poem may always have been loaded with self-irony. It makes sense, then, that the "guide" Williams discovered in "The Wanderer" is a semicomic Whitman in drag, by turns a crow and a seagull, a "marvelous old queen" (*CP1* 30), a slattern, an "old crone" (32), and a "beggar" (34).[10] Because she is a necessary ally to Williams in "seizing the precursor's power," she must also be a repressed version, or interpretation, of Keats. Thus she looks as Whitman might look if we could imagine him absurdly dressed as Keats's Moneta in "Hyperion."

This odd figure first appears in the poem as a crow watched by the ephebe:

I saw her eyes straining in the new distance
And as the woods fell from her flying
Likewise they fell from me as I followed—

So that I knew (that time) what I must put from me
To hold myself ready for the high course [*CP1* 27]

The woods here are the woods of the Romantic juvenilia that Williams had written hitherto. They represent all that he has already rejected so that he may approach the Scene of Instruction to learn really how to achieve clarity of poetic vision.

The Whitman influence immediately arrives to educate the poet. The ephebe has known what to reject; now he must be taught what to affirm. Whitman, in the form of the gull from "Crossing Brooklyn Ferry," appears as the ephebe is crossing the Hudson River ferry to Manhattan, "wearying many questions" (27), chief among them, "How shall I be a mirror to this modernity?" (28). At that moment the ephebe sees the gull who has flown out of Whitman's poem into his and joins her to fly above the river.

In finding the strength to reject overt English poetic influence, Williams has taken Whitman at his word that "you that shall cross from shore to shore years hence are more to me, and more in my meditations, than you might suppose" (Whitman 308). Williams's question about the poet's relation to modernity ponders Whitman's mystic faith in "the similitudes of the past and those of the future" (308). Similitude, however, is not identity. The quest in "The Wanderer" is to discover whether Whitman's methods can teach Williams about modernity. But if Whitman is clearly a better choice than Keats as a model for the modern poet, to what degree is the model of Whitman appropriate to modernity? The very need for Williams's question about modernity suggests the changes in American life that required a somewhat different kind of poetic self-consciousness from Whitman's.

The difference lies in "modernity" itself. As we have seen, modernity, to the belated post-Romantic Wanderer poet "crossing the ferry / With the towers of Manhattan before me" [*CP1* 27] is the skyscrapers of corporate America, with all of its unsettling implications for the self. The effects on the imagination of what Alan Trachtenberg has called the "incorporation of America" centers on a qualitative shift in the basic structure of economic life under capitalism; the shift from proprietary capitalist to corporate capitalist modes of production. These changes imply the modern metropolis—a city not only larger than earlier cities but differently arranged, because it embodies different social relations of production and distribution—namely, corporate relations.

These new corporate relations of production, and the resulting changes in social relations, mean that "Modernity" confronts the poet not only with new objective conditions, new facts like skyscrapers; modernity has produced new "I's" to mirror its accomplishments. One of the things that makes Williams different from Whitman is Williams's understanding that he is not simply a new poet but a new kind of person. He has a new kind of self, a "modern" identity. This self reflects the effects of the metropolis, with its anonymous crowds and mysterious financial superstructure, mirrored in the verticality of Manhattan.[11] The need for a new kind of self also addresses the resulting crisis for the individual no longer able to control, or even understand, his own economic and personal destiny in a society dominated by vast corporate associations whose inner workings are hidden from public scrutiny.

In the age of corporate capitalism, the modern poet must find a way to "mirror" mass phenomena and invisible forms of social control. These are exemplified by crowds, commerce, the metropolis. In the "Broadway" section of "The Wanderer," the influence of Whitman consequently forces the ephebe to confront the modern metropolis in its regimented anonymity:

> She struck!—from behind, in mid-air
> And instantly down the mists of my eyes
> There came crowds walking—men as visions
> With expressionless, animate faces;
> Empty men with shell-thin bodies
> Jostling close above the gutter,
> Hasting nowhere [CP1 29]

This vision strikingly anticipates the anomie in Eliot's vision of the crowd, like Dante's dead, flowing over London Bridge where "each man fixed his eyes before his feet" (Eliot 1962 39) in *The Waste Land* (1922).[12] Like Eliot, Williams is at first repelled by this vision, but at that instant, he is admonished by a vision of the modern muse:

> And then, for the first time
> I really scented the sweat of her presence
> And turning saw her and—fell back sickened!
> Ominous, old, painted—

With bright lips and eyes of the street sort—
Her might strapped in by a corset
To give her age, youth, perfect
In that will to be young she had covered
Her godhead to go beside me [29]

Only the imaginative confusion brought on by his confrontation with modernity allows the ephebe to see the Whitman influence for what she is. This itself is a kind of test. The "sweat of her presence" suggests labor and the problematic vulgarity of modern life for the poet who has trained himself in the Romantic sublime. Appropriately, the new muse is in the guise of an old whore; we see her as a member of the urban proletariat. She is "ominous, old and painted," yet still authentic beneath the shabby veneer of makeup, which only reveals her for what she is. Gathering his courage, the ephebe is inspired by his slatternly muse as "Silent, her voice entered at my eyes / And my astonished thought followed her easily" (29). Already in a kind of corporate bond, together they ask of the figures in the crowd: "do their eyes shine, their clothes fit?" (29). Their enthusiastic reaction is quite different from Eliot's later aversion: "These *live* I tell you / Old men with red cheeks, / Young men in gay suits! See them!" Williams cries (29). Where Eliot is always ready to deplore, Williams's instinct is to affirm. But he is still afraid. He begs the Whitmanian hag: "May I be lifted still up and out of terror, / Up from the death living around me" (30). But the muse has other plans.

It is not a sublime uplifting but a rigorous descent into the supposedly unpoetic social world that is necessary for the poet who would mirror modernity. The modern poet cannot be lifted up and over "the living death" of modern anonymity; rather he must plunge into that death in life and go through it to experience the social movements surging beneath. In "The Wanderer" the Whitman influence forces the ephebe to cover, like some cub reporter, the big Silk Strike in Paterson, New Jersey, a moment to which he will return in the epic *Paterson* (*P* 172–73). Hunkering in a bread line with the strikers, Williams finds himself singing the social body electric: "Nowhere / The Subtle! Everywhere the electric!" (*CP1* 31) he exults. He describes the working classes:

Faces all knotted up like burls on oaks,
Grasping, fox snouted, thick lipped,

Sagging breasts and protruding stomachs,
Rasping voices, filthy habits with the hands [31]

Despite the unpromising representation of the beastlike proletariat, Williams claims that he finds something wonderful, almost Dionysian, in this "electric," "Ugly, venomous, gigantic" breakdown of order, which "Toss[es] me as a great father his helpless / Infant till it shriek with ecstasy" (31). Williams wants to take a kind of sublime satisfaction in this. An initial alarm and disgust turning to delight in just such breakdowns of conventional order will mark his poetry for the rest of his life.

But the ephebe's tests are not over, he is not the figure we call Williams yet. The Whitman muse must teach him to sing America, not just the City. The City must be contextualized. The ephebe must be shown the costs of Modernity and the way the microcosm of the city relates to the macrocosm of the continent sprawling westward to and beyond the "Jersey mountains" (32). The ephebe must learn to sing nature a new way too.

His first attempt is a failure. The Whitman muse points out a rural landscape, a tree, a white house, and the sky and asks her pupil to

Speak to them of these concerning me!
For never while you permit them to ignore me
In these shall the full of my freed voice
Come grappling to the ear with intent! [32]

The ephebe does his best—but his voice is still fatally compromised by Romantic and "poetic" diction.

. . . I cried out with all the might I had,
"Waken! O people, to the boughs green
With unripe fruit within you!
Waken to the myriad cinquefoil
In the waving grass of your minds!
Waken to the silent Phoebe nest
Under the eaves of your spirit!" [32]

Imagining a symbol-filled, poetic realm of images, the ephebe produces a hackneyed, lyrical trill. The stance is Whitman's but the diction is Keats's. He tries again: "I shouted again still more loudly" but admits that "my voice was a seed in the wind" (32). The "old one,

laughing" takes him back to the city (32) where she forces the young
poet to attend to it:

> . . . the old one, laughing
> Seized me and whirling about, bore back
> To the city, upward, still laughing
> Until the great towers stood above the meadow
> Wheeling beneath, the little creeks, the mallows
> That I picked as a boy, the Hackensack
> So quiet, that looked so broad formerly:
> The crawling trains, the cedar swamp upon the one side—
> All so old, so familiar—so new now [32–33]

This aerial view of skyscrapers and crawling trains shows Manhattan
in relation to the countryside. The notion of a pure nature poetry of
"little creeks and mallows," which the poet still quite clearly wishes
to sing, is shown to be "old and familiar"—not a good thing—but also
the ephebe begins to see that nature is newly interesting for its prox-
imity and relation to the city. Pure little lyrics about nature such as he
had attempted to impress the muse with earlier in poem—"Waken! O
people, to the boughs green / With unripe fruit within you!" (32)—are
old hat. The marvels that the muse offers are related to the fact of met-
ropolitan space. The modern city organizes, stimulates, antagonizes
nature. The poet must learn to mirror this new relationship.

To do so, Williams must learn to locate his poetry in historical
time. He must abandon the ahistorical realm of poesy for a language
of experience derived from his own locality midway between the
down-at-the-heel regime of factory production represented by Paterson
and the fully financialized "culture of purchase" represented by Manhattan.

Between these very different cities we have a kind of symbolic history of production in the United States from its first corporate beginnings in Hamilton's Paterson to its financialized apotheosis in the
great glass towers of Manhattan. What links them is not just time, but
the river, which becomes, in "The Wanderer," the final site of Instruction, and in *Paterson* the cord that holds that narrativeless and anti-
chronological epic to some sort of progressive development.

To become a poet, Williams must somehow break the chronological
stranglehold of literary history. He must purge himself of Romantic
canonical ideals about truth and beauty and find another, pragmatic

kind of beauty in another sort of pragmatic truth. To do this he must swim in the river of time and place: "The Passaic, that filthy river" (34). The filth of the Passaic is specifically the filth of history, to which the poet is asked to sacrifice his youthful idealism in order to gain a mature and pragmatic appreciation of "meaning," which, as Dewey reminds us, "is wider in scope as well as more precious in value than is truth" because "truths are but one class of meanings, namely those in which a claim to verifiability by their consequences is an intrinsic part of their meaning. Beyond that island of meanings which in their own nature are true or false lies an ocean of meanings to which truth and falsity are irrelevant" (Dewey 1931 4–5). Poems are made out of meanings, not truth. To acknowledge this point is to know that poems are made, not found. When the poet begins to realize that his poems, like their "truths," are constructed, not inspired, he can continue to write poetry. By the final section of "The Wanderer," ("I knew the novitiate was ended," the poet says), his ephebe status will be sacrificed; "the ecstasy was over," he realizes, "the life begun" (34). The life launched here is the life of the poet, free for the first time to make the world meaningful, not just to adorn it with splendid but worn out truths.

> Then the river began to enter my heart,
> Eddying back cool and limpid
> Into the crystal beginnings of its days.
> But with the rebound it leaped forward:
> Muddy, then black and shrunken
> Till I felt the utter depths of its rottenness
> The vile breath of its degradation
> And dropped down knowing this was me now.
> But she lifted me and the water took a new tide
> Again into the older experiences,
> And so, backward and forward,
> It tortured itself within me
> Until time had been washed finally under,
> And the river had found its level
> And its last motion had ceased
> And I knew all—it became me [35]

At first the ephebe experiences the history of the river chronologically, from its "crystal beginnings" to the "utter depths" of its modern "rottenness" and "degradation" that is "me now." Indeed, the river *is* time.

But as the muse educates him, chronology loses its hold; remember his first impression of her: "indifferent, out of sequence" (28). At this moment, in an extraordinary image, the poet—ephebe no longer—is allowed to see his old novice-self depart downstream

> And I knew this for double certain
> For there I saw myself, whitely
> Being borne off under the water!
> I could have shouted out in my agony
> At the sight of myself departing
> Forever, but I bit back my despair
> For she had averted her eyes
> By which I knew well enough of her thoughts
> And so the last of me was taken [35]

The ephebe is now history. This baptism in what may be called the "historical sublime" meant giving up the sublime in the old sense ("ecstasy")—but for what? In 1914, Williams wasn't sure. But Williams later noted in *The Embodiment of Knowledge* that "to return to anything like values and clarity we have been forced into vulgarity. This is history" (*EK* 28). The second section of "The Wanderer" is titled "Clarity," so it seems likely that these sentences condense the lesson and importance of Williams's breakthrough poem. It is no accident that the structure of "The Wanderer" parallels that of the later, more elaborate epic, *Paterson*. In both poems the river serves as a kind of touchstone to which the poem returns. In both we have the Silk strike, the conundrum of Manhattan, and at the end, a ritual purging by water—in *Paterson* by the Atlantic Ocean. By the time of *Paterson* the filth in the Passaic has been historicized as the filthy industrial effluents of the city of Paterson, perhaps the first, certainly the most ambitious, corporation chartered by the new U.S. government in 1792.

Planning for *Paterson:* Dewey and the Problem of Form

In "The Wanderer" the Passaic River becomes History. In the more profound and accomplished *Paterson* it will become Language. In *Paterson* the river is eternal, both prior to, and outlasting history itself, even as it contains it, holding the sludge from Paterson's silk mills, dye works, and other manufacturing enterprises made possible by river power. The river is William James's "stream of thought," which breaks into speech as it goes over the Paterson falls (*P* 7–8). The poem enacts a kind of double fall—the fall of thought into the confusions of speech, and the further confusion of the spoken word when it is translated into writing, where, for example, "falls" can be misunderstood as "false":

> A false language. A true. A false language pouring—a
> language (misunderstood) pouring (misinterpreted) without
> dignity, without minister, crashing upon a stone ear. [*P* 15]

The river, or stream of thought, is also spoken language. This is the river Williams described when he wrote of *Paterson* in his *Autobiography* (1951), "The Falls let out a roar as it crashed upon the rocks at its base. In the imagination this roar is a speech or a voice, a speech in particular; it is the poem itself that is the answer" (*A* 392).

The river's different aspects reflect, in Bloomian terms, the different roles they play in repressing precursor poets. In "The Wanderer" the river is used to purge the ephebe of the wrong kind of historical influences, namely the historical burden of English Romanticism. In *Paterson,* Williams must reclaim the American language (not the English language) from its strongest poet, Whitman. In the service of this project the river becomes the torrent of the American language that Williams must possess as his own. In the final scene of the first, four-part version of *Paterson,* the poet arrives at the ocean. After a swim, he "turned again / to the water's steady roar, as of a distant / waterfall," then "heads inland, followed by the dog" (*P* 202). In Williams's own reading of this moment in his *Autobiography* (written immediately after *Paterson* was supposedly finished), he says the poet is turning inland, "toward Camden where Walt Whitman, much traduced, lived the latter years of his life and died" (*A* 392). To a Bloomian this statement can be read only as a confession of poetic weakness. Williams's admission already indicates the need for a fifth part of *Paterson,* which appeared in 1958.[13]

Having found himself as a poet in "The Wanderer," Williams constantly mulled over the idea of a *Paterson* poem. A longish poem of beginnings called "Paterson" appeared in 1927 (*CP1* 263–66). Williams gave an eighty-seven-page typescript called *Detail and Parody for the Poem Paterson* to his publisher James Laughlin in 1939 (*CP2* 448n). Fifteen short poems from this manuscript entitled "For the Poem 'Paterson' " appeared in Williams's pamphlet *The Broken Span* (1941).

Only the first of these fragments, consisting of only three crucial lines, appeared in the big poem:

> A man like a city and a woman like a flower—who are in
> love. Two women. Three women. Innumerable women,
> each like a flower. But only one man—like a city
>   [*CP2* 14]

These lines establish the corporate problem of unity in multiplicity that Williams wants his epic to address.

The most significant portion of the epic to be written and published before *Paterson* got underway was "Paterson: Episode 17" (1937), which becomes the "Beautiful Thing" episode in book 3 (*P* 98–99, 104–5, 127–28). It is in many ways the lyrical climax of the poem.

In *Paterson*, "Paterson: Episode 17" is transformed from a lyrical meditation of the poet watching a beautiful black woman, apparently someone's maid, idly beating the grass outside a church with a stick while the family she works for prays inside, to a densely mythologized Persephone/Orpheus story playing on the slave narrative. In both versions the "beautiful thing" can be construed as one of America's "pure products"—not an Elsie (*CP1* 217–19) exactly—but the embodiment of the inarticulate linguistic potential of the American language and thus the object of the poet's desire. This recurrent female figure in Williams's work, a working-class, usually nonwhite woman, culturally indigenous, the sublimely vulgar, untutored product of a purely local environment, is Williams's muse. "Beat hell out of it / Beautiful Thing" (*CP1* 439), the poem begins, and it ends:

> The stroke begins again—
>   regularly
> automatic
>   contrapuntal to
> the flogging
> like the beat of famous lines
> in a few excellent poems
>   woven to make you
>   gracious
> and on frequent occasions
>   foul drunk
> Beautiful Thing
> pulse of release

to the attentive
and obedient mind [*CP1* 442–43]

I quote these lines because they do *not* occur in *Paterson*. The fact that they do not suggests something important about the difference between Williams's conception of his epic project and the writing of lyric poetry. *Paterson* will be a poem about the struggle of that contrapuntal beat to be heard. Williams will break up "Episode 17" into several chunks and will disallow the pure closure these lines seem to give. In *Paterson*, the woman who embodies the "Beautiful Thing" is placed indoors, ill in a basement room ("—the small window with two panes, / my eye level with the ground, the furnace odor" [*P* 125]), where the Doctor visits her: Orpheus on a house call. It is an epiphany, an encounter with the goddess, with "Persephone / gone to hell" (*P* 126). Yet the final lines I have quoted above will be broken up, drowned out, by the intrusion of Billy Sunday's union-busting Evangelical singing, the religious antilyric, "BRIGHTen / the cor [we are supposed to hear "Kore' "] ner / where / you / are!" (*P* 128). The intrusion is the epic poet's acknowledgment of the oppressive historical, religious, and racist factors that keep the American equivalent of Persephone shut up in the maid's basement room. Insofar as *Paterson* is an epic, "the poem including history," the poet's Orphic quest must fail. He must be true to the cultural failure of America if he is to have any hope of resurrecting its buried virtues. Myths, he seems to say, ain't fairy tales, nor is history.[14]

Yet another poem, "Details for Paterson," appeared in 1941. Its purpose seems to have been a kind of self-exhortation: "If you talk about it / long enough / you'll finally write it—" (*CP2* 24). Next, a brief poetic prospectus, "Paterson: The Falls," was published in *The Wedge* (*CP2* 57–58). This poem suggested the four-part arrangement of the poem as it appeared in 1946–1951. This prospective Paterson poem states its problem in the first line: "What common language to unravel?"—an odd, double-edged sort of question. Does Williams propose to unravel a common language *from* some larger tangle, to separate a common language from another sort? Or does he want to unravel the common language of everyday speech into discrete strands to destroy it or even to deconstruct it? How we decide Williams resolved this question determines to a large extent how we will read *Paterson* itself,

the more so as these lines reappear near the opening of the final poem
(*P* 7).

I would argue from the lesson of "The Wanderer" that Williams resolves such a problem not in terms of either/or oppositions but rather
by "backward and forward" alternations of approach to what is, metaphorically, a knotty problem. The language is "combed into straight
lines" at the Falls itself, and here Williams proposes to "Strike in! the
middle of // some trenchant phrase, some / well packed clause" (*P* 57).
This statement alludes to the classical opening of the epic, in medias
res, and also creates the image of cutting the Gordian knot; Williams
sounds unsure that he wants to retangle what the falls have already
unraveled. Yet as the bearer of language, perhaps the poet has no other
choice.

Now Williams introduces "the archaic persons of the drama" (57)
First:

> An eternity of bird and bush,
> resolved. An unraveling:
> the confused streams aligned, side
> by side, speaking! Sound
>
> married to strength, a strength
> of falling—from a height! [57]

Then we hear

> The wild
> voice of the shirt-sleeved
> Evangelist rivaling, Hear
>
> me! I am the Resurrection
> and the Life! echoing
> among the bass and pickerel . . . [*CP2* 57–58]

The Evangelist, whom we will meet as Klaus Ehrens in *Paterson*, book
2, section 2, as a Christ-like money crank, seems here to be a sayer of
irrelevant Old World truths. His alternative language rivals the scene
of its saying with wild inappropriateness. His incongruity may serve
as an explanation for the unraveling that causes the stream of language
to run "confused . . . side by side," speaking at cross-purposes. The
joke ascribed to Winston Churchill, that England and America are two
countries divided by a common language, may be helpful here. Williams wants to complete this division within our shared but not com-

mon language. In so doing, he hopes to complete the American Revolution.

The impression is heightened by the third proposed section of *Paterson*, featuring "The old town" of Paterson and Alexander Hamilton—always, in Williams, a bearer of English values. In "Paterson: The Falls" there is the suggestion that Hamilton's story will be treated as a kind of poetic narrative in the final poem: "Alexander Hamilton / working up from St. Croix,"

> from that sea! and a deeper, whence
> he came! stopped cold
> by that unmoving roar, fastened
> there: the rocks silent [58]

Interestingly, none of this happens in the actual *Paterson*, in which Hamilton is given no dramatic part to play. In fact, this "section" of the final poem will be treated quite obliquely, and entirely by patching in documentary prose. Hamilton's presence is felt through his effects, not his acts. Williams's emphasis on "that sea"—the Caribbean, whence his own parents came to America, suggests a provocative identification with Hamilton. Like Hamilton, Williams is "stopped cold" by the "unmoving roar" of the Paterson Falls. Like Hamilton, Williams will use them for his own purposes. Unlike Hamilton, Williams will try to interpret the "whispers and moans" (58) of the falls, now drowned out behind Hamilton's legacy of clanging factory bells (58).

The fourth proposed section will try to deal with contemporary Paterson:

> the Modern town, a
>
> disembodied roar! The cataract and
> its clamor broken apart—and from
> all learning, the empty
> ear struck from within, roaring . . . [*CP2* 58]

The "disembodied, "broken apart" quality of the modern town is aptly represented by this shattered stanza with its sense-stopping line breaks. The style of this stanza is the only real clue we have as to the style of the eventual poem rather than its form.

In general, "Paterson: The Falls" fails to give much sense of the style of *Paterson*. It gives no hint that the planned poem will eschew narrative for odd blocks of prose and straggles of impressions. Williams's collagist use of newspapers, letters, and historical documents in *Paterson* owes much to the quirky alterations of prose and poetry that marked *Spring and All* (1923), and *The Descent of Winter* (1928), but in this prospectus we have no hint that he will revert to his earlier methods. *Paterson* will differ from his earlier Modernist experiments, however, in the *historical* nature of the documents that Williams will deploy. "Paterson: The Falls" reveals the historical theme of the proposed poem but not its historical method. As a record of Williams's intentions, however, "Paterson: The Falls" does show Williams puzzling out a form for his epic. He realizes that the form and structure of the poem are a single problem that he will have to unravel before it can take its proper shape.

The problem of form that Williams confronted in *Paterson* was, I am convinced, the conundrum of the corporate form. The relative shapelessness of the corporate form and the new shapes into which it cast society seemed formless only because they were not well understood. Williams strongly suspected that a form could be found if one could take the proper perspective on it. He tries to do so in *Paterson*, and as a result, *Paterson* itself seems frustratingly formless. The new forms that Williams was attempting to see and reproduce in his poem are "pragmatic"; that is, they do not already exist, waiting to be filled in by the poetic material, but rather are derived from it. The poem, in this sense, really is Paterson, New Jersey. Williams's task as "mirror" is to make the city meaningful by writing it. "Mirroring" apparently means more than somehow passively reflecting whatever is "out there" in the historical, actual world. Rather, Williams sees it as an active renovation of the world of actual experience. *Paterson* is his opportunity to update, renovate, and, in his own mind, reinvent American poetry.

Williams knew that the apparent formlessness of *Paterson* would be a problem even before it saw print. "Already I have been informed that *Paterson* will not be accepted because of its formlessness, because I have not organized it into some neo-classic *recognizable* context. Christ! Are there no intelligent men left in the world? Dewey might do something for me, but I am not worth his notice" (Williams's emphasis, *SL* 239).[15] The appeal to Dewey in this context is particularly interesting, because it suggests that Williams is thinking about *Paterson* in frankly pragmatic terms. In that case, he is not allowed to have a preconceived, a priori, neoclassical form for the poem. Is this why Williams thinks that Dewey, rather than, more definitively, literary critics or readers, might help make him understood? We will reach the answer by a somewhat roundabout method, but it is worth pursuing, for it will show why *Paterson* is, formally speaking, pluralistic and Pragmatic rather than a unified neoclassical poem.

The influence of Dewey on Williams begins with a brief essay called "Americanism and Localism,"[16] that Williams discovered "quite by chance" (*A* 391) in the summer of 1920. He had been reading the issue of the *Dial* that featured Pound's "Fourth Canto." The last page of "Americanism and Localism" faces the opening of Pound's poem, where Williams noticed it.

The five pages of "Americanism and Localism" are full of ideas that one associates with Williams, even though it becomes clear that for Dewey, "Americanism and Localism" is only a feuilleton. Dewey is not, he says, "essaying a political treatise. The bearing of these remarks is upon the literary career of our country" (686). Dewey writes more truly than even he knew. His observations about American newspapers became fundamental to Williams's poetics. Williams's prose directly echoes many of Dewey's points in "Americanism and Localism," especially the letters of the late 1940s, when Williams was composing *Paterson* and was much concerned with the problem of form.

Dewey begins his essay by remarking on the "momentary shock" one feels, when "one happens to receive a local newspaper from one of the smaller towns, from any town, that is, smaller than New York." "One is," he says, "brought back to earth" (684). "And the earth is just what it used to be. [The United States] is a loose collection of houses, of streets, of neighborhoods, villages, farms, towns. Each of these has an intense consciousness of what is going on within itself in the way of fires, burglaries, murders, family jars, weddings, and banquets to esteemed fellow citizens and a languid drooping interest in the rest of the spacious land" (684). "Very provincial?" Dewey asks rhetorically. "Not at all. Just local, just human, just at home, just where they live" (684). This "loose collection" of houses, streets, and neighborhoods is recognizably the topos of Williams's work throughout his life.

Dewey contrasts this ramshackle "localism" with "Americanism" or "Americanization." He notes, in examining small-town newspapers, "the strange phenomenon" that

> these same papers which fairly shriek with localisms devote a discreet amount of space to the activities of various Americanization agencies. From time to time, with a marked air of doing their duty, there are earnest editorials on the importance of Americanization and the wickedness of those who decline to be either Americanized or to go back where they came from. But these weighty and conscientious articles lack the chuckle and relish one finds in the report of the increase of the population of the town and of its crime wave. [684–85]

Dewey's conclusion is that "the wider the formal, the legal unity, the more intense becomes the local life" (686). The reason for this, Dewey speculates, is that "Americanization consists in learning a language strangely known as English. But perhaps they are too busy making the American language to devote much time to studying the English" (685). The notion that Americans don't speak English is, of course, one of Williams's pet themes: "We've got to *begin* by stating that we speak (here) a distinct, separate language in a present (new era) and that it is NOT English," Williams told a correspondent when he was writing *Paterson* (*SL* 268–69).

Dewey notes, "The newspaper is the only genuinely popular form of literature we have achieved. The newspaper hasn't been ashamed of localism. It has revelled in it, perhaps wallowed is the word" (*Dial* 686). Williams once called the newspaper "that unintentional parody of the modern epic" (quoted in Mariani 598). Insofar as a newspaper is a collection of disparate texts gathered together—incorporated—under a single name, we could say that a newspaper mimics corporate identity. In this sense *Paterson* is like a newspaper, and in fact it contains generous selections from newspapers. These selections, in turn, are decidedly local in content, full of the "fires, murders, and family jars" that constitute local news. In book 3, section 1, we have newspaperlike accounts (taken from the local historical publication *Prospector*) of the Paterson fire of February 8, 1902. In book 4, section 3, Williams includes a clipping from the *New York Herald Tribune* of September 18, 1950, detailing a murder investigation in Paterson: "Paterson N.J. Sept 17—Fred Goodell Jr., twenty-two, was arrested early this morning and charged with the murder of his six-months-old daughter, Nancy" (*P* 194).[17] We are supposed to think that Williams literally lifted this news from the morning paper—there is no reason to think otherwise. Other Passaic County murder stories, one dating from the American Revolution, are "clipped" from newspapers of the past (see *P* 186 197, 20).

Even "family jars" find their way into *Paterson* as "local news." Williams does the newspapers one better by including the private letters of people actively engaged in inventing the American language. Some of them are Literary people, poets such as Ezra Pound, Marcia Nardi, and Allen Ginsberg. Other letters come from Williams's non-literary correspondence. By far the most interesting one seems to have been left behind by Kitty Hoagland's maid when she "ran away in December of 1942" (*P* 283n). This letter, which Enalls received "from her friend Dolly" (*P* 283n), has a jazzy African-American energy that American writers since Twain have tried, usually in vain, to imitate. "But child, Nov[ember] 1, I did crack you know yourself I been going full force on the (jug) will we went out (going to newark) was raining, car slaped [*sic*] on brakes, car turned around a few times, rocked a bit and stopped facing the other way, from which we was going. Pal, believe me for the next few days. Honey, I couldn't even pick up a half filled bucket of water for fear of scalding myself" (*P* 124). The letter ends with a local example of a self-conscious attempt to invent a new language: "Tell Raymond I said I bubetut hatche isus cachute / Just a new way of talking kid. It is called (Tut) maybe you heard of it. Well here hoping you can read it" (*P* 125).[18] One can readily see why Williams saved this letter to use in his poem several years later. He recognized the voice of a kindred spirit. Enalls's friend Dolly is engaged in the identical project that Williams called *Paterson;* it's appropriate that she became one of the poem's many unwitting co-authors.

Finally, Dewey closes "Americanism and Localism" with a remark that Williams would repeat over and over in essays and letters: "We are discovering that the local is the only universal" (687). Dewey's brief essay ends by asserting that "the truth is first discovered in abstract form, or as an idea" (688). Once this discovery has happened, Dewey claims, it "creates a new poetry" (688). "When the discovery sinks a little deeper, the novelist and dramatist will discover the localities of America as they are, and no one will need to worry about the future of American art" (688).

The "universality of the local was," Williams repeated in "Against the Weather" (1939), what he had "all my life striven to emphasize" (*SE* 198). Twenty-four years after he first read it, we find Williams interpreting the remark for Horace Gregory in a 1944 letter: "There has to be a recognition by the intellectual heads (Eliot among them) of the work-a-day local culture of the United States. In fact there can be no general culture unless it is bedded, as he says, in a locality—something I have been saying for a generation: that there is no universal except in the local. I myself took it from Dewey. So it is not new" (*SL* 224).

Another, serendipitous virtue of Dewey's essay is that, as printed in the *Dial*, "Americanism and Localism" ends with Pound's "Fourth Canto" on the facing page. Perhaps nothing by an American poet could seem less local and determinedly less American than the poem that bears this deeply classical invocation of an epic muse:

Palace in smoky light,
Troy but a heap of smouldering boundary-stones
ANAXIFORMINGES! Aurunculeia!
Hear me. Cadmus of the golden prows . . . [689, 4:13]

With "Americanism and Localism" and "The Fourth Canto" in convenient juxtaposition, Williams had in his hands the ingredients of *Paterson*. This conjunction of the epic *and* the local would become the epic *of* the local he would finally undertake a quarter of a century later, after decades of preparation and thought. Dewey's "the local is the only universal" would become Williams's "local pride," authorizing his audacious "reply to Greek and Latin with the bare hands, [the] gathering up, [the] celebration" (*P* 2) that became *Paterson*. Williams's "reply" is, in part, an allusive critique of Pound's *Cantos* (especially Canto 4), which often strive for a self-consciously "classical" universality.

We can see, I think, that Dewey's essay "Americanism and Localism" exerted a formative influence, even a determining one, on Williams and *Paterson*. The literary model for the poem is to a remarkable degree that of a newspaper; the genre Dewey called "the only genuinely popular form of literature we have achieved" (*Dial* 686). *Paterson* is local news because Williams feels, like Dewey, that the heart of American literature is local news and because, like Dewey, Williams concluded that "the local is the only universal."

Paterson and the "Individual in Cultural Crisis"

Granted, then, that the newspaper is, in every sense, a kind of "corporate" literature, insofar as *Paterson* is like a newspaper it has a kind of corporate identity in its plurality of authors and texts. I have claimed more, however, for Dewey's influence on Williams. What about the mysterious "corporate self," the new "I," that Williams intuited in "The Wanderer"? The problem is immediately felt in *Paterson*, from the moment that its supposed hero or narrator is introduced. The "hero" of *Paterson* is "only one man—like a city" (*P* 7). Is he man or city? Which? Dr. Noah Faitoute Paterson (*P* 15) is a remarkably confusing plurality:

> Paterson lies in the valley under the Passaic Falls
> its spent waters forming the outline of his back. He
> lies on his right side, head near the thunder
> of the waters filling his dreams! Eternally asleep,
> his dreams walk about the city where he persists
> incognito. Butterflies settle in his stone ear.
> Immortal he neither moves nor rouses and is seldom
> seen, though he breathes and the subtleties of his
>   machinations
> drawing their substance from the noise of the pouring
>   river
> ⸳ animate a thousand automatons [*P* 6]

Apparently, man *and* city, Paterson has a corporate identity. Dream and dreamer, like the industrial corporation it historically is, Paterson "breathes" life into "a thousand automatons" of which he is also, necessarily, composed. These "automatons" are actually regular people whose selfhood has not yet been defined—they only *seem* like automatons. "Who are these people," the poet asks, "(how complex / the mathematic)" (*P* 9). Much of the epic is an attempt to find out.

The paradox of corporate personhood is what makes Williams's poem so strange. Not only is it an attempt to get a fix on the corporatized personhood of others; it also enacts the problem formally. Like a corporation or a newspaper, his epic is "a natural entity" that is entirely artificial, an impersonal person, a unity of unwitting components, a collage of texts seemingly pasted together. But precisely this constitutes a corporation: it is incognito behind its purely legal singularity.

The name Doctor Noah Faitoute Paterson is also corporate. First, we are supposed to understand that this is a pseudonym for the author, Dr. William Carlos Williams. Second, each component of the name, each division of the larger corporate entity, so to speak, carries with it a bundle of allusive expectations that we ourselves incorporate in our response to his presence in the text. Noah: carpenter, ark builder, flood survivor. Faitoute has been glossed as "the man who could do everything" (Mariani 470), Williams's sobriquet for David Lyle, the eccentric, Thoreauvian, "one-man information station" (Mariani 468), whose remarkable letters were part of the inspiration behind *Paterson*. Mike Weaver has read Faitoute as "the man doing all all the time" (Weaver 127). Faitoute also has another referent. Williams probably borrowed the name from the big steel fabrication company one can still see hard by the railroad tracks in Elizabeth, New Jersey—a modern corporation and also one engaged in the heavy construction trade. The last name, Paterson, we can figure, is the man, the city, and the poem itself.

One helpful text in understanding the corporate nature of Dr. Paterson is Dewey's "The Individual in Cultural Crisis" (1939).[19] The problem that Dewey wants to consider is how to lay the groundwork for "the creation of a new individualism as significant for modern conditions as the old individualism at its best was for its day and place" (1939 406). The essay begins: "Anthropologically speaking, we are living in a money culture. Our materialism, our devotion to money making and to having a good time, are not things by themselves. They are the product of the fact that we live in a money culture; of the fact that our technique and technology are controlled in the interest in private profit. There lies the fundamental defect of our civilization" (1939 405). The fundamental defect is a contradiction between the entrenched "economic system of private gain" and the "revolutionary" development of "industry and technology" (405). The result is "the American type," the materialistic, hedonistic American consumer. In Dewey's rendition of the American "type" or self, the "money question" covertly resurfaces. Dewey does not pursue this side of the problem he has set himself, however; I merely mention it to show that he could have. Instead, Dewey's attention is drawn to this "American type," perhaps made especially visible by the inflationary 1920s, and argues that this is a new type of person, with a new individuality.

This new individuality has to do with the ascendancy of corporate relations of production. In this "corporate age" the present "'socialization' [of the individual] is largely mechanical and quantitative. The system is kept in a kind of precarious balance by the movement towards lawless and reckless overstimulation among individuals. If the chaos and mechanism are to generate a mind and soul, an integrated personality, it will have to be an intelligence, a sentiment and an individuality of a new type" (407). What we must avoid in looking for this new person is any simple opposition between "the corporation" and "the individual," Dewey warns, as though the choice before us was simply between Positivism and Romanticism, the ant and the artist. If "the whole significance of the older individualism has now shrunk to a pecuniary scale and measure" (411), Dewey argues, the new is not some simpleminded conformity. In fact, we don't know who the new individual is, but the reason may well be that we don't know what we are looking for.

> The tragedy of the "lost individual" is due to the fact that while individuals are now caught up into a vast complex of associations, there is no harmonious and coherent reflection of the import of these connections into the imaginative and emotional outlook on life. This fact is of course due in turn to the absence of harmony within the state of society. There is an undoubted circle. But it is a vicious circle only as far as men decline to accept—in the intellectual, observing and inquiring spirit—the realities of the social estate, and because of this refusal either surrender to the division or seek to save their individuality by escape or sheer emotional revolt. [410]

If it is neither especially "harmonious or coherent," *Paterson* is very much an attempt to reflect on the import of these new associative connections on modern life. "The poem to me," Williams wrote of *Paterson*, "is an attempt, an experiment, a failing experiment, toward assertion with broken means but an assertion, always, to a new and total culture, the lifting of an environment to expression. Thus it is social— the poem is a social instrument—accepted or not accepted seems to be of no material importance. It embraces everything we are" (*SL* 286). So when dealing with the undereducated, uncivilized masses, Williams's concern was never with the "decline of the West," a subject that obsessed contemporaries like Eliot and Pound; rather, like Dewey, Williams was interested in detecting whatever it was that was being born and becoming in the modernity around him.

> Who are these people (how complex
> the mathematic) among whom I see myself
> in the regularly ordered plateglass of
> his thoughts, glimmering before shoes and bicycles?
> They walk incommunicado, the
> equation is beyond solution, yet
> its sense is clear—that they may live
> his thought is listed in the Telephone
> Directory— [P 9–10]

The half-thrilled dread of the masses we saw in "The Wanderer" has been replaced by a real curiosity: "Who are these people . . . among whom I see myself?" These are people defined, in part, by their relationship to commodities like shoes and bicycles, which reflect their desires back onto themselves. This clue is registered by Williams as a new development.

In his walk in the park in book 2 of *Paterson,* for example, the poet notices a couple sunning themselves by their "jalopy." "Semi-naked," "semi-roused," they lie in "frank vulgarity" while the woman speaks of buying a two-piece bathing suit: "just pants and a brassiere" (P 51). As his "semi" characterizations show, the poet is half voyeuristicly excited, half appalled by this glimpse into working-class Arcadia. The poet fussily concludes that "among / the working classes SOME sort / of breakdown has occurred" (P 51).

The "SOME sort of breakdown" is a "SUM" sort of breakdown, the cultural breakdown of Hamiltonian cultural discipline symbolized by the corporate Society of Useful Manufactures' monopoly over the Paterson Falls. The Federalist class barriers once thrown up by money power and repressive religion have evolved into the new consumption culture of modernity, with its casual sexuality, "flagrant beyond all talk" where "minds [are] beaten thin / by waste" (P 51). Yet for all these pejorative phrases, Williams seems finally reconciled to the "breakdown" he thinks he sees. He notices that

> Semi-roused
> they lie upon their blanket

face to face,
mottled by the shadows of the leaves

upon them, unannoyed,
at least here unchallenged.
Not undignified . . . [P 51]

The young couple in the Park, with the young woman covered in figleaf
fashion by a skimpy bathing suit, are a kind of low-rent Adam and Eve.
The Park, on Sunday, offers them a kind of halfway Eden, where they
can be "semi-naked" (P 51), their "jalopy half-hid / behind them" (P
51). They are attended by equivocal emotions, which Williams seems
to have a hard time registering accurately with his received vocabulary. They are "semi-roused," also "unannoyed," "unchallenged," and,
finally, "not undignified." Williams notes that "their pitiful thoughts
do meet / in the flesh—surrounded / by churring loves!" (P 52). The
tone, not unlike that of "The Wanderer" in its comic condescension,
is by no means bleak. Once the poet overcomes what he called in a
letter the "aesthetic shock occasioned by the rise of the masses" (SL
259), they become the source of a new poetry. The couple, existing in a
halfway position between Dewey's social mechanism—the industrial
mills of Paterson—and the "over stimulation" fed by the consumption of such reckless articles as two-piece bathing suits, are nonetheless recognizable as people, as representatives of a new class, with their
own style and their own claims to individuality.

In fact, Williams's tender tone suggests that the "frank vulgarity"
(P 51) of the couple may be just what the doctor ordered. We recall
Williams's dictum in The Embodiment of Knowledge quoted earlier:
"To return to anything like values and clarity we have been forced into
vulgarity. This is history" (EK 28). Indeed, often enough, vulgarity
is where the aging Williams will continue to go for aesthetic refreshment, as in "The Desert Music" (1954).

What in the form of an old whore in
a cheap Mexican joint in Juarez, her bare
can waggling crazily can be
so refreshing to me, raise to my ear
so sweet a tune, built of such slime? [CP2 281]

This stanza repeats Williams's unusual sense of sublimity and possibility in the frankly vulgar. The stripper's "bare / can waggling cra-

zily" is, believe it or not, a version of Williams's own poetics, of the naked affirmation pulsing in the "variable" feet of his idiosyncratic meter. Willams hears "so sweet a tune" for this reason. The imaginative "refreshment" offered by the exotic dancer in the sleazy lounge makes her the same muse who whispered sweet filthy nothings to him forty years earlier when he composed "The Wanderer."

The ascendancy of corporate modes of production meant that Williams became concerned with restoring "the self" because it seemed to have something important to do with the relation between art and artist. The extension of commercial monetary relations allowed by corporate modes seemed to be subtly mediating existence and coming between the artist and his work. In one of Cress's (Marcia Nardi's) letters that Williams included in *Paterson,* she complains about "that film, that crust, which has gathered there so fatally between my true self and that which can only make mechanical gestures of living" (*P* 76). Since she has been worrying earlier about her "economic and social malajustments" (*P* 64), it seems Williams wants us to understand that these are the source of her self-alienation.[20]

The duty of the artist, then, was to reestablish contact with reality, to recover the genius of the local from the alienations of modernity. Could this be accomplished, a form might be discerned, then used, by the poet to mirror modernity.

Throughout his career, Williams is obsessed with this problem of contact. His association with two magazines named "Contact" speaks to a fear he shared with others that contact was precisely what was being lost in the modern era. Like a good pragmatist, he insisted that "contact with experience, as evidenced in a man's work, [is] the essential quality in literature" (*SE* 32). He resisted the "bastardy of the simile" because it seemed to deny the importance of "that thing, the vividness which is poetry by itself," that "Makes the poem." "There is no need to explain or compare," Williams continues, "Make it and it *is* a poem. This is modern, not the saga. There are no sagas—only trees now, animals, engines: There's that" (*SE* 68). This sounds like James's "world of pure experience." We also know, however, that Williams wanted to write a modern poem of sagalike proportions. The ambition to write *Paterson* meant that Williams had somehow to create some sort of poetic scaffolding from which his saga of the pure experience of modernity could be constructed.

Perhaps the essayistic torsos that became *The Embodiment of Knowledge* are the remains of the scaffolding. Perhaps they remain unfinished because they seek to explain why explanation is unnecessary. "The first difficulty of the modern world is a difficulty of thought . . . , of the imagination of the world, the immediate" (*EK* 114). Williams's use of "immediate" in its root sense of "unmediated" and his stress on its importance, illuminates the significance of the all-at-onceness for which Williams strove in his work. Much of the confusion in his writing is due to his impatience with any forms of transition, of mediation—even with writing itself. The rude ardor one can often hear in Williams's writing, exemplified in this brusque scene from *Paterson*, comes from a wild impatience to be authentic, there, real, in touch:

> Your clothes (I said) quickly, while
> your beauty is attainable.
>
>
>   Put them on the chair
> (I said. Then in a fury, for which I am ashamed)
>   You smell as though you need
> a bath. Take off your clothes and purify
> yourself . .
> And let me purify myself
>   —to look at you
>   to look at you (I said)
>
> (Then, my anger rising) TAKE OFF YOUR
> CLOTHES! I didn't ask you
> to take off your skin . I said your
> clothes, your clothes. You smell
> like a whore. I ask you to bathe in my
> opinions, the astonishing virtue of your
> lost body (I said) .
>
>   —that you might
> send me hurtling to the moon
> . . let me look at you (I
> said, weeping)
>
> Let's take a ride around to see what the town looks like
>   [*P* 105–6]

This scene is less importantly a confrontation between a man and a woman than a confrontation between a pragmatic poet and the form of the pragmatic poem. "Immediacy" is, in every sense, the operative need here. The poet's frustration is over all that stands between him and his object: clothes, dirt, and money (the other "smells like a whore"). These get in the way of his need to reclaim the "astonishing virtue of [her] lost body," the virtue of which seems to be an unalienated self. Note the frequent irruption of the repeated parenthetical: "(I said)." These emphasize the frustrating space between then and now—the vision (or, maybe, experience) and the poem. Even saying itself is a mediation and therefore a problem. This is not by any means love poetry. Euphemism, which is part of that tradition, would interpose itself between the poet and the experience he wants to claim.

Only the female body, clean and naked, is pure, despite the poet's boorish raging, and it is thus honored with the power to purify the poet. But of course, the female body is not a female body at all. "Female body" stands here for "object of desire," that is, for the pure experience that the poem and the poet are groping for. She is female because she represents the intellectual alternatives that Williams has received from the Western philosophical and poetic traditions. She is at once the sublimated woman of the romantics and the unspeakable, antiphilosophical "eternal feminine," which has frightened philosophers in the West since Plato.

In contemporary life, mediation is a form of alienation. Burke could have been thinking of Williams when he noted that "People try to combat alienation by *immediacy,* such as the senses alone provide" (Burke's emphasis, 1937 218). Alienation, in turn, derives from a "loss of faith in the reasonableness of a society's purposes" (218). "We use it," Burke writes, "to designate that state of affairs wherein a man no longer "owns" his world because for one reason or another, it seems *basically unreasonable* (Burke's emphasis, 1937 216). Williams's figuration of immediacy as a woman's body reveals a desire for a possessable form, something he can, so to speak, "get his mind around." Yet her very silence, which serves as a stimulus for the poet's own speech, is part of what makes her seem graspable—silence is part of the very "virtue of her lost body." This scene is not an interaction but an occasion for the poet to express, without compromise, exactly what he wants, which is egocentrically to bathe her in his opinions and so to purify them and her. The implication, however, is that the woman is also a kind of reader. If she is the audience for his opinions, as well as the source of them, then, insofar as *she* provokes *them,* the poet is some kind of medium or mediator. He voices not rage against women but the frustration of a language user who wants language to be identical to the world it describes: "(I said), (I said), (I said)," the poet repeats in a kind of despair.

So why does the woman seem to propose that they "take a ride around to see what the town looks like?" If this is the woman speaking, we can interpret it to mean either that she understands riding around and looking at the town as a reasonable substitution for the poet's desire, that is, she believes that looking at the town is what he really wants; or she is resisting his advances by proposing the town instead of herself. This latter option cannot make much sense—if only because we are not dealing with a real woman and all of the speeches in this passage are spoken by Williams. A third possibility, that the proposal to ride around town is spoken by the desiring poet, suggests that to explore the woman's nakedness is equivalent to riding around town and vice versa. Perhaps language—and the woman, we have already decided, is language in a graspable, concrete form, the poem— then poetry is found just riding around town. Language cannot be isolated from the social interactions that give rise to it; the poet can never have language all to himself—he must have it impure or not at all. Nature and natural language is to be found no longer in the virgin landscape, or the wifely freehold, where Williams's eighteenth-century precursors found it, but in the vulgar authenticity of the commercial, lost body of a woman of the town.

In equating the poem with the town, Williams follows Dewey's advice in "Americanism and Localism." Williams wants to show that the object of his quest for poetic form is "attainable" only in comprehensible bodies. If these bodies become too large (like Manhattan) or too amorphous, like the modern industrial corporation, they lose their "reasonableness" and resist inclusion in the poem. The problem of form is the problem of how to turn the megalopolistic impulse to make a "saga" into manageable, reasonable proportions. It is a problem of scale.

The paradox within Williams's desire for a body sufficient for the form he wants to possess is that he is writing an epic poem in search of a form. In fact, the drama of the poem *is* its search for a form. Throughout the poem, form is achieved, but only locally; the overarching form that Williams promised himself in his prospectus, "Paterson: The Falls" is lost in the proliferation of localities and local observations within the poem.

The Money Question in *Paterson*: "Aesthetic Shock"

The populistic critique of "finance capitalism" is never far away in Williams's work. The "money question" in *Paterson* surfaces explicitly and at length in two scenes. The first is the "Klaus Ehrens" scene in *Paterson*, book 2, section 2 (*P* 64–74), one of the longest coherent scenes in the poem. The second is at the end of book 4, section 2. It includes a Social Credit "advertisement" and a meditation on money and credit (*P* 180–85).

Williams composed part 2 of *Paterson* during the spring and summer of 1947. In June, Babette Deutsch wrote Williams, wondering about the role of labor and labor unrest in Williams's poem. Williams replied,

> I must say that I have found little I wanted to say about the labor violence that has had Paterson as its scene during the past thirty, or, perhaps, hundred years. . . . However, in *Paterson* the social unrest that occasions all strikes is strong—underscored, especially in the 3rd part, but I must confess that the aesthetic shock occasioned by the rise of the masses upon the artist receives top notice.
>   In Part or Book II . . . there will be much more in the same manner, that is, much more relating to the economic distress occasioned by human greed and blindness—aided, as always, by the church, all churches in the broadest sense of that designation—but still, there will be little treating directly of the rise of labor as a named force. I am not a Marxian." [*SL* 258–59]

We have noticed Williams's "aesthetic shock" at the "flagrant" young couple in the park. A similar shock recurs in *Paterson*, book 2, as the poet follows the workers on their "Sunday in the park":

> the ugly legs of the young girls,
> pistons too powerful for delicacy!   .
> the men's arms, red, used to heat and cold,
> to toss quartered beeves and
>   Yah! Yah! Yah! Yah! [*P* 44]

One doesn't expect Williams, of all poets, to continuously portray the working classes as so many yahoos on holiday, but it is part of the program of *Paterson* that he should do so. Williams's attitude toward these people is doubly complicated in that these lines have been lifted from "The Wanderer" as though to suggest that nothing has changed in the social climate or in the Williams's poetic project, in the intervening thirty years. The self-plagiarism suggests that "The Wanderer," in a sense, *is Paterson*. But perhaps Williams wants to remind us that, even as his initial aversion to the proletariat as a subject for poetry still exists, the role of the poet in the twentieth century is to resist such feelings and understand them for what they are, that is, as ideological reactions, not real feelings. Williams seems to follow James and others in "identifying the moral personality with the liminal figures who had hitherto appeared only at the margins, as the Other, in modern political theory"—that is, with "figures of the proletariat" (Livingston 1994 275). Failure to account for such people threatens to make a modern epic poem irrelevant.[21] But if Williams needs to stage his own impulse to caricature the masses, he wants also to contrast these people with the view of the financial superstructure that he sees from the top of Garret Mountain. Williams's pragmatic impulses are underwritten by his dyed-in-the-wool Jeffersonianism. There the poet

> Arrives breathless, after a hard climb he,
> looks back (beautiful but expensive!) to
> the pearl grey towers! [*P* 44]

These are the towers of Manhattan, visible from the high ground—the moral high ground—of Williams's Populist feeling and Pragmatic understanding. These are the same towers that made such an impression on the poetic ephebe in "The Wanderer." We are to remember that these expensive, beautiful things have been bought with the profits made, sweated, from the beefy and (provokingly) "red-armed" workers—possibly a hint of the "indirect treatment" that "Labor" receives in *Paterson*.

Williams's emphasis on "human greed and blindness" in his letter to Deutsch, rather than, say, contradictions within capitalism and the class struggle, mark Williams not only as a Populist but also—at least in the anticlerical context of the letter—reveal a radicalism of the old Christian Socialist type. The remarks about "churches," and thus orthodoxies of all kinds, in his letter explain the opening lines of book 2, scene 2:

Blocked.
> (Make a song out of that: concretely)
> By whom?

In its midst rose a massive church . . . And it all came
to me then—that those poor souls had nothing else in the world,
save that church, between them and the eternal stony, ungrate-
ful and unpromising dirt they lived by. . . . .

> Cash is mulct of them that others may live
> secure
> . . and knowledge restricted

> an orchestral dullness overlays their world. [*P* 62]

Williams's anticlericalism stems from his belief that "all formal reli-
gions," based as they are on "the immanence of religious experience,"
tend to become "monopolies using religion to bring a man under an
economic yoke of one sort or another" (*SE* 215–16) as he wrote in
"Against the Weather" (1939). He continues, "The simple teaching,
'Give all thy goods to feed the poor' was in spite of great examples,
such as that of St. Francis, turned into—the draining of every cent
from the Russian serfs, the Mexican peon and the Spanish peasantry
to their everlasting misery and impoverishment" (216). Williams is
a quixotic opponent of orthodoxy in any form, and orthodoxy—especially economic orthodoxy—is what he means by the image of the
massive church, rising like an iceberg over the huddled roofs of impoverished Paterson.[22] Most important here, however, is the method that
Williams ascribes to the church of corporate economic orthodoxy; the
mulcting of cash and the restriction of knowledge. These "concretely"
cause the writer's block.

Marcia Nardi's letters play an important role in this part of *Paterson*. Williams has spliced them in in such a way that they highlight the
difficulty of writing. Much of this difficulty has to do with the poet's
apparent indifference to her work; other reasons, though, are her "economic and social maladjustments" (*P* 64). Her description of "the
crust" and "film" that comes between herself and her work ends book
2, section 2 of the poem (*P* 76). The whole section, in fact, is largely
about the difficulty of writing in the shadows of the oppressive church
of economic orthodoxy.

This reading confirms every reader's sense that the St. Francis–like
Klaus Ehrens scene is a parody of Christ's "Sermon on the Mount."

Despite the ironic treatment of Ehrens, it indicates, if we hadn't taken the hint already, that we are to take his prescription—"give up your money"—pretty seriously. A Christian who invokes the Father, Son, and Holy Ghost (P 71), Ehrens is decidedly outside the church. This Sunday finds him preaching in the park at "the base / of the observation tower near the urinals" (P 63); "This," Williams adds pointedly, "is the Lord's line" (71). Given the ideological—even frankly political—rhetorical situation within which Ehrens is presented to us, it is likely that Williams thinks of him as a version of himself—a man who has renounced worldly success for a deeper integrity.

Ehrens is a Christ-like "money crank" preaching in the wilderness, "A Protestant! protesting" (P 65). His German, "Dutch" name links him to the godly seekers who first settled so many parts of the east coast of North America. But we are not to link Ehrens with the puritanism that Williams disparaged in *In the American Grain*. Ehrens's revelation came *after* he arrived in the New World from the "Old Country" (P 66). In fact, he seems to have come to America to enjoy himself after making money in Europe (P 67). In America, he made even more money, but he was unhappy. It was here that Ehrens heard the voice of the Lord urging him to "Give up my money!" (P 70). Ehrens has been preaching the lesson ever since.

Ehrens's discourse is punctuated by the story of Alexander Hamilton, told in chunks of prose[23] that set forth an aggressively Jeffersonian interpretation of Hamilton's career. Hamilton is edited into the scene in such a way that he is forced to play the hackneyed role of Populist anti-Christ. The "Scandal of the Assumption" (of the Revolutionary War debt), always the equivalent of original sin in Jeffersonian Populist circles, is foregrounded (P 67).[24] These moments in the poem are not as much about Hamilton as about Jeffersonianism; they are straight political ideology. Williams is blaming the difficulty of writing on the legacy of Hamiltonianism: finance capitalism.

Hamiltonianism, like "the church," is made present throughout this part of *Paterson* by passage after passage deployed in resistance to it. Portions from contemporary anti–Federal Reserve Bank propaganda are inserted into the poem in such a way as to bracket a prose description of Hamilton's planned Society for Useful Manufactures (P 73–74). The effect is to make the prose passages appear as one document cut up—so that Hamilton becomes the literal, not simply the ideological, father of the Federal Reserve System, also known as the "National Usury System."[25]

The first of these anti-Fed pieces is followed by a parodic vision of the American eagle, probably the one we see on the U.S. seal as printed on the one dollar bill.

> The bird, the eagle, made himself
> small—to creep into the hinged egg
> until therein he disappeared, all
> but one leg upon which a claw opened
> and closed wretchedly gripping
> the air, and would not—for all
> the effort of the struggle, remain
> inside . [P 73]

The eagle is the true spirit of America—its Jeffersonian idealism. The "progress" of America is here savagely imagined as a struggle to pretend it was never born in the first place, to stuff it back into the egg from which it has emerged. The shell is the shell game of finance, the usury system promoted by bankers through a national debt and the taxes necessary to pay it off. In context, it allegorizes Hamilton's almost entirely successful plan to subvert the American revolution and re-establish the English financial system in the United States. But for the one grasping claw, he has almost succeeded. This shell is the same as the "crust" that causes the writer's block that opens this section of *Paterson,* to which "Cress's" (Marcia Nardi's) letters refer. Williams's image of the eagle is an image of the resistance his poem exemplifies. It is ineffectual, unsuccessful, "wretchedly gripping the air,"[26] but at least resistance is there. The shell remains open, and so a few poems like *Paterson* and some wretched self-published pamphlets are allowed to reach the world to tell the truth about America.

At another moment in the middle of Ehrens's sermon, the poem suddenly breaks into a populistic parody of "America the Beautiful":

> America the golden!
> with trick and money
>   damned
> like Altgeld sick
>   and molden
> we love thee bitter
>   land

Like Altgeld on the
    corner
seeing the mourners
    pass
we bow our heads
    before thee
and take our hats
    in hand   [P 68]

George Zabriskie (a friend of Williams), in what is still the best reading of this passage, pointed out its affinities to the Populist poetry of Vachel Lindsay; Zabriskie wrote Weaver that its opening derived from Bryan's "Cross of Gold" speech (Weaver 208). Its Populism is revealed in its critique of America's ills: "With trick and money / damned." The poem suggests that the system (capitalism) itself is not at fault; it is being manipulated by a corrupt clique of profiteers.

The reference to Altgeld, onetime Mayor of Chicago in the 1890s, is synonymous with an allusion to the Haymarket Riots, the Pullman Strike, and Populism. Altgeld was not technically a Populist (he was a Democrat), but he certainly adhered to political principles held by the Populists (Wiebe 6). Altgeld's pardon of the "anarchists" charged with the Haymarket bombing and his refusal to call out federal troops to quell the railway strike made him a Populist hero. Despite his popularity with the workers—or, more likely, because of it—Altgeld paid for his decisions at the polls. He sacrificed his political career to his principles. In showing Altgeld mourning (the Pullman strikers killed by President Cleveland's troops? the victims of the Haymarket bomb?), Williams is really showing Altgeld mourning for himself and for a vision of America that has been violently suppressed by what Bryan called "the money power."

The son of German immigrants, Altgeld is linked by his background to Klaus Ehrens. Williams's use of parody to turn "America the Beautiful" into a kind of elegy for Altgeld and his political philosophy is analogous to the parodic "Sermon on the Mount" preached by Ehrens in this part of Paterson. Throughout the poem, Williams uses parody to represent positions that are dear to him. In America the undertaking itself amounts to a parody of its own ideals—an upside-down America that begins as an eagle and retreats to an egg. Parody may be Williams's only way of representing sincerity.

Williams means something like this pardodic reversal, when, in the next section of *Paterson*, he states that the poem is

> illuminating [the scene] within itself, out of itself
> to form the colors, in the terms of some
> back street, so that history may escape
> the panders
>
> . . accomplish the inevitable
> poor, the invisible, thrashing, breeding
> . debased city
>
> Love is no comforter, rather a nail in the
> skull
>
> . *reversed in the mirror* of its
> own squalor, debased by the divorce from learning,
> its garbage on the curbs, its legislators
> under the garbage, uninstructed, incapable of
> self-instruction . [my emphasis, *P* 81]

In order to accomplish what it needs to, the poem must appear to be "reversed as in a mirror." This is not passive reflection but active interpretation. "Back streets" become center stage, "the invisible, thrashing, breeding / debased city" and its inhabitants step up from the background to become the important figures of the tale. Onetime star players, like Hamilton, appear secondarily (as prose) in the populistic poem. This kind of reversal means that parody can do the duty of elegy through parodic subversion, as in the parody of "America the Beautiful"—a song considered by some to be the national anthem. Likewise Ehrens's devilish preaching (*P* 65) parodies the "Sermon on the Mount" in order to pay homage to Christ's gnomic teachings. In this passage, Williams implies that order can be derived only from a poetry of disorder that strictly mimics the squalor, vulgarity, and the ignorance, within which, and from which, the historical Paterson, its people, and its American language are to be rescued.

This is both a Populist and a Pragmatic aesthetic. It assumes that salvation lies in abandoning imposed forms, a priori solutions, and good taste. "Poetry," in the old sense, is to be replaced by a poetry that reproduces the "aesthetic shock" that Williams continues to receive from the "rise of the masses." This poetry is ad hoc, "formless," and fiercely "protestant" in regard to all established orthodoxies, whether they are poetic conventions or economic "realities."

The second irruption of the "money question" in *Paterson* occurs in the second section of book 4. Thinking in terms of the "newspaper epic" he culled from Dewey, Williams places a Social Credit "advertisement" (lifted from *Money: A Mass Appeal Social Credit Paper,* published by August Walters of Newark, New Jersey; Weaver 215n) in the midst of a passage devoted to the creative powers of women, notably exemplified by Marie Curie's discovery of radium (*P* 175–79). Williams compares the discovery of radioactive energy to Columbus's discovery of the New World by quoting the diary passage of his landfall (177) and by comparing uranium's nuclear energy to "Trade winds that broached a continent [which] drive the ship forward" (*P* 181).

The discovery of radium is also likened to a reformation of the credit system. This, in turn, is linked to "win[ning] the cold war" (180) through Walters's broadside, which advocated building cost-effective weapons (airplanes) through the use of "national credits." The new "order" of nature that Madame Curie discovered is praised as being "perfect and controlled." At the same time it is regretted as that sort of discovery, "on which empires, alas, are built" (178). With this section of *Paterson,* the "money question" enters the nuclear age.

The gist of the "money question" hangs on the difference between money and credit. Williams's dissonant beginning: "MONEY : JOKE"[27] starts what will turn out to be a longish meditation on just this difference (*P* 182). Using the same sense of parodic reversal that he used earlier in the Ehrens passage, Williams explains how the joke works: "(i.e., crime / under the circumstances : value / chipped away at an accelerated pace.)" (*P* 181). The money system is a criminal system. "Crime" just destroys value more quickly than the bankers do already.

In "The American Background" (1934), Williams had written in a similar radical, unmistakably Jeffersonian, vein:

> It is clear that the racketeer, the hired assassin, the confirmed perjurer, the non-office-holding boss, is the same person as the higher agent of the class holding the money, who by their cash in turn keep the whole range of false cultural agencies in line. Money being power and the power to move at will, it has always been the prime agent of decay in the world. But in America, whose resources made Golconda look like a copper penny, it would run, a fire through the grass, more wildly than anything the world had ever seen before. The organization of the

underworld would be exactly the replica, the true picture, of the national government—until finally they fused actually into one in the early years of this century. [*SE* 152]

This conspiracy theory history of the United States explains why this section of *Paterson* contains the cryptic and paranoid: "Reuther [a UAW organizer]—shot through a window, at whose pay?" (*P* 183)—a sudden fact that explodes, like a gunshot, from the world outside the poem.

Williams had also worked this paranoid line before in "An Early Martyr" (1935) (*CP1* 377–78), a poem (based on a true story) about John Coffey, a Romantic thief who stole valuable furs from department stores, then wrote to the police telling them where to find him so that he could speak on behalf of the poor at his trial. A onetime lover of Louise Bogan, Coffey was romanticized by a number of writers (including Max Bodenheim and Conrad Aiken) for making a statement against the hypocrisy of the social system. Coffey was railroaded to a mental hospital, however, apparently in order to prevent him from making whatever statement he had planned (*CP1* 536–37). In a criminal system, "criminals" are "martyrs." If Williams's money/joke equation reminds him of his own earlier poem, it must also remind him of Pound, whose case is in some ways similar to Coffey's. I expect that Williams did make the connection, for in the ensuing discussion of credit and money in *Paterson*, the voice of Pound is allowed to speak more than once.

And so we see the kind of "joke" we are dealing with. The joke's on us—the same kind of "trick" mentioned in the satirical anthem to Altgeld earlier in the poem—and, Williams asks rhetorically, "do you joke when a man is dying / of a brain tumor?" (*P* 181). The "tumor" in this case is "the cancer, usury" attended by the incompetent "brain surgeon" economists (*P* 181–82).

The cure for this cancer is credit. Credit in turn is compared to the gamma rays released by uranium or radium: "release the Gamma rays that cure the cancer," Williams writes, "Let credit out . out from between the bars / before the bank windows" (182).

Williams sounds like a Gesellite when he complains about "Money sequestered enriches avarice, / makes poverty: the direct cause of / disaster" (181). Also, "credit, stalled / in money, conceals the generative / that thwarts art or buys it" (182). What Williams is prescribing for the sick economy is a separation of credit and money. (This is exactly what Walters, with his plan for "NATIONAL CREDIT CERTIFI-CATES" is also proposing.) The difference between credit and money is imagined as the difference between "the Parthenon," which, we are told, is a kind of credit, and "money," which is "the gold entrusted to Phideas for the / statue of Pallas Athena, that he 'put aside' / for private purposes" (183). "You can't steal credit . the parthenon," Williams claims with splendid innuendo, "skip[ping] any reference, at this time, to the Elgin marbles" (183).

By associating credit with the supposedly permanent value of works of art, Williams implies that *Paterson* itself has better credit than gold. In fact, it does, because the poem cannot be abolished—as the gold standard could—by any laws or act of Congress.

> Money : joke
> could be wiped out
> at stroke
> of pen
> and was when
> gold and pound were
> devalued [P 184]

Williams makes it clear the money (in whatever form) is only the sign of credit, and credit is based on permanent works of culture, works with the enduring power of the Parthenon, not on certain legislated signifying money systems—gold, or the English pound. Here Williams is also punning on the monetary meaning hidden in the names of Mike Gold, former editor of the *New Masses,* and Ezra Pound, embodiments of Left and Right. Williams implies that their contributions have been devalued since the 1930s, because they joined the red and white churches of political orthodoxy.

By reminding us that money can be (and is) wiped out with the stroke of a pen, that it is, by its nature, purely textual, Williams reasserts the power of the poet, whose own pen strokes create credit by producing culture itself. Money is always secondary to the primary facts with which poetry alone can come into contact, because poetry is not the sign of the thing but the thing, the action, the process itself.

Williams argues that money, as currently constituted, is a "small time / reciprocal action relic" outdated by the "stream-lined turbine : credit" (184). Credit, which "drive[s] the ship forward" (181) is, as usual for Williams, connected to the images of the machine, which Williams likes also to use as a figure for the poem. The "turbine" should be connected to the waterfall at Paterson, which has stood throughout *Paterson* both for Dr. Paterson's dreams (*P* 6) and for thoughts (*P* 7–8). (There is an irony here, since the turbines driven to this day by the Paterson falls are the last vestigial property owned by Hamilton's SUM franchise.) The turbine is constant—as constant as the falls that drive it. The turbine-driven economy does not depend on a crude series of actions and reactions, huffing and chuffing like a simple reciprocal steam engine, contrived by an economy ineptly trying to keep up with the realities of what Social Creditors called "the power age."[28] It is constantly spinning in response to "natural" market forces, just as the SUM turbines turn "naturally" under the Paterson falls. The old moneymaking mechanism, which now benefits the few at the expense of the many by monopolizing credit, should continuously distribute credit throughout the republic as a form of energy.

The turbine metaphor becomes all the more pronounced as an image for creative power when Williams couples it with nuclear energy. (Even though "peaceful" nuclear power did not yet exist when Williams composed this part of *Paterson*, it is interesting that nuclear power is used to make steam to drive turbines to create electricity.) "Somewhere in some piece of art resides a radioactive force," Williams told a correspondent prophetically in July of 1945 (*SL* 239). So that we get the following equations:

Uranium : basic thought—leadward
Fractured : radium : credit

Or restated:

Curie : woman (of no importance) genius : radium [*P* 184]

Williams means that Curie's gender is not important—her "genius" is. Genius is equivalent to "fractured" because it breaks through "the crust," which forms the "impenetrable substance" (*P* 45), which makes the poem (credit) possible.[29] Curie's genius, like Williams's, was to realize that "Dissonance / (if you are interested) / leads to discovery" (175). Curie's understanding of the order within the fracture made her realize that uranium is always "breaking down / to lead" (*P* 177).

This "dissonance," the recognition of a new order within "breakdown," brings us circling back to the scene of the two modern lovers with their jalopy in book 2 of *Paterson*. There Williams marveled that "SOME sort / of breakdown / has occurred" (*P* 51). We also remember that this was precisely the moment of "aesthetic shock" (*SL* 259) that (Williams told Deutsch) was so important for his poetry.

Underneath the "breakdown" lies some impervious "gist" of meaning or order that Williams equates with credit. "Credit : the gist," he writes—almost as though he were an Einstein writing $E = MC^2$. Having reduced his variables to this profound but rather obscure equivalence, Williams invokes Pound by inserting part of a letter that Pound had written in response to Williams's imitation of the "Usura Canto" (Canto 45) in book 2 of *Paterson* (*P* 292, *P/W* 267–68). There Williams had chanted affirmatively "Without invention nothing is well spaced" (*P* 50). Pound's reply now surfaces in the poem:

IN
   venshun
O.KAY
     In venshun

 and seeinz how yu hv/ started. Would you consider
a remedy of a lot:
             i.e. LOCAL control of local purchasing
                   power   .
                      ? ?
Difference between squalor of spreading slums
and splendour of renaissance cities. [*P* 184–85]

In the original note Pound had written "renaissance *italian* cities" (*P/W* 268), Williams's change reveals his hopes for his poem *Paterson*, which is a sort of renaissance city, but also for the real, and American, Paterson. The splendor that Pound finds in the Italian city (by Siena made wealthy by the same lending policies of the Monte dei Paschi, for example?) is, implicitly, connected here to the radiant gist of credit and the "local control of purchasing power" that Williams seems to be endorsing as a kind of fusion between Deweyan aesthetics and Social Credit economic remedies. This position is, I might add, strictly Jeffersonian—it echoes the "Resolutions of Congress on Lord North's Conciliatory Proposal" (1775) written by Jefferson, which resolves that "the colonies of America are entitled to the sole and exclusive privilege of giving and granting their own money" (Jefferson 331). Pound's consonance with Jefferson, and Williams's implicit endorsement of Jefferson's proposal, amount to a renewal of revolutionary claims made at the very inception of the American republic. Credit is linked to the ongoing American revolutionary struggle:

> Credit makes solid
> is related directly to the effort,
> work: value created and received,
> "the radiant gist" against all that
> scants our lives [P 185]

At the beginning of this long chapter, I tried to show how Williams attempts to evolve a Pragmatic position for poetry by entering it as a category of discourse that might resolve the dispute between Romanticism and Positivism, which James Livingston sees as the terms of the argument "between pragmatists and their critics" (1994 77). By the end of *Paterson* book 4—that is, by the end of the "original" *Paterson*—Williams has managed a rather unexpected reconciliation with Positivism—or Science. Nuclear physics becomes commensurate with his theory of the poem *and* his program for economic reform. If this is pragmatism, it is a pragmatism with a distinctly Romantic flavor.

The "radiant gist," which becomes Williams's ultimate synonym for "credit" (P 185), veers close to a reinstatement of ideal Platonic forms. What rescues it is the labor theory of value. Williams's credit is based on work, effort. It is not a static preexisting ideal. Credit is something that must be laboriously constructed, like the Parthenon, or *Paterson*. The radiant gist that is credit is an ongoing process. Williams's emphasis on making and process link his gist to pragmatism. He is proposing not a theory of ideal forms but a theory of meaningful processes sanctified by the labor of making one's own forms out of one's own meanings. It is not the gold standard of Platonic truths that Williams is after but the flexible credit of the Pragmatic truth, which is meaning. This thoroughly Pragmatic approach to "the money question" and the poem is, as always in Williams, couched in terms of Jeffersonian revolutionary rhetoric. "The mutability of the truth, Ibsen said it. Jefferson said it. We should have a revolution of some sort in America every ten years. The truth has to be redressed, re-examined, re-affirmed in a new mode. There has to be a new poetry. But the thing is that the change, the greater material, the altered structure of the inevitable revolution must be *in* the poem, in it. Made of it. It must shine in the structural body of it" (*SE* 217). The inseparable bond that Williams always sees between the American Revolution and the "new poetry" is a crucial assumption behind his epic, *Paterson*. Without a clear understanding of the economic implication of his Jeffersonian-ism, we cannot grasp "the joke" that *Paterson* first appears to be.

7

OVERCOMING MODERNITY
Representing the Corporation
and the Promise of Pluralism

WILLIAM JAMES CALLED the problem of unity and multiplicity "the most central of all philosophic problems, central because so pregnant" (James 1977 405). In "The One and the Many," his lecture on the problem, he challenges the then current definition of philosophy "as the quest or the vision of the world's unity," arguing that "what our intellect really aims at is neither variety or unity taken singly, but *totality.* In this, acquaintance with the world's diversities is as important as understanding their connexion" (James's emphasis, James 1977 406). James's Pragmatism is a deeply (some might say hopelessly) pluralistic philosophy because it is derived from his "radical empiricism," which is mainly concerned with the connections and transitions between things or states rather than with the things themselves. Jamesian Pragmatism is all about how things do, or perhaps do not, "hang together" (407). It is determined to account for "plain conjunctive experience," to insist that experience simply is conjunctive (Livingston 1994 289–90).

The moral problem of the corporation we have been discussing is the institutional form of this one/many problem. As a collective entity, the moral status of the corporation reflects the moral problem of the self in the corporate age. For this reason Dewey became very interested in it in the 1930s. Its promise to incorporate the corporation within the State, and thus to conquer modernity, partly explains why Fascism enjoyed political success in Italy, Spain, and Germany during the same period. It also explains why Pound and Williams construct their epic poems as corporate bodies of heterogeneous materials that forgo traditional narratives. The absence of such narratives forces us to examine the conjunctive relations between the matter in the poems and to address the question that Pound raises directly at the end of *The Cantos:* do they "cohere" or not? (116:810–11).

The Cantos and *Paterson* are both corporate poems. But they have different attitudes toward the corporation—or, as I now want to broaden the terms—they have different attitudes toward the one and the many. In their search for totality, their search, that is, for a poetic form sufficiently large to include the corporation and "history," Pound and Williams take different tacks. Temperamentally, Pound is for unity, Williams for multiplicity. *The Cantos* reflect the anxieties of a monist in the corporate age; Pound has staked his version of the self on the eighteenth-century model, the farmer/freeholder, and he intends to make it new by adapting the order they represent to the corporate age. Williams's *Paterson* is a determinedly pluralist poem, anxiously so. They are both founded on Jeffersonian critiques of capitalism, but the differences in their authors' respective temperaments are reflected in the way that the poems represent the corporation, which both writers understand as the predominant institutional and social form of the twentieth century.

Representing the Industrial Corporation

The representation of the corporation in any form is no easy task. It is made difficult by the collective individuality peculiar to corporations; although they are huge group enterprises, corporations are legally individual persons, "right and duty bearing subjects," with implicit corporate interests, needs, desires, and responsibilities. Nonetheless, they resist personification. The responsibilities of corporations are, as Burke emphasizes, the murkiest aspect of their organization. The beauty of the corporate form from the business point of view is that it can act with the firmness of an individual, but its liabilities are absorbed by the corporation. Individual members of the board of directors, or the managing partnership, are not individually liable for any unpleasant consequences of a corporate action. Corporate board members are (almost by definition) "faceless." They have no personality. They are not "captains of industry" in the Marxist sense. They are much more like a general staff, more or less anonymous planners and decision makers. These kinds of people are not very readily amenable to literary treatment of the usual kind, they register as *functions*, chief executive officers, accountants, and so forth, not as persons with temperaments, character, or individual motivations.

In personifiying the Ford Motor Corporation as Henry Ford, say, the poet risks trivializing the organization's peculiar leverage over the structure, shape, and texture of modern life. Simple personification is in danger of becoming facile impersonation if the all-important collective identity is absorbed, so to speak, into the figure of the capitalist, the very fellow who is now merely a figurehead. In truth, he is only a symbol of the corporate whole. Williams seems to understand this problem very well in *Paterson* when he meditates on the fate of the "Castle" ("soon too to be razed") built as a symbol of success by the old-style capitalist, the spinning magnate Lambert

> —the old boy himself, a Limey,
> his head full of castles, the pivots of that
> curt dialectic (while it lasted), built himself a
> Balmoral on the alluvial silt, the rock-fall skirt-
> ing the volcanic upthrust of the "Mountain" [P 99]

This sort of Horatio Alger rags-to-riches capitalist has been superseded. His dreams and their expression, his "castles," all derived from literature, are razed because "in- / comprehensible; of no USE!" (P 99). Under the rules of the "curt-dialectic" of modernity, which has already moved on to the new corporate forms that Williams's poem seeks to understand, Lambert's romantic capitalism, his vision of himself as a kind of industrial king, has become an incomprehensible and absurd anachronism. Lambert has built his dreams on the alluvial silt of quick-moving modern history, on the detritus of the thought stream, on the romances of Sir Walter Scott, not the more permanent rock of Garret Mountain, which ("female to the city," P 43) has become in *Paterson* the embattled site of human "re-creation," freedom, and possibility, where, on Sundays, the new class can sunbathe beside its jalopies.

Pound confronts this identical captain-of-industry problem in trying to use Sir Zenos Metevsky, based on the notorious arms dealer Sir Basil Zaharoff, to personify the multinational armaments firm Vickers Limited in Cantos 18 and 38. Metevsky is Pound's allegorical figuration of corporate identity and its motives. Metevsky says,

Don't buy until you can get ours.
And he went over the border
   and he said to the other side:
The *other* side has more munitions. Don't buy
   until you can get ours . . . [38:187]

Yet it is "Akers" (read "Vickers"), not Metevsky, who systematically "made a large profit and imported gold into England / Thus increasing gold imports" (38:187). Here the corporate identity seems to flow naturally from its agent to the firm as though they were one. The satanic Metevsky is reduced to a rather comic figure unless we read him, and Pound hopes we shall, as the allegorical will of Vickers Limited.[1] We must read him as a puppet in some revolutionary theatrical, or as an allegory of the profit motive, not merely as a historical individual. As a result, the figure of Metevsky is necessarily a caricature because he appears to be the cause, not the symptom, of international corporate capitalism at its most satanic. The truer, deeper story lies in Vickers as an organization, but this story does not have the zip of Metevsky's exploits, which are, in fact, "a true story" based on the real life adventures of the historical Zaharoff.

Certainly "the International Arms Dealer" as an allegorical figure does suggest the crucial role that arms manufacture plays in an industrialized economy, a role that remains immediately relevant in the world after the Iran-Contra scandal. (The Iranian arms dealer Manucher Gorbanifar is another Metevsky.) But like Oliver North's Gorbanifar, Pound's Metevsky distracts attention from the underlying, structural role of what Eisenhower aptly called "the military industrial complex." The Arms Dealer is only a salesman; he is a modern Mephistopheles, not Satan himself. In this sense, Metevsky is a tragicomic figure, not the embodiment of modern military/industrial evil. This initial problem of adequately representing the armaments industry in poetry is caused by the enigma of corporate personality, which wants to be taken as a person and so lends itself to a convenient but dangerous allegorical oversimplification.

The animus behind Pound's critique of the military industrial complex is contained in Metevsky's cosmopolitanism and his satanic ubiquity. Metevsky, who is seemingly everywhere, is at home nowhere. The ingredients, if not the fact, of Populistic anti-Semitism lie latent in this uprooted Other.[2] As with the usurers who recur throughout *The*

Cantos, Metevsky's allegorization conforms to the Populist critique of corporate capitalism, which regards "exogenous factors" (Sklar 1988 54), such as satanic individuals, or cabals like the Rothschilds, as corrupting an otherwise workable economic system. Unlike the Socialist critique, the Populist position (which also recognizes contradictions in capitalism) sees the structural inequities in industrial capitalism not as inherent but instead as "accidental" distortions of a market that would function fairly if it was not "rigged" by "illegitimate monopolistic or corrupt political power" (1988 54).

Like Williams, Pound seems to have realized that the problem of the corporation exceeded the use of an allegorical figure. His alternative presentation, and a far more sophisticated one, later in Canto 38, is a more successful attempt to express corporate iniquity without relying wholly on any realizable single human figure:

> 1900 fifty thousand operai,
> 53 thousand cannon, about half for his country,
> Bohlen und Halbach,
> Herr Schneider of Creusot
> Twin arse with one belly,
> Eugene, Adolph and Alfred "more money from guns than from tractiles"
> Eugene was sent to the deputies;
> Saone et Loire) to the Deputies, minister;
> Later rose to be minister,
> "guns coming from anywhere,
> but appropriations from the Chambers of parliaments"
> In 1874 recd. license for free exportation
> Adopted by 22 nations
> 1885/1900 produced ten thousand cannon
> to 1914, 34 thousand
> one half of them sent out of the country [38:191]

Here Pound ably presents the corporate gist of the armaments industry by means of a corporate presentation. We read of the corporation's history, of its interconnection with government, of its international character, and of its principals, Gustav Krupp von Bohlem und Halbach, Eugene Schneider (directors, respectively, of Krupp and Schneider during World War I), and Adolph and Alfred Schneider, the founders of Schneider-Creusot. The strophe is loaded with economic data: numbers of employees ("operai"), figures of rates of production, and licensing agreements. As the Canto continues, we are told that Schneider-Creusot pays out millions to control important French newspapers, and how "Our bank [presumably the Banque de France] "has bought us / shares in Mitsui / Who arm 50 divisions, who keep up the Japanese army / and they are destined to have a large future" (38:192). All in all, we see the corporation as the nexus of a variety of economic and political maneuvers, and we also see that it has corrupted the State, which it uses as an investor. It is not the Japanese army, but the shares of stock invested in the Mitsui corporation that arms them, that are destined to have a very large future.

I know of no other poetry that so ambitiously undertakes to suggest the tangled web of contemporary twentieth-century business practice. Half German, half French, fully committed to profiting from French and German enmity but also deeply interested in the global arms market and world wars, Schneider-Creusot is represented as the quintessential example of the military-industrial complex.

This is a new kind of poetry, obscure by traditional poetic standards, but after all, the virtues of corporate flexibility and opportunism are equally obscured by old-fashioned models of personhood. Pound's method also has real virtues. Representing the corporation in verse means anatomizing it so as to suggest the intricacies of the corporation's relation and responsibilities both to the state and to the individual. Furthermore, the corporation must be presented historically and in action, for the corporation is (like any other individual) both a historical creature and an actor. It has agency, as Pound's verse shows. The result of Pound's version of the corporate may seem cryptic on the page, but it is no more so than the true state of defense contracting. Pound's lines are certainly no harder to understand than our current proposition that the national interest demands a huge armaments industry, which, unfortunately, can be kept afloat only by encouraging arms sales abroad and even to potential enemies.

One thing makes Pound's very different representations of the corporation commensurate: his moral outrage at the "gun-buzzards," as he liked to call them, and the corporate structures that give them power and offer them legal protection. In this sense, both Metevsky and Schneider-Creusot are "twin arse with one belly." Pound cannot stomach the immorality sanctioned by the corporate industrial form even as he is forced to acknowledge its all but determinative power. He cannot incorporate the corporation because it threatens his sense of order, the ethical rock on which his theory of self is founded. Quite simply, Pound's sense of social order was based on the ideal of social harmony, not competition. The industrial incorporation, the business firm, the banks, saw social order as competitive, as *power over* expressed in the deification of the profit motive.

Because of his Jeffersonianism, Pound's attitude toward the corporation, which is finally his attitude toward modernity itself, is instinctively one of resistance. He is interested not so much in getting rid of the corporation as in redefining its motives. It is too easy to call such a stance reactionary; what Pound really wants is to rewrite the history of capitalism so as to reduce the role of the profit motive to one among many. A true Jeffersonian, he thinks markets are, first and foremost, places to distribute goods and not, as capitalists seem to think, places to make money. In following this line of resistance to markets through the ascendancy of the corporation, *The Cantos* increasingly becomes a sourcebook for a Jeffersonian alternative. Under the sign of Jefferson, both Confucius and Mussolini are invoked to do battle against Geryon and Usura. Using the will to order to control profiteering, Pound wants to reestablish an economy of abundance over one of scarcity. He wants to replace the spirit of capitalism with a will to order derived from natural values, premised on the abundance of nature.

We know that Pound is not a simple reactionary, because Pound's epic work shows that he understands one aspect of the problem of the self in the corporate age: it is an epic without a hero. *The Cantos* are frequently compared to the *Odyssey*, but there is no Odysseus, except in those moments, and, admittedly, they become more noticeable from *The Pisan Cantos* (1947) on, when we sense the presence of Pound himself. But he presents himself never as an epic hero or even as a poet but rather as editor, redactor, composer, of a poem that is fundamentally about not himself but his arrangement of heteroclite preexisting texts. My reading of *The Cantos* discounts the odyssean reading except to say that reading *The Cantos* is, itself, an odyssey. "The epic figure of the wandering hero" (Sicari 1991 x), which Stephen Sicari is the most recent critic to propose as "the unifying principle of *The Cantos*" (xi), does not, to my mind, have a coherent existence within the poem; rather, the poem turns and wanders. The odyssean figure is a trope, not a hero, and stages, but does not undertake, the epic *periplum*. Consider

Pound's remarks in Canto 99: "The State is corporate / as with pulse in its body" (99:721). He continues, "This [*The Cantos*] is not a work of fiction/ nor yet of one man" (99:722). Even allowing for the subliminal reverberations of the discorporate odyssean "no man," underneath "one man," the hero as an individual, as a "unifying principle," seems to be firmly discounted. As far as Pound is concerned, the best that can be done is to steer the poetic project. The heroism of *The Cantos*, if there is any, lies in Pound's willingness to let the collective entity of the poem resist the motivation that liberal economists assume underwrites contemporary history. Its heroism lies not in resolving, but in confronting, the problem of the competitive many with the possibility of the harmonious (if autocratic) one.[3] *The Cantos* are an epic of Jeffersonian dissent, but in this regard they are necessarily Absolutist, in proposing a natural harmony, they offer a vision of "the good" as such. In their campaign against a market for money, they require state control of the economy. The poem's tragedy lies in Pound's eventual realization that a will to believe in unity is insufficient in a corporate age: "And I am not a demigod, / I cannot make it cohere" (116:810). The poem's triumph lies in the nearly simultaneous assertion that, "it coheres all right / even if my notes do not cohere" (116:811). The difference between these remarks lies in the referent for "it": in the first quotation "it" refers to *The Cantos*, in the second, "paradise," another way of saying "the universe."

By the end of *The Cantos*, Pound sounds a great deal like Henry Adams, a writer with whom he shares a surprisingly complex affinity. Like Adams, Pound fears that history is making the human will obsolete, replacing it with abstract forces. Like Adams, Pound has tried to resist force actively through the creative will. Unlike Adams, the greatest ironic sensibility America has produced, Pound, who after 1930 exhibits almost no irony at all, is surprised, hurt, and half crazed by the encounter with modernity.

> That I lost my center
> > fighting the world
> The dreams clash
> > and are shattered—
> and that I tried to make a paradiso
> > terrestre [118:816]

The utopic motives in *The Cantos*, finally, cause them to shatter into what Randall Jarrell called in a review "notes on the margins of the universe" (*Kipling, Auden, and Company* 265). Pound would no doubt have seen it differently. He might have proposed that industrial civilization is itself nothing more than some notes on the universal margin and that his ethical economics, derived from nature itself, is closer to the center than his critics believe.

Williams and the Pluralistic Poem

Williams's Pragmatism helps explain why he and Pound could arrive at such different political and poetic conclusions from nearly identical Jeffersonian premises. Pound seeks to impose his "will to order"—actually a brand of Enlightenment Reason—on Modernity and, failing that, accedes to its conquest by a yet more willful Fascism. Williams, having absorbed the lessons of American Pragmatism, tries through *Paterson* to understand modernity as a conjunctive experience. His new measure is finally an attempt to identify a new mode of conjunction adequate to the new corporativeness. And it is based on his own brand of radical empiricism: "The poet does not . . . permit himself to go beyond the thought to be discovered in the context of that which he is dealing: no ideas but in things. The poet thinks with his poem, in that lies his thought, and that in itself is the profundity. The thought is *Paterson* to be discovered there" (*A* 390–91). By not going beyond the thought, the poet refuses the rationalist temptation to impose some unifying significance on it. This statement does not mean that he gives up the right to express his opinions and politics. It means that the significance of the thought (or thoughts) that make up the poem is totally historical—a function of placement in the poem. Each thought's local context on the page, added to the poet's local context when putting the thought on the paper, conspires to create conjunctive relations, which the reader must take into account. One way of doing so, and that which I have chosen in this book, is to give in to a lower rationalism, to emphasize the Jeffersonian strain, or tendency, in Williams's sense of conjunction. It has therefore been necessary to focus on Williams's rewriting of American history, not only in *Paterson* but in prose works like *In the American Grain* and "The American

Background." To understand the conjunctive relations in *Paterson* one must rediscover the history into which the poem makes its Jeffersonian intervention. It is like testing the current in a river.

When I call Williams a radical empiricist, then, I am not saying that his poem is incapable of making an argument or that it does not reflect any ideological position or political opinions. It obviously does. I am saying that *Paterson* makes its "argument," or, more accurately, that it hangs together, by virtue of transitions that sometimes seem like mere juxtapositions, or no transitions at all, but that are in fact new kinds of transitions waiting to be recognized. The paradox is, however, that in order to recognize Williams's transitions, we must understand the poem's tendency, its stance, toward the history to which it replies. The title "Jeffersonian" permits some of the transitions to come forward.

Paterson, like Pound's "Malatesta" and "Adams" Cantos, is partly built with the voices of others as recorded in their letters, literary people like Pound himself, Edward Dahlberg, Alan Ginsberg, Marcia Nardi, Josephine Herbst (who supplies a letter used in book 5 of *Paterson*), and regular folks like Gladys Enalls's friend Dolly. The difference between the two poems is that Williams uses letters from contemporaries, even allowing these other voices to talk about his poem in the poem. *Paterson* includes its own criticism. This feature helps give it its peculiar "pluralistic" character. Williams's pluralism is his way of getting at corporateness, which he, like other pragmatists, sees as fundamentally dialogic.

The dialogic effect is most strikingly evident in Williams's conversation with Pound throughout *Paterson*. *Paterson* is, of course, always implicitly in dialogue with Pound via the influence of *The Cantos*. *Paterson* is "a reply" from the get-go. But Williams goes further: he invites Pound into his poem as a speaker commenting on his project.

The dialogue begins with Williams's revision of Canto 45, the chant against Usura: "With Usura hath no man." Williams makes a counterproposal:

Without invention nothing is well spaced
unless the mind change, unless
the stars are new measured, according
to their relative positions, the
line will not change, the necessity

will not matriculate, unless there is
new mind there cannot be a new
line, the old will go on
repeating itself with recurring
deadliness . . . [P 50]

By itself, Williams's allusive reply is simply an intertextual reference, not pluralistic. It becomes so when, later in *Paterson*, Williams includes the letter from Pound, quoted earlier, that comments on Williams's lines: "IN / venshun / O.KAY / In venshun" [P 184]. Pound is not just agreeing, he is taking Williams at his word by the inventive and "well spaced" arrangement of his agreement on the page. His agreement then becomes part of Williams's poem, not just an assent to Williams's idea. The second "stanza" of Pound's letter, about "purchasing power," directly responds to the idea behind Williams's "invention" stanza; that is, Pound responds to Williams's proposal that having made the critique of Usura, it is now time to invent a way out from under it. Responding to Williams's own fierce sense of locality, Pound suggests "LOCAL control of local purchasing power" (which I take to mean the supplementing of the local money supply by the use of Gesellite *Schwundgeld* on the model of the Woergl monetary experiment). Williams's inclusion of Pound's letter in his poem is a pluralistic moment: Williams copies Pound's reply to Williams about his answer (the lines on "invention") to Pound's Usura canto. There is nothing comparable in poetry.

In book 4, part 2 of *Paterson*, "The Run to the Sea," we find the speaker (obviously Williams himself) saying parenthetically to one of his sons "(What I miss, said your mother, is the poetry, the pure poem / of the first parts .)" (P 171]. In part 3, we hear Williams's wife saying it herself, "Haven't you forgot your virgin purpose / the language?" [P 186]. If, as critics have long acknowledged, Pound's "Malatesta Cantos" represent a technical breakthrough by destroying the distinction between prose and poetry, here Williams stages a comparable breakthrough in terms of poetic voices. Forget "pure poetry," he seems to say, poetry has no "virgin purpose"—no purpose that lies outside history; it traces no primal warblings. By means of such ongoing commentary, we are made aware of *Paterson* as a living process, as a work in the process of becoming.

Furthermore, we must accept the possibility that the poem has no plan—it is susceptible to events. The poem stages its own contingency. Apparently completely comfortable with the abandonment of its own autonomy as a "work of art" or "pure poetry," it reflects on its own madeness. Susceptibility *is* its plan. *Paterson* may be, to use William James's phrase, "a world of additive constitution," a poem "in which some parts are connected so loosely with some other parts as to be strung together by nothing but the copula *and*" (James's emphasis, James 1977 418).

Is that statement enough? Is *Paterson merely* a world of additive constitution, unrolling through time? If *Paterson* is contingent in the sense that it includes its own commentary, then it should be contingent in other ways as well. Indeed, throughout the poem there are moments when we seem to be given the dates on which it was written. In book 3, part 3, in the midst of the lines that tumble drunkenly down the page, we read a date, "January sunshine. / 1949 / Wednesday, 11" (*P* 137). In book 4, part 3, we are confronted by a story out of Williams's morning paper, the *New York Tribune,* a story about the murder, by Fred Goodell, Jr., of his "six-month old daughter Nancy" with the dateline "Sept. 17" (*P* 194–95). Actually, as Christopher MacGowan has informed us, the story ran on September 18, 1950; so the Goodell murder happened on September 17, Williams's birthday. This fact only heightens our uneasy sense of Williams's self-consciousness about his poem as a mirror of events (*P* 294n); he seems to be taking literally Pound's injunction "Literature is news that STAYS news" (*ABCR* 29).

The feeling is reinforced when the Goodell murder is joined by the account of another murder, by one "John Johnson, a laboring farmer" (*P* 197). Johnson was apparently the first murderer in Passaic county (297n). We sense that nothing changes, or that history repeats itself, an impression that mingles uneasily with the additive quality that the daily newspaper seems to represent. If history is unrolling forward through the poem, it also seems to be rolling up behind it.

A few pages later, weeks have gone by. *Paterson* seems to be drawing toward what Williams remembered in his *Autobiography* as its final image, the figure of a man who appears to be an Odysseus-like avatar of Walt Whitman, emerging from the ocean and "turn[ing] inland towards Camden where Walt Whitman, much traduced, lived the latter years of his life and died" (*A* 392). Yet concurrently, the Korean War is threatening to become World War III. Images of the recent Pacific war keep intruding into Williams's consciousness. He makes, or recalls, an image of "Twenty feet of / guts on the black sands of Iwo" (*P* 198). He "cannot believe / that it can begin again, here / again . here" (*P* 198). "Turn back I warn you," he writes, "(Oct. 10, 1950 / from the shark, that snaps / at his own trailing guts, makes a sunset / of the green water" (*P* 195). At this point it seems fair to ask, is Williams writing the poem, or are events writing it? Insofar as *Paterson* is a Pragmatic poem, aren't its Pragmatic truths "being made by events" (James 1977 430) in the most arbitrary way? Furthermore, is the poem truly additive, or is there a concealed narrative circularity that is suggested by the shark's eating its own guts?

However we answer these questions, *Paterson* is certainly not "coming together" as one expects an autonomous work of literature to do. Instead it seems to be coming apart. As his poem nears the sea, Williams engages in a debate with himself about what the approach means, for it seems to signal the poem's death, rather than its birth. This thought is less radical than it sounds when applied to the work of art that is about its own making: the finishing of the work is also the end of it. Williams sees that the poem is about to enter a different phase: "You will come to it," he says to himself, "the blood dark sea / of praise. You must come to it" (*P* 202). The poem, in short, is about to become Literature, and at that moment it will change. Williams worries what this will mean, for even though the first three books of *Paterson* have already been published, book 4 will complete the epic project and will turn it into something definitive, something with a beginning, middle, and end that is to take its place among the epic poems and literary monuments of the past. "The sea is *not* our home," one part of him insists anxiously. "The sea *is* our home whither all rivers / (wither) run," he replies (*P* 199).

The Korean War intrudes on this debate, and out of it we expect the poet, somehow, to resolve his poem. But it does not do so. Instead, we are treated to some enormously suggestive conjunctions. The sea imagery regresses to the Homeric origins of the epic: "The nostalgic sea / sopped with our cries / Thalassa! Thalassa!" (199) but simultaneously inoculates us against it, "Put wax in your / ears against the hungry sea it is not our home!" (200). Finally, as the Homeric (or pseudo Homeric) pressures become more insistent, and the poem's resistance more strident, the poem breaks into the moment of the stranger from the sea coming to land—a moment heavily dependent on Odysseus's meeting with Nausicaa in book 6 of the *Odyssey*. And just here, perversely, the diction changes to a deliberately prosy American:

> What's that?
> —a duck, a hell-diver? A swimming dog?
> What a sea-dog? There it is again.
> A porpoise, of course, following
> the mackerel . No. Must be the up-
> end of something sunk [201]

Eventually, a man steps out of the water to be greeted by his dog. He sleeps. Some girls play ball just like Nausicaa and her maids. It is another day at the Jersey shore. Then this Odysseus wakes up and "walking a few steps got into a pair of faded / overalls, slid his shirt on overhand (the / sleeves were still rolled up shoes / hat where [the dog] had been watching them under / the bank and turned again / to the water's steady roar, as of a distant / waterfall" (202). Prosaic enough, until, taking Williams's hint, we see that the Odysseus figure is dressing himself in the rough workingman's costume in which Whitman portrayed himself on the title page of the original *Leaves of Grass*.

Yet the overdetermined literary images of an Odysseus/Whitman, which seem such a fine ending to the poem that Williams himself chose to remember it in this way are then ruthlessly juxtaposed with the newspaper account of the hanging of poor John Johnson on Garret Mountain "in full view of thousands" (202). As the account of the crime has been full of baffling inconsistencies (197), and since we learn that Johnson was convicted after only twenty minutes of deliberation, Williams makes us suspect that Johnson was a victim of a terrible miscarriage of justice made by thoughtless people who sought a public spectacle and a tidy story more eagerly than they did the truth. Is this a preemptive strike by the poet against the criticism of people like us, who expect Literature to supply cathartic endings and moving verbal spectacles? Even if it is, how do we square this account of criminality and injustice with the figure of the questing poet, reborn, as it were, to sing again?

This is the problem behind an artistic model based on the "additive constitution" of the universe, the "world of mere *withness*," which, James argues, "the pragmatist is unable to rule out of serious consideration" (James 1977 415, 418). An additive universe by definition must be open-ended; if Williams is staging such an additive performance, then he is writing something not like art at all but like experience. But if experience is what Williams wants, then doesn't *Paterson* baldly succumb to events, to everything that Pound's *Cantos* manfully resists, the anonymous whatever-comes-next-comes-nextness of economic forces informed by technological change? Our suspicions on this score are not helped by the fact that Williams's promise at the end of book 4, "This is the blast / the eternal close / the spiral / the final somersault / the end" (*P* 202) is belied by a book 5, now staring at us on the next page. At least Pound laments the fact that his poetic universe cannot cohere, Williams appears to be at the mercy of the flux even as he argues with himself. So the end of *Paterson* seems to be radically discontinuous. Yet I do not believe that discontinuity is Williams's aim. To find a way out of this impasse, and a way back into Williams's poem, I will turn again to Livingston's account of James's radical empiricism.

In *Pragmatism and the Political Economy of Cultural Revolution, 1850–1940*, Livingston has suggested that we take James's radical empiricism as the basis for a reconsideration of the continuity, as opposed to the discontinuities, of historical time and that we use it as the basis for a reconstruction of moral personality in the corporate age. The continuity of historical time, he argues, is that rarest of endangered philosophical species, a "concrete universal," and it implies a "transhistorical standard of rationality" (289). Contemporary philosophy and historiography have focused on discontinuity: "revolutionary" events (Lenin), "epistemological breaks" (Foucault), "paradigm shifts" (Kuhn), and so on because both radical and conservative intellectuals, from the old leveler Gerard Winstanley to Edmund Burke and on to Kuhn and Derrida, have accepted that "the goal of revolution as such is to break with the past by repudiating received political tradition" (286). "But the fact remains," Livingston observes, "that revolutionary movements have always been larger than their 'cutting edges' on the Left, and have faltered or failed insofar as their leaders have forgotten that" (286). Richard Rorty, in reviving Deweyan Pragmatism as one basis for "social hope" by contrasting Dewey with Foucault, shows he is a captive to this revolutionary view by veering to the opposite side of the revolutionary dialectic in (quite gratuitously) identifing that hope with "bourgeois liberalism" (Rorty 1982 207). But if Livingston is right, Rorty could have found a firmer basis for his hopes by rereading "A World of Pure Experience," especially by reconsidering a passage that Livingston quotes and that incidentally sheds some light on Williams's unusual procedures in closing, or rather stopping, his first four-book version of *Paterson*.

> in passing from one of my own moments to another the sameness of object and interest is unbroken, and both earlier and the later experience are of things directly lived. There is no other *nature*, no other whatness than this absence of break and this sense of continuity in that most intimate of conjunctive relations, the passing of one experience into another when they belong to the same self. And this whatness is real empirical "content" just as the whatness of separation and discontinuity is real content in the contrasted case. Practically to experience one's personal continuum in this living way is to know the originals of the ideas of continuity and sameness, to know what the words stand for concretely, to own all that they can ever mean. [James 1977 198, quoted in Livingston 1994 292–93]

Continuing to quote James, Livingston argues persuasively that James's account authorizes the integrity of the self in "the retrospective integration of these moments, in the knowledge that is 'made by relations that unroll themselves in time' " (293). We live "prospectively as well as retrospectively," says James. "Life is in the transitions as much as in the terms connected . . . , as if our spurts and sallies forward were the real firing line of the battle, were like a thin line of flame advancing across the dry autumnal field" (James 1977 212–13). For Livingston, the upshot is that "the integrity of the self—the ethical principle that serves as premise and purpose of all moral philosophy— now appears as the consequence, not the casualty, of historical development" (293).

Livingston's sense of the consequences for the self in James's radical empiricism allows us to revisit the end of Williams's *Paterson* with renewed understanding. We don't have to choose between Johnson's hanging and the poet returning inland. We don't have to measure Williams's anxieties about the Korean War against his nostalgic yearning for the resources of Greek tragedy (*P* 200). We may read these moments not necessarily in the spirit of contradiction but in the spirit of conjunction. We are asked to understand them in terms of not either/or but and/with. One image does not cancel the other. In fact, Williams wants us to understand that they cannot do so. They are inevitably related by their placement on the page. By that placement they become historical: we experience first one image and then the next. None of them is autonomous. To experience the end of *Paterson* fruitfully, then, is to experience it conjunctively—"out of sequence, marvelously," as Williams said in "The Wanderer," which is to say, in a new sequence, making a new history.

Conjunctive experience is a broader way of indicating what is important about the corporate experience. Williams comes closer than Pound does to understanding the corporate age and corporate capitalism because he is able to overcome his own almost visceral dismay at what corporate capitalism stands for—the valorization of abstract values. He realizes that his task is not to rescue civilization but to represent it. He is able to do so because he is able to experience the city of Paterson and *Paterson* as a continuum in a living way, without the need of any mediating narrative except time itself. To paraphrase James, in Williams's conception of the Passaic River, derived from James's image of the stream of thought, presents the original of the ideas of continuity and sameness. In short, he is able to "know what [those] words stand for concretely, to own all that they can ever mean." By referring to the river and "the roar of the falls," Williams anchors his poem in historical continuities that he can then render concretely.

I suspect that Williams intuited this problem of continuity, without understanding all of the Pragmatic implications, as early as "The Wanderer" of 1914, when he felt the utter depth of the Passaic's filthiness and the vile breath of its degradation and "sank down knowing this was me now" (*CP1* 35). Insofar as the river is time, and the polluted water of the Passaic is history, Williams shows how the self is immersed in and created by time-in-history. There is no other useful self nor any purer poem.

Williams is most emphatically *not* trying to write a "paradiso terrestre." He does not think of poetry in this way. Poesis, "making," or, to enrich it with Heidegger's sense of the term, "bringing forth" (1977 293), means trading on continuity and sameness, that which is there to be brought forward. Paradise is like "pure poetry," or virgin purposes, a concept that cannot exist in any concrete form. It cannot be said, because we live and speak prospectively and retrospectively, not transcendently. As a result, poetry is nothing if not concrete particulars. The particulars include the experience of language, written accounts of the past, such as the hanging of Johnson, and anxiety about the future ("I cannot believe / that it can begin again"). They include the present: "What's that? / —a duck, hell diver?" Finally, they include the mythic, which we might regard, with Pound, as the recurrent present. Whitman is our Homer, not our Odysseus, but insofar as Williams himself is our Whitman (as Pound is our Dante?), it seems right that Whitman should play Odysseus in an epic that is determined to sound much more like a local newspaper (our daily epic of the quotidian)—or a fire advancing across a field than like any other epic poem.

Conclusion: Worshiping the Dynamo

In the nineteenth century, people became aware of modernity in the chronic sense that they were being determined by abstract, inhuman forces, especially the struggle for economic existence.[4] Whether associated with Darwinian "social evolution," or with Marx's forces of production, with the death of God and the Nietzschean flux, with "progress," capitalism, and narratives of decline and decadence or with continuous scientific revolution and political visions of abundance, modernity was also accompanied by the sense of outrage and loss. Individuals feel helpless in the face of historical and technological change.

The history of Modernity, then, is largely the history of the human will pitted against abstract force. "Modern politics is, at bottom, a struggle not of men but of forces," wrote Henry Adams. "The men become every year more and more creatures of force, massed about central power houses. The conflict is no longer between the men, but between the motors that drive the men, and the men tend to succumb to their own motive forces" (421–22). Martin Sklar comments on this passage, "History now not only proceeded independently of human will, but was proceeding to abolish it" (Sklar 1992 201).

"History," in this sense, is simply modernity. "History" in the first half of the twentieth century as in the latter half, is virtually just another expression of economic determinism. The problem for individuals was, and is, how not to be abolished. Yet if the fact of economic determinism was the inescapable conclusion of thinking people in the first half of the twentieth century, a conclusion that led thinkers like Henry Adams to a profound skepticism about the study of history, it was not the end of the story. For economic determinism is not in and of itself a political program; it is not even an adequate diagnosis. At best it is a theory of causation, at worst a philosophy of despair. We may understand historical events as more or less determined by economic forces and "objective conditions" without wanting to sit by and be determined by them. Yet having accepted economic determinism as a working hypothesis, having derived a working model based on economic causation, how are we to exempt our own lives from the buffeting of impersonal forces? One answer is to will something different. How else to change the world?

As Sklar says about Henry Adams, "Adams knew that intellectually and politically you either stayed with the assertion of historically conscious human will as against the drift of things as they seemed to be dictated by 'economics' and technology, you either held to Marx's formulation such as expressed in his *Theses on Feuerbach* that the point is to change the world, and understood that this was the essence of science, or you threw in your lot with evolutionary positivism and the insistence of human adjustment to, accepting or suffering, that which was" (Sklar 1992 203). Adams himself noted that if he had ever wished to be intellectually consistent, he would have been a Marxist.

There is a third alternative that would have been unthinkable for Henry Adams but became an option for the younger generation of Pound and Williams: "political modernism," those ideologies that Emilio Gentile describes as arising in connection with modernization. These are ideologies that seek to render human beings capable of mastering the processes of modernization that are changing them, allowing them to make their own way within it (Gentile 58). One such ideology was the Italian-based art movement of "Futurism."[5] "Futurism glorified modern life with a dionysian exaltation of everything generated by modernity and its continuous explosion of energies, even its most violent and brutal aspects. 'For the first time,' wrote [the Futurist painter] Boccioni,'we Futurists are giving an example of an enthusiastic human adherence to the form of civilization that is forming itself before our eyes. . . . We are ecstatic in the face of modernity and feel the innovative delirium of our epoch' " (Gentile 630). Futurism's nationalist cousin, Fascism, would harness these revolutionary energies to the chariot of the state.

If Ezra Pound's Fascism has been the major scandal in literary modernism, Fascism as a political philosophy is the major embarrassment for modernity generally, and Pragmatism in particular. In asserting the will against impersonal forces in a way that can easily be misconstrued as being like William James's turn "towards action and towards power" (James 1977 379), Fascism solves the problem of the moral personality by endowing it with a corporate body, the State—personified by the physical body of the Leader. The Leader and his State simply assume all of the burdens of individual morality, effortlessly combining the social and the individual, the public and the private. "Fascism sees in the world not only those superficial, material aspects in which man appears as an individual, standing by himself, self-centred, subject to natural law which instinctively urges him toward a life of selfish momentary pleasure," Mussolini writes; it also sees nation and country, within which "individuals and generations are bound together by a moral law, with common traditions and missions which . . . build up a higher life, founded on duty." Properly disciplined, instinctive urges are trained to become a national will. Theoretically, the Fascist is able, "by self-sacrifice, the renunciation of self-interest, by death itself [to] achieve that purely spiritual existence in which his value as a man consists" (Mussolini 1935 8). It goes almost without saying, though Mussolini says it most emphatically, that this conception of life is a religious and ethical one (9). The Fascist is "complete," because he is no longer merely the "economic man" posited by liberal economists. "Man is complete. He is political, he is economic, he is religious, he is a saint, he is a warrior," Mussolini asserts (1936 24).

Fascism is a religion of the will, a secular religion of self-renunciation and public duty. It solves the problem of modernity by mobilizing the will collectively, which gives the Fascist (the word "individual" no longer quite applies) a fighting chance against the instinctive life, "natural law," and, presumably, the naturalized laws of economic forces. Rather than trying to recover reason, it "renounces reason," not merely for "barbarism," as John Diggins claims (281), but for what it takes to be higher values, that is, the collective will of the State, which functions like that of a purely earthly church—but an earthly church cognizant of the economic problems and opportunities of a modern industrial society. Fascism, one might say, fights fire with fire by incorporating itself against the corporate combinations of industrial capitalism. Rather than the military industrial complex swallowing the state, as Pound shows it doing in Canto 38, the State absorbs the complex.

By virtue of its monopoly of the will, Fascism is able to reject the Socialist "science of history," which itself had become one of those morally disabling "forces" threatening the moral personality. Fascism doesn't need God (although Mussolini cagily claimed that the Catholic church completed Fascism) Fascism obviates the class struggle. It even, as Dewey himself noticed, trades on certain democratic-sounding virtues like "community, personality and collective activity" (Diggins 281) and endorses some Jamesian values, especially action and the will to believe.

Fascism also illustrates the problems of the will to believe when separated from a truly radical empiricism and founded on "bad *a priori* reasoning" (James 1977 379). Obviously Mussolini, who read James, had no trouble mobilizing the will to belief; just as obviously, James would have rejected the things that Mussolini persuaded people to believe in. The will to believe, in and of itself, is no moral guarantee of anything unless one is willing to complete Jamesian moral philosophy by understanding the moral importance of pluralism.[6] Under the sign of moral absolutism, James's will to believe is just old-fashioned evangelism—here mobilized to worship the dynamo, rather than the virgin.

The Fascist worship of the dynamo has something in common with the Romantic worship of art. This connection became, for Pound, a faith in a politicized version of the Romantic poetic imagination, or the artist's will, which might, with sweat and study, exceed or transform the economic world at large. By invoking the will, Pound could reaffirm the artist's position in the new "volitionist" economic order he projected. This approach uses the positive side of the Populist critique of capitalism by endorsing the possibility of historical individuals who can manipulate the sytem for good as well as ill. The idea of the poet-king, "making" history while bending the forces of production to his will, was, for Pound, a compelling, if dangerous, way to make sense of modernity.

Pound, like Zukofsky and Williams (and Mussolini himself), took the model of this figure to be Lenin. Thus the seeming ideological confusion of the "Fascist" Pound complaining to his Communist friend and protégé Zukofsky, "WHY, is the only communism the American reds will accept precisely the non-marxian anti-leninite abstraction IN VACUO?" (January 7, 1936, *P/Z* 174). Why, that is, are Communists afraid of the concrete body of the leader? Any ideological paradox is resolved once we see that, for Pound, the political problem of "acceptance" is framed in artistic terms.

The revolutionary leader is like an artist: "treat him as *artifex* and all the details fall into place. Take him as anything save the artist and you will get muddled with contradictions," as Pound said of Mussolini (*JM* 33–34). As I observed earlier, in this sense Pound was unconcerned about any ideological differences between Lenin and Mussolini. The history that they were making looked different only because they were confronting different historical canvases. Pound cared less about their ideological differences than he did about their styles, the way their wills manifested themselves in action. Like other great artists, like the charismatic Renaissance figures that Pound admired, the two leaders were trying to impose their will on the times. In his unlikely comparison of Jefferson and Mussolini, Pound stressed "the opportunism of the artist, who has a definite aim, and creates out of the materials present. The greater the artist the more permanent his creation. And this is a matter of WILL" (*JM* 15–16). By this standard of simple duration, Jefferson was a greater artist than Lenin, and Lenin was greater than Mussolini. The more important fact is, however, that Pound believed he had found a way to judge these revolutionaries by the same standard—the same standard he would use to judge himself.[7] Pound's hero worship, then, has a peculiar quality—he judges these men by their work in such a way as to be able to compare his own ambitious poetic undertaking with theirs directly, as though they were commensurate. In *Guide to Kulchur* (1937) Pound rates artifex and dux in the same list: Brancusi, Picabia, Mussolini, and Arthur Balfour ("a fake") (*GK* 105). "Human Greatness," Pound decides—in terms that can apply to the individual or to a society, to the artist as well as to the politician— "is an unusual energy coupled with straightness, the direct shooting mind, it is incompatible with a man's lying to himself, it does not indulge in petty pretences" (*GK* 106).

Pound did not, could not, distinguish between public policy and private expression. This inability led to a real confusion, however, at the level of self. Pound's ideal statesman was simultaneously Jefferson *and* Mussolini, a kind of collective individual, who, as the embodiment of the will of the people, had become therefore a corporate, or at least collective, self. In this sense, the totalitarian leader that Pound admired should have been the opposite of the artist, who remains for Pound, the arch-individualist of the Romantics, a man who makes his own rules. But as *The Cantos* show, Pound saw the modern artist as an editor of tendencies and texts, and Mussolini, as Pound saw him, was "an EDITORIAL eye and ear—precisely—an editor, who will see through the bunkum" (*JM* 74). The transformation of himself and of Mussolini from Romantic icons of self-sufficient individualism to corporate artists—editors—reflects Pound's ingenious attempt to "incorporate" his thinking, to bring it up-to-date so that Mussolini might produce the corporate state and so that he himself might produce the epic poem the corporate age demanded.

Williams's reaction to modernity was no less radical but much more "American." True to his pluralistic temperament, he remained committed to the ideal of democracy. Williams's Jefferson is the democrat, not the autocrat, the "anti" of the Washington and Adams administrations, not the willful executive of his own presidencies. One might say that "experiment," not "utopia," was Williams's principal concern. He knew what he didn't like about modernity more than he knew what he wanted it to become, and this knowledge was a strength. If Pound's watchword was "order," Williams's was "form."

"A Foot-Note" is the last of a group of poems that Williams published in *Poetry* in 1934:

> Walk on the delicate parts
> of necessary mechanisms
> and you will pretty soon have
> neither food, clothing, nor
> even communism itself,
> Comrades. Read good poetry! [*CP1* 370]

A complicated linkage of both poetry and Communism, this poem seems to me to be, in its quiet way, as powerful a statement about poetry and politics as one can imagine. As a reaction to modernity, it suggests that poetic form, rather than individual or collective will, is the better answer. A future worth affirming depends on poems, not poets, on political form, not political will.

Coda

Paterson did not end where Williams thought it would, at book 4. "In old age" the poet's mind "cast off / rebelliously / an eagle / from its crag" (*P* 205), book 5 of *Paterson*, which was published in 1958. Included is a letter that Pound had sent Williams from St. Elizabeth's, one of his by now tiresome rants on "the money question." As though Williams had never heard it before, Pound repeats with unflagging urgency that "wars are made to make debt" and that "sovereignty inheres in the POWER to issue money, whether you have / the right to do it or not" (*P* 216, *P/W* 302–4). Yet Williams placed the letter in *Paterson* (*P* 215–16).

Its inclusion is partly a gesture of friendship (although Pound was alarmed that the publication of the letter, with its comments about Roosevelt ["an ambulating dunghill"] and "the stink that elevated / him" might preclude any possible release from his hospital prison [*P* 302n]). Williams wanted the letter primarily, I think, as an example of "the American idiom" (*P* 222).[8] Pound's letter is a radical example of the American idiom not only in its orthographic Pound-ese but in its fanatical populistic politics. The money question *is* the American idiom, one might say.

As it happens, Thirwalls's edition of Williams's *Selected Letters*, for many years the only accessible introduction to their correspondence, ends with Williams's original reply to Pound's letter, which has the welcome effect of highlighting the poets' Jeffersonian conversation. Williams reacts impatiently to Pound, understandably so, for he has been bombarded with just such letters for many years. But his impatience is all with Pound's hectoring tone and method. He agrees with Pound that "we may have saved ourselves 2 or 3 billion dollars debt during the recent war [World War 2] with a valid banking system," but he asks, "in the rush of financing our money supply," what else could have been done? "We weren't governed by crooks," he insists pragmatically, but "by men who had to employ the instruments that were ready at hand." Softening, Williams adds, "I 'feel' that much that you say is right," and he reminds Pound that he too has "tried to follow the teachings of Major Douglass [*sic*]" (*SL* 339).

Nevertheless, Pound's problem is that he knows nothing about the

> IMPLEMENTATION of what you THINK you are saying . . . YOU DON'T EVEN BEGIN TO KNOW what the problem IS. . . . You don't even know the terms you are using and have never known them. . . . You are too damned thickheaded to know you're asleep—and have been from the beginning. You are incapable of recognizing what you mean to present and to hide your stupidity resort to name-calling. . . . Do you think you are going to get anywhere that way—but in jail or the insane asylum where you are now? Mussolini led you there, he was your adolescent hero—or was it Jefferson. You still don't know the difference" [*SL* 338].

Exiled, incarcerated, cut off, Pound *has* been asleep. He's become a cranky Rip van Winkle and a bore. Williams is absolutely right in charging that Pound no longer knows, and perhaps never did know, the difference between Jefferson and Mussolini. To be ignorant of this difference is to be unaware of difficulties—difficulties with adjusting eighteenth-century ideas of economy and of the self to the postwar, Cold War, thoroughly incorporated world. These difficulties are what Jamesian pragmatism, founded on a really radical empiricism, can help us resolve. They are one reason why Livingston's recent work is unexpectedly useful to readers of poetry. Above all, they are why *Paterson* is such an important poem—perhaps as important a poem for the second half of the twentieth century as *The Cantos* were for the first half. Williams tried to to use a radically empirical method to make visible the Jeffersonian and Social Credit ideas that determine in many ways the conjunctive relations in the poem. By showing that the key to the corporate age in which we live is conjunctive relations—that corporate means conjunct—Williams anticipates later corporate poems of late capitalism like John Ashbery's *Flow Chart*. But that is a subject for another book.

NOTES

Introduction

1. In *The Age of Reform* (1955), Hofstadter was concerned with the "ambiguous character" of the Populist and Progressive Movements (18). In phrases that could easily be applied to the career of Ezra Pound, Hofstadter notes how "the frequent recurrence of demand for reforms, many of them aimed at the remedy of genuine ills, combined with strong moral convictions and with the choice of hatred as a kind of creed," characterizes the history of American reform and the personal lives of reformers (1955 21). He adds: "The precise line between useful and valid criticism of any society and a destructive alienation from its essential values is not always easy to draw. Some men, and indeed some political movements, seem to live so close to that line and to swing back and forth across it more than once in their lives. The impulses behind yesterday's reform may be put in the service of reform today, but they may also be enlisted in the service of reaction" (21). See Hofstadter, *The Age of Reform.*

2. As I write, the reactionary and even totalitarian side of Modernism is becoming a more acceptable interpretation. For Pound, "totalitarian" was a positive quality, suggesting an integrated culture (*GK* 121). On reactionary Modernism, see: Redman, *Ezra Pound and Italian Fascism*; Stead, *Pound, Yeats, Eliot, and the Modernist Movement*; Frederic Jameson, *Fables of Aggression: Wyndham Lewis, the Modernist as Fascist* (Berkeley: University of California Press, 1979). Arguably, Jameson himself is a totalitarian thinker; see *The Political Unconscious* (Ithaca: Cornell University Press, 1981), 20, 34.

3. See especially Christopher Lasch's final work, *The True and Only Heaven: Progress and Its Critics* (New York: W. W. Norton, 1991), which extols the populism of the small producer as the true answer to a culturally imperialistic "Liberalism" that seeks to bury the particular, the ethnic, the useful, and the local in the pyramid of "limitless progress." Unaccountably, Jefferson's name appears only three times in its 521 pages. Pound's appears once, and Williams's not at all. It is precisely the lack of these figures in Lasch's seemingly comprehensive survey that makes interdisciplinary study so important.

4. Forrest McDonald calls Jefferson and the Jeffersonians "reactionary." The problem with the epithet "reactionary" is that it allows us to pass over, rather than to reconsider, the possibilities opened up by the Jeffersonian critique of modernity and especially modern finance. See *The Presidency of Thomas Jefferson*, 161–62.

5. There is no question that all of these men, born in the Midwest, were formed by their personal contact with Populist agitation, "the money question," and Bryan. Parrington had actually been a member of the People's party (Hofstadter 1968 368–70). Though not notably "political," Turner voted for Bryan in 1896 (106), and Smith was a Bryanite and money radical who wrote a "heretical" doctoral dissertation entitled "The Multiple Money Standard" (387–88). As a young man, Beard

read Marx in college and heard the socialistic "labor-populists" Debs and Altgeld, as well as Bryan, speak in Chicago. Later, as a graduate student at Oxford, Beard became a Ruskinian labor agitator (170–79). See Hofstadter, *The Progressive Historians.* Claude Bowers, a self-styled Jeffersonian, also fell under Bryan's spell and later became an important Democratic spokesman. Bowers gave the keynote speech at the Democratic national convention in Houston in 1928. See Claude Bowers, *My Life,* 42–43, 192–97.

6. I am using the term "Populist" following the lead of Hofstadter in *The Age of Reform* (1955); that is, I am not restricting it to members of the People's Party. Hofstadter says: "By 'Populism' I do not mean only the People's (or Populist) Party of the 1890's; for I consider the Populist Party to be merely a heightened expression, at a particular moment of time, of a kind of popular impulse that is endemic in American culture. Long before the rebellion of the 1890's one can observe a larger trend of thought, stemming from the time of Andrew Jackson, and crystallizing after the Civil War in the Greenback, Granger, and anti-monopoly movements, that expressed the discontents of a great many farmers and businessmen with the economic changes of the nineteenth century" (Hofstadter 1955 4–5).

7. The phrase "second financial revolution" sounds exaggerated. Nonetheless, the 1890s were a period of intense financial crisis. The Panic of 1893, the challenge of Bryan and "free-silver" in 1896, the "political economic and cultural stalemate" between labor and capital, and "the marginalist revolution" in economics (Livingston 1987 70), mark this decade as decisive for the future of capitalism." The successful negotiation of these difficulties by the financial elite created "consumer culture" by radically altering the basis of credit.

8. Whether the Populists and their allies constituted a true revolutionary movement is, of course, debatable; it is perhaps more acccurate to see them as having resisted a "revolution from above," led by the financiers; this, surely, is how they saw themselves. Nonetheless, the title of the first important history of Populism, John Hick's *The Populist Revolt* (1931), and Lawrence Goodwyn's *The Populist Moment: A Short History of the Agrarian Revolt in America* (1978), hint at the radical flavor that many historians have identified in Populism. See also Alan Trachtenberg, *The Incorporation of America* (1982), 173–81. For a contrasting view, see Hofstadter, *The Age of Reform* (1955). Hofstadter nonetheless speaks of the "revolt of Populism" in *The Progressive Historians* (1968), 47, 48.

9. Also its betrayal; see Goodwyn, *The Populist Moment* (1978), chap. 9.

10. See Jefferson's famous 1813 letter to John Eppes (Jefferson 1280). The terror of debt informs the thinking of both Jefferson and Madison. "Indeed, a special mentality with regard to debt of any kind was the heritage of almost any Virginian, running the borderline between thought and feeling" (Elkins and McKintrick 90).

11. The case of Masters reveals how unhelpful the term "Fascist" is in understanding Pound's work. Because Masters has a secure reputation as a significant regional writer, few seem to care about his anti-Semitism or the treasonous sentiments scattered throughout his work. He wrote poems praising John Wilkes Booth and denounced Jews as plutocrats. "The Spooniad," an unfinished epic by one of the Spoon River characters, was to have been a Populist *Iliad* about the failure of a bank and resulting popular insurrection. In his epic *The New World* (1937), Masters accuses Alexander Hamilton of being a Jew who brings financial evil to the new world. See Edgar Lee Masters, *The New World* (New York: D. Appleton-Century, 1937), 107–8, and *The Spoon River Anthology* (New York: Collier, 1962), 283.

12. See Martin J. Sklar, *The Corporate Reconstruction of American Capitalism*.

13. Whitman's connection to Pragmatism is often acknowledged but is not well understood. He was William James's favorite—or at least most quoted—poet. Tapscott links Whitman and Dewey in relation to Williams in *American Beauty*, 97–99.

14. Pound's Populism was first discussed in articles by Victor Ferkiss, in the 1950s. Wendy Stallard Flory touches on it in *The American Ezra Pound* (39–41), where she argues that Pound attempted to convert his grandfather, Thaddeus Coleman Pound, into a Bryanite money radical. See Victor Ferkiss, "Populist Influences on American Fascism," 350–73, and "Ezra Pound and American Fascism," 173–97. The best and, as far as I know, only recent treatment of Pound's Populism occurs in the latter half of David Murray's "Pound-Signs: Money and Representation in Ezra Pound," 50–77, especially 70–77. For Williams and Populism, the best source is still Mike Weaver's *William Carlos Williams: The American Background*, 89–114.

1: Jeffersonian Economics: Debt and the Production of Value

1. See Guillory, *Cultural Capital*, chap. 5, "The Discourse of Value." Pages 303–17 speak to my discussion here. As Guillory acknowledges, Howard Caygill's *Art of Judgement* (London: Blackwell, 1989) lies in the deeper intellectual background.

2. The term "cultural capital," now an academic commonplace, originated with Pierre Bordieu. See Pierre Bordieu, *Distinction: A Social Critique of the Judgement of Taste*, trans. Richard Nice (Cambridge, Mass.: Harvard University Press, 1984).

3. Hamilton never pretended that financial capital equaled real wealth. He saw it as a motive force, a fictional energy. In arguing for a "funded [National] debt" in the "Report on Manufactures," he is very careful to distinguish "between an absolute increase in capital, or an accession of real wealth, and the artificial increase of capital as an engine of business, or as an instrument of industry and commerce. In the first sense, a funded debt has no pretentions to being deemed an increase in capital; in the last it has pretensions which are not easy to be controverted" (*Works* 4:124). The "pretensions" of debt are the creation of credit. Hamilton's claims for credit, like William James's for "truth," are, indeed, incontrovertible. Credit works, and it functions as though it were real wealth: "serving as a new power in the operations of industry, it has, within certain bounds, a tendency to increase the real wealth of a community in like manner as money" (124–25). See *The Works of Alexander Hamilton*, vols. 1, 4 (first published in 1904).

4. See, for example, Whitman's "The Eighteenth Presidency" (1856), in Walt Whitman, *Complete Poetry and Collected Prose*, 1307f.

5. "I even gave the Phi Beta Kappa poem at Harvard on June 11. Quite an experience taken all in all. From the faces of some (not all) of the faces of those on the platform I think they must have fumigated Memorial Hall after I left. The student body was, on the other hand delighted and showed it by their tumultuous applause after I finished my '15 minute' poem" (WCW to Robert Lowell, 1951, *SL* 302).

6. This famous passage seems to draw freely on one by Cicero in *De officiis*

that coincidentally turns up in a note to the "third edition" of Quesnay's *Tableau économique* (1758). See Kuczynski and Meek, *Quesnay's "Tableau économique,"* 15, 22–23n.

7. There are examples in Crèvecoeur, John Taylor, and Pound, some of which I will address in the course of this book. The persistence of this wordplay through time might be accounted for by the yearning for an older "gift economy" that has been supplanted by the market economy of capitalism. This gift economy is clearly libidinous, as Lewis Hyde shows, in that it assumes the idea that giving brings more in return. In such an economy giving *is* taking; as in sexual love, giving is part of the process of receiving. Venereal disease is the curse of the marketplace on the gift economy of love. See Lewis Hyde, *The Gift*, 21–22, and Pound, Canto 45.

8. In suggesting that New Englanders like Thoreau, or Emerson, are Jeffersonian, I'm not suggesting they voted for Andrew Jackson, who most New Englanders, and most obviously J. Q. Adams, detested as proslavery.

9. Pound's passage is startlingly similar to one by Brooks Adams in the conclusion of *The Law of Civilization and Decay*: "Art, perhaps, even more clearly than religion, love, or war, indicates the pathway of [economic] consolidation; for art reflects with the subtlest delicacy those changes in the forms of competition which enfeeble or inflame the imagination. Of Greek art, in its zenith, little need be said; its greatest qualities have been too fully recognized. It suffices to point out that it was absolutely honest, and that it formed a vehicle of expression as flexible as the language itself. A temple apparently of marble, was of marble; a colonnade apparently supporting a portico, did support it; and, while the ornament formed an integral part of the structure, the people read it intelligently as they read the poems of Homer. Nothing similar ever flourished in Rome" (372).

The Roman builders, by contrast, used "a cheap core of rubble, bricks and mortar" with a veneer of marble over it. "That gaudy exterior had nothing whatever to do with the building itself, and could be stripped off without vital injury. From the greek point of view nothing could be falser, more insulting to the intelligence, or, in a word, more plutocratic" (373). Brooks Adams's criticism suggests once again how total an economic criticism may be.

Adams's work is not a source for Pound's criticism, however. Pound didn't read Brooks Adams until 1940: "We have been orful MUGGS not to read Brooks Adams twenty years sooner," he wrote to Douglas (May 15, 1940, YCAL 43, Beinecke Library, Yale University).

10. For a discussion of Pound and *virtu* in relation to Neoplatonism and Pound, see Peter Nicholls, *Ezra Pound, Politics, Economics, and Writing*, 66–69.

11. In 1802 Jefferson wrote regretfully to the Physiocrat Pierre Dupont de Nemours, a recent immigrant to the United States, "When this government was first established, it was possible to have kept it going on true principles, but the contracted, English, half-lettered ideas of Hamilton, destroyed that hope in the bud. We can pay off his debt in 15. years; but we can never get rid of his financial system" (Jefferson 1101). See Thomas Jefferson, *Writings*.

12. It could be conjectured that Hamilton, a native of the West Indies who had been born out of wedlock to an aristocrat English father, needed a constitution to legitimate himself. Jefferson, a hereditary landowner intimately connected with the great families of Virginia, needed no such legitimacy. Endowed with land by his birth, he was integrated into the political elite at an early age; he was a member of the Virginia House of Burgesses at twenty-six. One could argue that Jefferson could

afford to choose democracy as his political philosophy because he was ensconced in real political and social power and surrounded by real property in land and slaves. Hamilton, born in the opposite circumstances, possessed only his own talents, was a brilliantly successful self-made man, and was obliged to use democracy to achieve a position consistent with his aristocratic expectations. "Hamilton's audacious mission in life was to remake American society in accordance with his own values," a biographer writes (McDonald 1979 4). Indeed, there is something Napoleonic in Hamilton's republicanism, which fits well with his lifelong urge for military glory. Jefferson, by contrast, longed for the luxury of study. Despite his thousands of acres and hundreds of slaves, Jefferson spent much of his later life paying off his family's debts. Hamilton seemingly always understood that the key to political power and social acceptance in "the world aborning" was control of finance; he regarded money as "oblivious to class, status, color and inherited social position" and as "the ultimate, neutral, impersonal arbiter" (McDonald 1979 4) of all social questions.

13. This is essentially Beard's thesis in his seminal *Economic Interpretation:* "The Constitution was essentially an economic document based upon the concept that the fundamental private rights of property are anterior to government and morally beyond the reach of popular majorities." And the final words of the book: "The Constitution was not created by 'the whole people' as the jurists have said; neither was it created by 'the states' as Southern nullifiers long contended; but it was the work of a consolidated group whose interests knew no state boundaries and were truly national in their scope." This group was the financial elite, the class that became the Federalist Party of Alexander Hamilton. See Charles A. Beard, *Economic Interpretation of the Constitution of the United States,* 324–25 and passim.

14. Pound and Williams never opposed a credit economy. What bothered them was that the credit system was monopolized by a creditor clique. Pound and Williams wanted to democratize credit. They understood that the basis of credit is the society as a whole—not those private individuals or (their legal equivalent) corporations (including banks) that rent out credit for private profit by using public moneys as private funds. When you use a credit card to buy a commodity, for example, the credit card company advances no money. That money is, in effect, created at the instant of transaction. Yet you must pay the debt, plus interest (often between 17 percent and 21 percent) to the credit card company, with real money gotten somewhere else. The credit of Amex, however, is based on its access to public money, not on its "assets," which are, in any case, debts.

15. In a note Lewis Hyde remarks, "I use 'value' and 'worth' when I want to make this distinction [between use value and exchange value]. I was therefore delighted to find the following footnote in Marx: 'In the seventeenth century, many English authors continued to write "worth" for "use-value" and "value" for "exchange-value," this being accordant with the genius of the language which prefers an Anglo-Saxon word for an actual thing, and a Romance word for its reflexion' " (Lewis Hyde 60n).

16. William James makes this point explicitly. Arguing for the power of the Pragmatic method in resolving (if not solving) metaphysical problems, he writes: "If you follow the pragmatic method you cannot look on any such word ['God,' 'matter,' 'reason'] as closing your quest. You must bring out of each word its *practical cash value* [my emphasis], set it at work within the stream of your experience. It appears less as a solution, than as a program for more work, and more particularly

as an indication of the ways in which existing realities may be *changed.*" See "What Pragmatism Means," in James 1977 380.

17. But see Nicholls 143–46.

18. In the *Grundrisse,* see also "On the Jewish Question." See Karl Marx, *Early Writings,* 239.

19. This is still true. The "prime rate" determines the money supply, we are told, as though money existed in a kind of reservoir. There is no such supply—only the manipulation of demand by setting a price on money via the interest rate determined by the Federal Reserve. In fact, credit is what determines how much money there is in circulation. In a letter to John Adams, Jefferson said: "Destutt-Tracy is, in my judgement, the ablest writer living on intellectual subjects" (October 14, 1816). He continues: "He has lately published a . . . work on Political Economy, comprising the whole subject . . . in which all its principles are demonstrated with the severity of Euclid. . . . I have procured this to be translated, and have been 4 years endeavouring to get it printed. But as yet without success" (Jefferson to Adams, October 14, 1816, in *The Adams-Jefferson Letters,* 491–92).

20. It seems that Jefferson did not know the person who was eventually commissioned (via Joseph Milligan, the editor) to translate the work. He writes to Adams: "I never knew who the translator was: but I thought him someone who understood neither French nor English: and probably a Caledonian, from the number of Scotticisms I found in his MS. The innumerable corrections of that cost me more labor than would a translation of the whole de novo; and made at last but an inelegant altho' faithful version of the sense of the author" (March 21, 1819, in Cappon 539). Jefferson's word "published" in the earlier letter (see note 19 above) apparently simply means "made available." Jefferson's translation was published in 1817, the French version not until 1822 (Cappon 492n).

21. This "forward" appears as a letter dated "Monticello, October 25, 1818." How it could find its way into a "first edition" dated 1817 is unclear. I am working from the reprint published by August M. Kelley of New York in 1970, which claims to have been offset from a first edition.

22. Despite the inflationary bias of Jeffersonianism generally, Jefferson was as worried about inflation and a ruinous devaluation of the currrency as Destutt de Tracy. See his famous letter to John Eppes of 1813 (Jefferson 1285–86).

23. The words are assigned to the "American farmer's" unnamed wife in Crève-coeur's text.

24. See Thoreau's parable of the reception of his first book, *A Week on the Concord and Merrimack Rivers* (1849) in *Walden* (1854). See Henry David Thoreau, *A Week, Walden, Maine Woods, Cape Cod,* 337–38.

25. I am using the male pronoun on purpose, because the discourse of Jeffersonianism is much concerned with "manhood." For the relation between the ownership of commodities and the problem of sale, see Marx's *Capital:* "The leap taken by value from the body of the commodity into the body of the gold is the commodity's *salto mortale.* . . . If the leap falls short, it is not the commodity which is defrauded but rather its owner." (See Karl Marx, *Capital,* 1:201.)

26. These questions surface in the correspondence between James Laughlin and Williams. Laughlin's "New Directions" publishing venture was designed to rescue "literature" from "merchandise" (14). The objective underlying Laughlin's "'New Classics Series'—dollar books like the Modern Library, of which you [Williams] and

Ezra [Pound] will be the backbones" (23) is clearly to eliminate the problem of price. Laughlin succeeded. The New Directions authors—especially Pound and Williams—have probably had more comprehensive distribution in cheaper editions over a longer time than any other American poets. See Hugh Witemeyer, ed., *William Carlos Williams and James Laughlin: Selected Letters* (New York: Norton, 1989).

27. Williams makes the same allusion repeatedly in *The Embodiment of Knowledge*. See *EK* 86, 136, 142, 143.

28. No one seems to know whether Crèvecoeur actually read the Physiocratic writings of Quesnay. Later, in France, he certainly knew many people who were influenced by Physiocracy and were thoroughly conversant with its principles: the Abbé Raynal (to whom the *Letters from an American Farmer* was dedicated), Etienne-François Turgot, the brother of the Physiocrat finance minister of Louis XVI, Benjamin Franklin, and Jefferson. See Gay Wilson Allen and Roger Asselineau, *St. John de Crèvecoeur* (New York: Viking, 1987), esp. 77.

29. For a discussion of the complexities of Native American notions of property and the confusion they caused Europeans, see William Cronon, *Changes in the Land*, 54–81.

2: Three Aspects of the Jeffersonian Political Aesthetic

1. This political/aesthetic vision predates American independence. It descends directly from the Puritan conception of America as a "special providence" and, as it were, a second chance to reform mankind. Later it became part of American revolutionary ideology; Bernard Bailyn notes that America was supposed to be "the refinement of all that was good in England" and quotes Voltaire's judgment from afar that American Quakers actually lived "that golden age of which men talk so much and which probably has never existed anywhere except in Pennsylvania." See Bernard Bailyn, *The Ideological Origins of the American Revolution*, 84, and Livingston, "How to Succeed in Business Without Really Trying: Remarks on Martin J. Sklar's *Corporate Reconstruction of American Capitalism, 1890–1916*" (paper presented at the Business History Conference, Pasadena, March 1992), 9.

2. Pound's version is in Canto 99:

Let a man do a good job at his trade:
        whence is honesty
        whence are good manners,
           good custom . . . [99:714]

3. Perhaps the most flagrant and moving example of Berry's nostalgic Jeffersonianism is his essay "Two Economies" (1983) in *Home Economics*, 54–75.

4. Nicholls is aware of the importance of Hofstadter's thesis but does not pursue it. See Nicholls 52.

5. In his *Autobiography* (1951), Williams recalled: "Then out of the blue *The Dial* brought out *The Wasteland* and all our hilarity ended. It wiped out our world as if an atom bomb had been dropped on it and our brave sallies into the unknown were turned to dust. To me especially it struck like a sardonic bullet. I felt at once that it had set me back twenty years, and I'm sure it did. Critically Eliot returned us to the classroom just at the moment when I felt that we were on the point of

escape to matters much closer to the essence of a new art form itself—rooted in the locality which should give it fruit. I knew at once that in certain ways I was most defeated. Eliot had turned his back on the possibility of reviving my world. And being an accomplished craftsman, better skilled in some ways than I could ever hope to be, I had to watch him carry off my world, the fool, to the enemy" (A 176). The "new art form rooted in the locality which should give it fruit" is *Paterson;* note the agrarian metaphor.

6. See, for example, the Knights of Labor anthology *The Voice of Labor,* edited by S. M. Jelley. The tone of this passage is representative of the Jeffersonian stance of resistance to finance: "No nation can prosper with our limited circulation [of money], cornered as it is by demogogues, to raise the interest, cramp the people, and to sell their homes" (Jelley 118).

7. See Pound's unpublished essay "Notes on Douglas C.H." (c. 1934): "I admit that I am a Jeffersonian; I [was] a Douglasite before there were any . . . and I am strong for Mussolini" (YCAL 43, Box 88, Beinecke Library, Yale University).

8. On luxury and American ideology in the Revolutionary and Federalist periods, see Drew R. McCoy, *The Elusive Republic,* esp. 21–32 and 90–104, and Gordon S. Wood, *The Creation of the American Republic, 1776–1787,* 48–53 and 413–25.

9. Julius Caesar is a most interesting figure for American republicans, as was Napoleon, who in some sense modeled his career on Caesar, just as Mussolini would later do. In their correspondence Jefferson and Adams heap scorn upon both men, and Adams compares Hamilton (and Burr) to them (see Cappon 549–51). Pound never saw his interest in Mussolini as Caesarism, although he knew the Jefferson/Adams correspondence intimately and was fervently recommending it to an American audience in *The North American Review* in the winter of 1937–38, at the height of his admiration for Il Duce (SP 117–28). I discuss the complicated reasons in chapter 7. Briefly, Pound's sense of Mussolini is mediated through the figure of Lenin. Pound seems mistakenly to have assumed that Jefferson was like the two modern revolutionary dictators, who took not the Roman republic but the Roman empire as models (Gentile 74). See Emilio Gentile, "The Conquest of Modernity," 55–87.

10. I am reacting here, not only to James's "The Stream of Thought" but also to Richard Poirier, *Poetry and Pragmatism,* chap. 3, "The Re-Instatement of the Vague," 129–68.

11. "Pragmatism," notes Poirier, "especially the Emersonian-Jamesian version, seems to me essentially a poetic theory" (Poirier 1992 135).

12. Cushman, *William Carlos Williams and the Meanings of Measure.*

13. Stand at the rampart (use a metronome
    if your ear is deficient, one made in Hungary
    if you prefer)
    and look away north . . . [P 55]

14. Mangan later copied it and sent it on to Ezra Pound with his dissenting marginalia—the copy is in the Pound/Williams correspondence, YCAL 43, Box 49, Beinecke Library, Yale University.

15. The word "character" is a dead metaphor derived from the Greek word for "the upper die used by the coin maker or impressed mark upon the coin" (Shell 1978 64). Pound was well aware of the word's etymology. See his early poem

"Hystrion" (*CE* 71). For a discussion of this poem, see Maud Ellman, *The Poetics of Impersonality* (Cambridge, Mass.: Harvard University Press, 1987), 147.

16. "The truth about economics has had no warmer welcome than had a few simple and known facts about the tradition in metric and poetry during a couple of preceding decades. The parallel would be comic were it not freighted with tragedy, death, malnutrition, degradation of the national health in several countries. No intelligent man will be content to treat economics merely as economics, and probably no writer could write anything of interest in so doing" ("The Individual in His Milieu" *Criterion* [October 1935] *SP* 250). Flory has quoted this passage. See her discussion in *The American Ezra Pound* (New Haven: Yale University Press, 1989), 82–130.

17. The source for this phrase can be found in Pound's copy of Jeffery Mark's *The Modern Idolatry* (1934); Pound had marked and remembered it. Mark quotes Kitson's testimony to the Macmillan Committee on Finance and Industry on May 15, 1930: "Kitson testifies: 'I put this question to him: "Mr. Bryan, do you think that bimetallism is going to solve the economic problem?" He said, "No, certainly not. Metallism is merely a symbol; the real fight is for control of the national credit. If McKinley (the nominee of the Republican Party) wins, this country will be governed by the most unscrupulous set of speculators the world has ever known. If I win the Government will control its own credit" ' " (Mark 339–40). See Mark, *The Modern Idolatry*.

3: The Virtues of Distribution:
A Genealogy of Poundian Economics

1. According to Ronald L. Meek, "Smith, Ricardo and Marx . . . tended to visualise production and distribution as two aspects of a single economic process in which production was regarded as the dominant and determining factor" (Meek 1975 246). It is tempting to suggest that the reification of Marx's emphasis on production in Bolshevik practice is what perverted and eventually destroyed twentieth-century state Socialism. The Soviet Empire seems to have succumbed, finally, because of problems of distribution, not of production.

2. Readers of William Faulkner's *The Sound and the Fury* (1929) will remember Jason Compson, an angry man full of nativism, Populism, and naked greed who plays the stock market like a gambler and who in turn is played upon by that market in his obsessive fears and dreams of gain. The last Compson, Jason is also (not unlike Pound) a late, perverted Jeffersonian. He is the twisted spiritual descendant of John Taylor of Caroline. Dispossessed of land, slaves, real property, and a positive ideology, he exhibits its negative: racism, anti-Semitism, a pathetic fascination with a financial order he can never understand. A dogmatic realist, Jason is nonetheless completely entangled in paranoid fantasies, most of them monetary. He winds up living with a whore in Memphis, alienated from his birthright in the fictional (but aptly named) town of Jefferson, Mississippi (Faulkner 224–36). Jason Compson is a useful figure of Jeffersonianism because he embodies its dark, defensive side; he has something in common with the Ezra Pound of the 1940s and 1950s. See Faulkner, *The Sound and the Fury*.

3. Douglas and Pound were fond of quoting Charles Ferguson, who noted that

"control of credit and control of the news are concentric." See *The Monopoly of Credit* 3 and *Jefferson and/or Mussolini* vii.

4. Sklar's vision of the "corporate reconstruction" of American capitalism depends on his notion of "corporate liberalism," a consensus (reached after a protracted struggle) that regulation of capitalism was essential to its survival. That liberalism "among the different views of what constituted legitimate property rights, the public interest, salutary innovation, and optimal efficiency, that which defined them in terms of regulating, affirming, and legitimizing the corporate-capitalist order came to dominate all the rest. It came to be identified in social thought with what was progressive and liberal in the nation's political life, with . . . 'corporate liberalism' " (Sklar 1988 19).

5. For the more radical and distinctively Poundian view, see Eustace Mullins, *The Secrets of the Federal Reserve* (1952) (Staunton: Bankers' Institute, 1984). Mullins's book appears in the bibliography of Pat Robertson, *The New World Order* (Dallas: Word Press, 1991). For the history of the Federal Reserve, see Livingston 1986 and Greider 1987.

6. One example of a shrinking money supply that tragically affected American farmers in the latter half of the nineteenth century is discussed in Goodwyn, *The Populist Moment*, 12.

7. See *The Great News*, chap. 7, "Transplacement of the Centre of Social Credit." In all probability, C. H. Douglas's "Social Credit" movement found its name here in Ferguson.

8. It is interesting to see how would-be reformers of capitalism, like Ferguson, but also Arthur Kitson and Major Douglas, formulate the same diagnosis as Lenin in *Imperialism: The Highest Stage of Capitalism* (1917). As reformers, not revolutionaries, they have quite other ideas about the cure for capitalism's contradictions.

9. Ferguson's Jeffersonianism is not, of course, about Jefferson as much as about contemporary politics. Ferguson's view of Jefferson complemented his view of Alexander Hamilton. "It was an incalculable misfortune," Ferguson wrote, that Hamilton and his contemporaries "were so much more concerned about the indispensable shell and integument of the new order than they were about the vitality of the kernel. To conceive of the government of the modern free state as merely a powerful set of conventions of property, was to sterilize the seed of democracy" (Ferguson 1915 31). This view of Hamilton was surely colored by the association of Hamiltonianism with Theodore Roosevelt, inspired by Herbert Croly's influential *The Promise of American Life* (1909). Ferguson's book, it could be argued, was a reply from the Wilson camp. See Herbert Croly, *The Promise of American Life*.

10. As William Greider puts it: "The ultimate purpose of the central bank was to control the society's overall expansion of debt—to decide, in effect, what level of hopes and promises the future could reasonably fullfill. . . . The Federal Reserve's estimates of the future were calculated by scientific reasoning, of course, but the function closely resembled the prophetic role of the ancient temple priests who were given divine license to look into the future and foretell whether lean or abundant years lay ahead. The Federal Reserve governors also made prophecy, but they had the ability to make their own predictions come true" (Greider 60). See William Greider, *Secrets of the Temple*.

11. On Orage and *The New Age*, see Flory 1989 chap. 2; Redman 1991 esp. chap. 1, and Michael Coyle, " 'A Profounder Didacticism.' "

12. Kitson mentions his contributions to the Bryan campaign in a letter to Homer Pound of June 10, 1936, and in his testimony of May 15, 1930, to the Macmillan Committee on Finance and Industry, a parliamentary body. Part of his testimony is quoted in Jeffrey Mark's *The Modern Idolatry* (1934), 239–40. Pound marked the page "Bryan" on the back leaf of his copy of the book, which is at Brunnenburg (see note 17 to Chapter 2 above). As Kitson wrote Homer Pound, he was convinced that Bryan had been cheated of victory in 1896: "There is no doubt that Bryan was defeated solely by corruption" (June 10, 1936).

Oddly, despite their mutual connection to Orage's *The New Age*, Kitson and Pound never met, though they had read each other's work. By the time they began to correspond in 1933, Kitson had become a rabid anti-Semite (though he may have been one earlier). In a letter of December 5, 1933, he complained of "this rotten Jew-controlled commercial age." Pound retorted: "I think the yarn about the jews / is just the old game of trying to discredit anyone who is inconvenient" (December ? 1933). Kitson replied, "I think you are wrong about the Jewish menace. It is becoming very serious here" (December 12, 1933). Kitson sent Pound *The Protocols of the Elders of Zion* with the encomium: "I doubt there has ever been a more complete programme for World conquest as set forth in these volumes" (February 2, 1934). Kitson closes that same letter by observing, "A friend of mine is writing "Germany 1934" He is in close touch with Hitler and is staying in Berlin. He went there a very rabid anti-Hitlerite, but he has been converted by the marvellous improvement in German affairs since Hitler took the helm" (February 2, 1934). By 1936 Kitson is hoping that "Mussolini will shake hands with Hitler and that Germany and Italy will unite for the advance of Christian civilization. Our so-called 'statesmen' are entirely controlled by the Money Power and they represent nobody but themselves and the international-Jew-financiers" (June 10, 1936).

It is instructive to compare Pound's anti-Semitism with the more full-blown example of Kitson. It seems clear that Pound's bigotry "evolved" throughout the 1930s. In 1933 Pound resists Kitson's paranoia about a global Jewish conspiracy. Ten years later, over Rome radio, he will sound much like Kitson. The Kitson/Pound correspondence is in YCAL 43, Box 25, Folder 905, Beinecke Library, Yale University.

13. "The money power preys on the nation in times of speech and conspires against it in times of adversity. It is more despotic than monarchy, more insolent than autocracy, more selfish than bureaucracy. It denounces as public enemies, all who question its methods, or throw light upon its crimes. It can only be overthrown by the awakened conscience of the nation" (vi). Pound would later quote this same passage in one of his speeches over Rome radio, July 26, 1942 (*EPS* 218), a speech that also cites Jefferson. See Flory 1989 39–40.

14. Pound's involvment with Social Credit is well known and dates from the serialization of Douglas's first book, *Economic Democracy*, in A. R. Orage's *New Age* in 1918. As Flory and Redman have recently shown, however, Pound's interest in the movement was hardly orthodox, as is clear by his later interest in the work of Sylvio Gesell and finally by his illusion that Italian Fascism was effactually achieving Social Credit goals. Williams's involvment is less publicized, but he was "actively committed" by early 1934 (Flory 1989 79). See Williams's "Revolutions Revalued," a lecture given July 11, 1936, printed in *A Recognizable Image*, 97–118. See also Coyle 1988 and Mariani 1981 (348–407).

15. Leon Surette points out, however, that Pound reviewed "Douglas's second book, *Credit Power and Democracy*, in Williams's short-lived periodical *Contact*" in the summer of 1921 (Surette 1983 449).

16. The term is Martin Sklar's, from a 1969 essay called "On the Proletarian Revolution and the End of Political-Economic Society." The revised version that is my source appears as chapter 5 of *The United States as a Developing Country* (1992). My description of capitalist accumulation and disaccumulation draws on Sklar and Livingston 1994 3–23.

17. Part of Douglas's scathing analysis is worth quoting: "Great Britain, which was one of the nations very vocal in asserting that Germany must pay, is feverishly searching for methods either by tariffs or otherwise, which will prevent German goods, which are by common consent the only method by which Germany can pay, from entering this country, and is providing Germany with credits—in order that she may *import* British coal" (Douglas's emphasis, 1933 158).

18. Arthur Kitson complained in *Unemployment* (1921): "For a nation to sit still and starve because foreigners are unable to buy its products—the use of which would bring health and prosperity to its people—is the very acme of stupidity. A visitor from Mars would surely view with amazement the spectacle of a Leicester or Northampton shoe manufacturer incurring the expense of sending travellers to the North Pole and the Far East, and advertising in foreign journals, whilst hundreds and thousands of English people are going about half-shod and millions more are striving to make one pair of shoes do the work of two pairs. Similarly he would wonder at the shabby costumes of women who throng our manufacturing towns, whilst the Lancashire and Yorkshire mills were either closed down or running on half-time" (35). It is in this book that Kitson announces his conversion to Douglasite economics (45f.).

19. British libel laws led to a systematic garbling of proper names throughout *The Cantos*. The poem's obscurity is not always willful; it was often required. Surette also quotes this passage. Compare *A Light from Eleusis* 85–86. See also Redman 46.

20. "Jesus Christ / Standing in the Earthly Paradise / Thinking as he made himself a companion of Adam." See Carroll F. Terrell, *A Companion to the Cantos of Ezra Pound*, 1:90.

21. "A factory or other productive organisation has, besides its economic function as a producer of goods, a purely financial aspect—it may be regarded on the one hand as a device for the distribution of purchasing power to individuals through the media of wages, salaries and dividends; and on the other hand as a manufactory of prices—financial values" (Douglas 1920 21). See Douglas, *Credit Power and Democracy*.

22. Yet we have noticed how money as ration tickets worked, or rather (in the long run) how it failed to work, in the Soviet Union. Unable to measure value, money lost its unique power to call value forth in the shape of goods. The result was that value manifested itself negatively, in the form of chronic shortages and sudden gluts of goods, as pent-up demand, belatedly released through the central pricing bureaucracy, threw goods onto the market. Douglas's Social Credit economy would avoid this kind of problem because it still contains a market apparatus to determine prices. On Soviet money problems, compare Sergei Nikolaenko, "Soviet Consumers: Problems of the Transition to the Market Economy" (New Brunswick: Rutgers Center for Historical Analysis, December 3, 1991).

23. To be consistent with Douglas, Pound must mean work in the largest sense, that is, the cultural, technological work that has been done in the past to make possible production in the present. Pound can't mean that "money is a certificate for the work any individual has just finished." Nonetheless, Pound often sounds as if this is exactly what he means.

24. Williams too saw the language and monetary problem as the same. Both were the result of the destructive economic forces unleashed by modernity. Williams attributed the lack of progress in resolving these difficulties to

> the special interests
> which perpetuate the stasis and make it
> profitable.

> They block the release
> that should cleanse and assume
> prerogatives as a private recompense [P 34]

And later on in *Paterson:*

> Money sequestered enriches avarice, makes
> poverty: the direct cause of
> disaster .
>   while the leak drips
> Let out the fire, let the wind go!
> Release the Gamma rays that cure the cancer

The "release" will later be explicitly linked to credit and a "cure" for cancerous social ills—allegorized here as a brain tumor killing a patient while the hospital "penalizes him with surgeon's fees / and accessories at an advance over the / market price" (P 182). This is surely a gibe at the "brain surgeon" economists who serve those "special interests."

> . the cancer, usury. Let credit
> out . out from between the bars
> before the bank windows
>   [P 182–83]

Williams suggests that credit, like the cure for the tumor, is being consciously withheld by special interests and "avaricious" forces inimical to human life. Again, as Pound shows in his cantos about the Monte dei Paschi, the accumulation of capital is contrary to health and fertility and the "generative" impulse. The release of credit is thus connected to the value of art and, by implication, to the cultural values that art embodies.

> . credit, stalled
> in money, conceals the generative
> that thwarts art or buys it (without
> understanding), out of poverty of wit, to
> win, vicariously, the blue ribbon [P 183]

Under Social Credit, credit is not "stalled in money," which distorts credit's true basis in the "generative" power of invention—one of Williams's privileged terms. Douglas understood that the steady increase in productive power, and the invention of new things and processes, was made possible by the cultural heritage, that is, the real capital inherited from prior generations working with nature—the same basis that has long been accepted for art and poetry.

25. To Social Credit people like Munson, Pound's economic syncretism was not so much one step further as one step off the track preparatory to going off the rails altogether. Munson mistakenly believed that "in the nineteen thirties [Pound] began to mix [Social Credit] with Gesellism and finally with Fascism. The result of this veering to the Right was that Pound became an out-and-out fascist propagandist, the Social credit point of view disappeared from his writings, and he was finally indicted for treason in the United States. *By the same token that the Right, the Left and the center are unable to pick up Social credit because it will transform them completely, so Social creditors are unable to join Right, left, or center without ceasing to be Social creditors*" (my emphasis; Munson 372). This truth exposes the mortal weakness of the Social Credit movement: it could not survive compromise. See Gorham Munson, *Aladdin's Lamp*.

26. Surette points out that Pound reviewed *The Natural Economic Order* in *New English Weekly* on January 31, 1935 (Surette 1986 87). The edition at the Brunnenberg with Pound's notes is the translation by Philip Pye, published by the Free-Economy Publishing Company of San Antonio in 1936; it must be a different edition from the one Pound reviewed. This translation is dedicated "to the memory of Moses-Spartacus Henry George and all those who have striven to create an adequate economic basis for peace and goodwill among men and nations" (no page number). I suspect that the dedication is Pye's. Pound began, but apparently never published, another long rambling review of Gesell's book. See YCAL 43, Box 95, Beinecke Library, Yale University.

In the back of *The New Economic Order* are several advertisements for works by E. S. Woodward, with whom Pound corresponded for over thirty years (from 1933 to 1964). There is also an advertisement for a book by Hans Cohrssen, Irving Fisher's assistant, entitled *The Story of Woergl*. Pound corresponded briefly with Cohrssen also and probably found out about the *Schwundgeld* experiment in Woergl from him.

27. See the excellent discussions of this passage in Sieburth, "In Pound We Trust," 153–55, and in Lewis Hyde's *The Gift*, 258–59.

28. I take barter to mean the direct face-to-face exchange of two real goods of equal value. The exchange of goods for labor, or indirect exchange of goods through some intermediate party, brings us into a debt-and-credit system—a system of promises and obligations—that is to say, of signs, which leads to money.

29. Pound probably took all his Nietzsche and much of his sense of continental philosophy generally from his reading of Wyndham Lewis. These epithets closely echo Lewis's satire of Nietzsche in *The Art of Being Ruled*, 113–18.

30. American philosophy has never seen the will in the radically pessimistic light of the Europeans, William James speaks of Schopenhauer's "incurably vicious will-substance" (James 1977 328). Both James and Nietzsche learned much about the affirmative powers from reading Emerson, but Schopenhauer's pessimism seems to have had a decisive effect on Nietzsche.

31. Secondary sources that have influenced my understanding of the will, modernity, and its relationship to the Enlightenment project principally include Art Berman, *Preface to Modernism*; Emilio Gentile, "The Conquest of Modernity";

Jürgen Habermas, *The Philosophical Discourse of Modernity;* Wyndham Lewis, *The Art of Being Ruled;* and Karl Loewith, *From Hegel to Nietzsche* (London: Constable, 1965).

32. Fascism, we could say, following Wyndham Lewis's characterization of the thought of Sorel, is about the production of the hero and the heroic (Lewis 1926 121). Romantic heroes are disorderly persons almost by definition. They do not make systems; they break them. Fearless, active, violent, irresponsible geniuses of action, they transcend reason. The Fascist hero, on the other hand, like his Soviet counterpart, is built on the paradigm of self-sacrifice. His will is identified with the will of the state, which is theoretically the supreme expression of the will of the people.

33. I'm thinking of the "Preface" of *Beyond Good and Evil* (1886), in which Nietzsche warns us of "the dogmatist's error" (Nietzsche 1886 3), that is, the dangers of Platonic idealism and the transcendental "good."

34. The essay does not have numbered pages. For convenience I have assigned the pages numbers here.

35. The essay seems to have been written before Pound had read Gesell but after he had read Fisher; Pound mentions the Gesellite experiment in Woergl without seeming to understand exactly what it was (seventh page).

36. Leon Surette has also commented on this point. See Leon Surette, "Ezra Pound's Fascism: Aberration or Essence?"

37. This is probably a misprint for eight—the number of points in Pound's "Volitionist Economics" program. In a letter to Dewey Pound mentions Mussolini's reaction to his scheme: "He said 'Ugh, these aren't things to answer straight off the bat. No, this one (no. 4) about taxes Ungh! Have to think about THAT.' " Pound continues, "This contrasts happily with our own national administration. I admit I have some official stationery stating that 'the administration is giving respectful attention to all points raised in yr. letter' " (November 13, 1934, YCAL 43, Beinecke Library, Yale University).

4: Fertility Rites/Financial Rites: Pound, Williams, and the Political Economy of Sex

1. See Carlo Ginzburg, *Night Battles: Witchcraft and Agrarian Cults in the Sixteenth and Seventeenth Centuries* (1966)(New York: Penguin, 1983), and *Ecstasies: Deciphering the Witches' Sabbath* (New York: Penguin, 1991).

2. Surette has now revised his earlier belief that such mysteries actually existed, as he strongly argued in *A Light from Eleusis.* The connection between fertility cults and the courtly love tradition he now regards as a fantasy of occult neo-Platonism. See Leon Surette, *The Birth of Modernism,* 96–122. According to Ginzburg, however: "Present research now establishes, in an area such as the Friuli [the region of Italy from which the inquisitorial testimony in *Night Battles* has been drawn], where Germanic and Slavic traditions came together, the positive existence at a relatively late date (from c. 1570) of a fertility cult whose participants, the benandanti, represented themselves as defenders of harvests and the fertility of fields. On the one hand this belief is tied to a larger complex of traditions (connected, in turn with the myth of nocturnal gatherings over which female dieties named Perchta, Holda, Diana, presided) in an area that extends from Alsace to Hesse and from Bavaria to Switzerland. On the other hand it is found in an almost

identical form in the lands which once comprised Livonia (present day Latvia and Estonia). Given this geographic spread it may not be too daring to suggest that in antiquity these beliefs must once have covered much of central Europe" (1983 xx).

3. See *Speculum of the Other Woman,* trans. Gillian C. Gill (Ithaca: Cornell University Press, 1983). The term "economy of the same" is pervasive throughout Irigaray's work because it is opposed to her master term "sexual difference." The most extended discussion can be found in Luce Irigaray, *An Ethics of Sexual Difference,* trans. Carolyn Burke and Gillian C. Gill (Ithaca: Cornell University Press, 1993).

4. Kevin Oderman's *Ezra Pound and the Erotic Medium* focuses on Pound's interest in the " 'mediumistic' potentialities of sexuality; its ability to stimulate visions" (xi). Richard Sieburth's *Instigations* concerns Pound's relation to Rémy de Gourmont, his *Physique de l'amour* was Englished by Pound as *The Natural Philosophy of Love* in 1922: "Gourmont's work . . . provided scientific evidence of the phallic synthesis" between Amor and Eros, love and sex "towards which Pound was . . . striving" (129). Surette calls the relation between Amor and Usura "the imaginative heart of [Pound's] poem" (1979 67). All of these works depend heavily but to varying degrees on the chapter "Psychology and Troubadours" in Pound's *Spirit of Romance* (1910) and the "Translator's Postscript" to Rémy de Gourmont's *Natural Philosophy of Love* (1922) and numerous cantos. See Kevin Oderman, *Ezra Pound and the Erotic Medium* (Chapel Hill: Duke University Press, 1986), and Richard Sieburth, *Instigations* (Cambridge, Mass.: Harvard University Press, 1978).

5. I choose these terms without prejudice to try to suggest the economic bearing of sexuality for Pound. In his agrarian scheme there can be no significant difference between production and reproduction. His brief against homosexuality and the historical tropic links between homosexuality and usury, which date from Aristotle, will be discussed later in the chapter. Incidentally, Brooks Adams linked the ascendancy of the aristocracy of bankers to a "marked loss of fecundity among the more costly [i.e., money-using as opposed to wealth-producing] races." See Brooks Adams, *The Law of Civilization and Decay,* 349–51.

6. The actual lecture that Pound mentions having heard (*SR* 91n) is lost, but Surette publishes a passage from G. R. S. Mead's *Simon Magus* (1892), which, he argues, must have been like the kind of thing that Pound probably heard: "Of the universal Aeons there are two shoots, without beginning or end, springing from one Root, which is the Power invisible, inapprehensible Silence. Of these shoots one is manifested from above, which is the Great Power, the Universal Mind ordering all things, male, and the other (is manifested) from below, the great Thought, female producing all things" (quoted in Surette 1979 60–61). How Pound justified these ideas via a long detour through Gnostic philosophy is described by Surette (1979 57–65).

7. This phrase is a chapter title in Munson's *Aladdin's Lamp* (1945), a brilliant look at American history from a Social Credit viewpoint. In this book, dedicated to A. R. Orage, Munson seems to have taken on the task of writing a Social Credit version of Keynes's *The Economic Consequences of the Peace* for World War II. He succeeds. It is a pity that this rare book, long out of print, is not better known.

8. The documents of incorporation from which Pound "translates" in his poem date the Monte to December 30, 1622. Timothy Green says that the Monte dei Paschi "was founded by the city-state of Siena in 1472" (60). The earlier date

seems to refer to the Monte in its original form as another Monti di Pietà. According to his article in the *Smithsonian*, the current Monte has assets of some $72 billion; compare "From a Pawnshop to a Patron of the Arts in Five Centuries," *Smithsonian* 22:4 (July 1991), 59–69.

9. The documents from which Pound worked have been printed and translated in *Paideuma*. See Ben Kimpel and T. C. Duncan Eaves, "The Sources of Cantos XLII and XLIII," *Paideuma* 6:3 (Winter 1977), 333–58, and "The Sources of the Leopoldine Cantos," *Paideuma* 7:1–2 (Spring-Fall 1978), 249–77.

10. Unfortunately, as Hugh Kenner points out, Pound doesn't say this so plainly in the actual canto (Canto 42) when he introduces the Monte. In Canto 42 Pound leaves out any mention of sheep, so an important point is obscured (Kenner 1971 427).

11. The controversy is laid out in Benjamin Nelson's *The Idea of Usury*, chap. 1. Lewis Hyde cites Nelson's work as the basis for his chapter, "Usury: A History of Gift Exchange," in *The Gift*, 109–40.

12. The linkage of the ideas "Mount" and "fund" in one word is like the "ideogramic method of . . . heaping together the components of thought" (*SP* 209).

13. Pound wants us to translate *luoghi*, "places," as "lots" or "shares." See Canto 42:

> And that whoso puts in money shall have lots in the Monte
> that yield 5% interest
> and that these shareholders shall receive their due fruit
> [42:211]

14. The notion that a "five-percent contract" is not necessarily usurious has a long history. Interest of 4 or 5 percent was considered by Luther and Melancthon, among others, to be allowable and even necessary for the emergent capitalism of the Reformation period. See Nelson 43–47, and Lewis Hyde 123–25.

15. Not the same William Paterson who was governor of New Jersey and for whom Paterson, New Jersey—and thus Williams's *Paterson*—are named. According to Terrell, Paterson's statements came to Pound via Christopher Hollis's *Two Nations* (London: n.p., 1935), 30 (Terrell 181 26n).

16. So does Arthur J. Penty, the English economist who gave us the word "post-industrial." In a brief chapter entitled "Usury and Prices," Penty expresses the belief that "society has been brought to the edge of a precipice over which it certainly will go, unless in the meantime measures are taken to remove the cancer that is exercising such a disintegrating and disrupting influence" (*Protection and the Social Problem*, 229–30).

17. This statement opens a really bizarre "review" of John Buchan's *Oliver Cromwell*, which Pound wrote for the *New English Weekly* in 1935.

18. See Norman O. Brown's classic *Life Against Death*, 2d ed. (Middletown: Wesleyan University Press, 1985).

19. It shows up in the poems of the Populist poet Edgar Lee Masters. Take, for example, the poem "Ralph Rhodes" in *The Spoon River Anthology*:

> All they said was true:
> I wrecked my father's bank with my loans
> To dabble in wheat; but this was true—

I was buying wheat for him as well,
Who couldn't margin the deal in his name
Because of his church relationship. [154]

20. Banks continuously insist that they help money "grow" as though they were deliberately confusing procreation with the supplementation of interest. My bank, National Westminster, or "Nat West," has been handing out free kits on growing coleus. You get a little pot of soil with some seeds and instructions on how to plant the seeds. "Nat West/Advantage Banking/Watch Your Money Grow," it says on the white plastic pot. My coleus is doing nicely, but contrary to the advertising, watching it grow is nothing like watching my money grow—because money can't grow. Money can only be supplemented with more money.

21. One can hear Whitman in this as well: "The president," he charges, in "The Eighteenth Presidency!" "eats dirt and excrement for his daily meals, likes it, and tries to force it on the States. The cushions of the Presidency are nothing but filth and blood" (Whitman 1310).

22. This scene may also have something to do with Williams's bitterness over the rich British socialite and novelist Bryher (Winifred Ellerman), H. D.'s lesbian lover and the wife—via a marriage of convenience—of Robert McAlmon, Williams's "closest friend" (Mariani 51). Williams makes clear in his *Autobiography* that he believed the impecunious McAlmon made a "disastrous" mistake in marrying Bryher, which according to Williams destroyed both his talent and his life (*A* 178).

23. Butler, this "vain and imperious President of Columbia University" (Hofstadter 1968 285), may have been remembered by Williams because, among other things, he had condoned the investigation of his faculty for possible disloyalty after America's entry into World War I (Hofstadter 1968 285). The firing of two faculty members for pacifism had caused Charles Beard, then chairman of the Department of Political Science, to resign in protest (Hofstadter 1968 285–86). One of the professors fired was Henry Wadsworth Longfellow Dana. In 1911 he had lived in the same *pension* in Paris as T. S. Eliot and Jean Verdenal—to whose memory Eliot would dedicate "The Love Song of J. Alfred Prufrock." See *The Letters of T. S. Eliot*, vol. 1, edited by Valerie Eliot (New York: Harcourt Brace Jovanovich, 1988), 17, 20.

5: Poesis Versus Production: The Economic Defense of Poetry in the Age of Corporate Capitalism

1. The concept of "Corporate Capitalism" and its periodization come from William Appleton Williams, *The Contours of American History* (Cleveland: World, 1961). In a note to *The Corporate Reconstruction of American Capitalism, 1890–1916*, Sklar, one of Williams's most important students, notes: "It may be fairly said that William A. Williams established the concept of corporate capitalism as an essential periodization of United States political, social, and intellectual, not only economic, history since the 1890's. Williams's phrase (*Contours* 343–478) was 'The Age of Corporate Capitalism,' and he dated the period from 1882 to the 1960's (and presumably beyond)" (1988 18n). If Sklar is right, then the social and intellectual, and therefore cultural, manifestations of the new Corporate Age ought to be evident in American poetry.

2. Burke recalls this in an addendum to the 1953 reissue of *Counter-state-*

ment. The essay, "Curriculum Criticae," is rehearsed in a letter to Malcolm Cowley dated May 3, 1950. Burke never worked up his notes, but what he learned informs much of *Permanence and Change* (1935) and *Attitudes Towards History* (1937)—especially the fascinating footnotes. See also Paul Jay, ed., *Selected Correspondence of Kenneth Burke and Malcolm Cowley* (Berkeley: University of California Press, 1990), 290–93.

3. Important exceptions are Earle Davis's *Vision Fugitive,* Flory's *The American Ezra Pound,* and Richard Sieburth, "In Pound We Trust: The Economy of Poetry/The Poetry of Economics," *Critical Inquiry* 14 (Autumn 1987), 142–72. Redman's *Ezra Pound and Italian Fascism* is a fair and balanced account of the trajectory of Pound's political economics. In *The Pound Era,* Hugh Kenner is something of an apologist. Two of the most strident attacks on Pound's politics, economics, and anti-Semitism are Robert Casillo's exhaustive and fascinating *The Genealogy of Demons: The Myths of Ezra Pound* and Andrew Parker's morally confused "Ezra Pound and the 'Economy' of Anti-Semitism."

4. On Zukofsky and economic poetry, see my "Poetry and the Age."

5. The argument anticipates Heidegger's "The Question Concerning Technology" (1954). There Heidegger invokes poesis as a "bringing-forth" and tries to make it commensurate with "modern technology and, implicitly, mass commodity production. He sees this latter sort of enterprise as a "challenging" (*Herausfordern*) and proposes that hidden within the challenge is a "granting" (*gewähren*), which, properly understood, might allow us to confront the essence of things and thus of ourselves. Heidegger's notion of granting, which invokes the idea of the gift, is therefore consistent with Lewis Hyde's "gift economy." See Martin Heidegger, *Basic Writings,* 287–317.

6. Other poets were trying to do the same thing but not within Modernism. Edgar Lee Masters, Vachel Lindsay, and Carl Sandburg were actively promoting Populist ideology throughout the 1930s. See Michael Yatron, *America's Literary Revolt* (1959) (Freeport: Books for Libraries Press, 1969). Dozens of poets on the Left were also announcing the coming victory of the proletariat, but they were not Modernists either.

7. This acceptance of modern industrial life as an irrevocable fact is one aspect of these poets' Modernism. Other contemporary poets—I'm thinking particularly of Masters—were not Modernists precisely because they rejected modern life along with Modernist ways of putting poems together. Pound and Masters were both profoundly influenced by Browning, for example. The difference is that Pound wanted to go beyond him, to exceed the lessons of the master. Pound realized as early as Canto 2 that there could be only "one Sordello" (2:6), and *The Cantos* are wholly his own from that moment. Masters could only do a good job of repeating Browning in his *Domesday Book* (1920). The inquest into the death of Eleanor Murray is a skillful appropriation of Browning's technical discoveries in *The Ring and the Book* (1868–69) as well as an analysis of "what's wrong with America" circa 1920, but it speaks constantly of returning to halcyon Jeffersonian days. Pound was affected by the same longing, but his poetry by its method acknowledges that such a return does not mean going back. Rather, a long circle *forward* is the only answer. Modernism in this sense is more than a matter of style. It is an acceptance of the conditions of modernity and the priority of history, technical developments, above all the pressures of the political economy that has created and has been created by modernity.

8. *Poetry* 46:4 (July 1935), 222–27.

9. Burke's own offering at the "First American Writer's Conference," entitled "Revolutionary Symbolism in America," exposed him to stinging criticism and accusations of treason and even Nazi sympathies. For a full discussion of this paper and its implications, see Frank Lentricchia, *Criticism and Social Change*, 21–38.

10. Here Burke points toward the deconstruction of the privileged place of "use value" and labor in Marxism recently undertaken by Jean Baudrillard. See "The Concept of Labor" in *The Mirror of Production*, chap. 1.

11. *Poetry* 44:4 (July 1934), 210–15.

12. *Poetry* 44:6 (September 1934), 351–54.

13. Burnshaw recalls this exchange in *Robert Frost Himself*, 51–53. For another, similar exchange, see Edmund Wilson's account of the debate over Mike Gold's views on Thornton Wilder in the pages of the *New Republic* during the autumn of 1930. See "The Economic Interpretation of Wilder" (500–3) and "The Literary Class War" (534–39), reprinted in *Shores of Light*.

14. On the impact of these issues on British poets during the same period, see Samuel Hynes, *The Auden Generation* (Princeton: Princeton University Press, 1976).

15. See "In Time of War," Canto 16, which ends:

And maps can really point to places
Where life is evil now:
Nanking: Dachau [1979 72]

16. The justification for mass murder in the Third Reich or Stalin's Russia was "History." Hannah Arendt quotes one of Himmler's speeches to his troops: "To have stuck it out and, apart from exceptions caused by human weakness, to have remained decent, that is what has made us hard. This is a page of glory in our history which has never been written and which is never to be written" (105). As in Auden's "Spain," the "struggle" requires sacrifices—here the "decent" sacrifice of conscience made by the murderers doing their difficult duty to history! See Hannah Arendt, *Eichmann in Jerusalem* (New York: Penguin, 1963).

17. This is a question asked in a questionnaire circulated by *New Verse* in 1934. Wallace Stevens answered, "Not consciously. Perhaps I don't like the word *useful*" (1989 307).

18. Ron Loewinsohn says that the essays, notes, and fragments in *The Embodiment of Knowledge* were written between "1928 and 1930" (*EK* xix).

19. See Burke: "The great influx of information has led the artist also to lay his emphasis on the giving of information—with the result that art tends more and more to substitute the psychology of the hero (the subject) for the psychology of the audience. Under such an attitude, when form is preserved, it is preserved as an annex, a luxury, or, as some feel, a downright affectation. It remains, though sluggish, like a human appendix, for occasional demands are still made upon it; but its true vigor is gone, since it is no longer organically required. Proposition: The hypertrophy of the psychology of information is accompanied by the corresponding atrophy of the psychology of form" (Burke 1931 32–33).

20. On the importance of "Build Soil" and Frost's potential alliance with the Left, see Stanley Burnshaw, *Robert Frost Himself*, 49–69.

21. See the discussion in Poirier, *Robert Frost: The Work of Knowing*, 235–43.

22. This last sentence apparently inspired the subtitle of Longenbach's superb critical biography.

23. Filene's *Successful Living in the Machine Age* (New York: Simon and Schuster, 1931), begins with a definition of "mass production." It reads, in part: "Mass production . . . is *production for the masses.* It changes the whole social order. It necessitates the abandonment of all class thinking, and the substitution of fact-finding for tradition, not only by business-men but by all who wish to live successfully in the Machine Age. But it is not standardizing human life. It is liberating the masses, rather, from the struggle for mere existence and enabling them, for the first time in human history, to give their attention to more distinctly human problems" (Filene's emphasis; 1).

24. C. H. Douglas was one of the first to see this point. See *Social Credit* 108–28. See also Stuart Chase, *The Economy of Abundance* (New York: Macmillan, 1934), 208–34. For a discussion of structural unemployment and the problem of self, see Livingston 1994.

25. *Poetry* 44:4 (July 1934), 220–25. It is reprinted in *Something to Say,* 55–59.

26. Williams's whole polemic on measure in poetry is predicated (as all such quantitative discussions must be) on this fundamental distinction between a poem's matter and its manner. Williams understands the poem to be "primarily" its form or manner, not the "secondary" information it carries (*EK* 141). For the same reasons Williams waged war on the sonnet. See *EK* 17, *SE* 291. In the "Introduction" to *The Wedge* (1944), he would repeat his comparison of the poem to the "machine made of words" (*CP2* 54).

27. *Paterson* does not, of course, explicitly deal with religious questions—Williams surely has Eliot's recent *Four Quartets* (1943) in mind (*SE* 289).

28. I have no doubt that, had Williams chosen to put a leaflet of the Socialist Workers Party in his poem, it would have been considered "Communist" by many in 1951. Williams may have wanted to expose such attitudes.

29. Flory opens her first book on Pound and *The Cantos* with the declaration that "the poet's personal struggle is the most dramatic part of *The Cantos,* and is finally responsible for its unity." This observation perhaps applies even more obviously to *Paterson,* where the difficulties of writing, highlighted by Cress's (Marcia Nardi's) letters, quite consciously become subject matter within the poem (Flory 1980 7).

6: Dewey, Williams, and the Pragmatic Poem

1. Auden believed that people thought they wanted to be artists or writers in part because the artist is seen as the last self-reliant producer: "A man can be proud of being a worker—someone, that is, who fabricates enduring objects, but in our society, the process of fabrication has been so rationalized in the interests of speed, economy and quantity that the part played by the individual factory employee has become too small for it to be meaningful for him as work, and practically all workers have been reduced to laborers. It is only natural, therefore, that the arts which cannot be rationalized in this way—the artist still remains personally responsible for what he makes—should fascinate those who, because they have no marked talent, are afraid, with good reason, that all they have to look forward to is a lifetime of meaningless labor. This fascination is not due to the nature of art itself, but to

the way in which an artist works; he, and in our age, almost nobody else, is his own master." See W. H. Auden, *The Dyer's Hand*, 73.

2. Livingston's argument is in the tradition of Rorty's "neo-pragmatism," even as it augments, revises and heavily criticizes Rorty for his anti-historicism. In effect, Livingston uses William James against Rorty's Dewey. Rorty proposes (Deweyan) Pragmatism as the bearer of "social hope" over and against the Nietzschean line then being taken by Foucault in a 1980 paper (see Rorty 1982 191–210 esp. 207). John Patrick Diggins criticizes what he sees as the false promises of Pragmatism in *The Promise of Pragmatism*. "Dewey," he says, "should be regarded as a half-way modernist, a brilliant philosopher who, sensing the implications of modernism, did everything possible to avoid its conclusions" (1994 5).

3. James says: "I believe that consciousness (as it is commonly represented, either as an entity, or as pure activity, but in any case as being fluid, inextended, diaphanous, devoid of self-content, but directly self-knowing—spiritual in short), I believe, I say, that this sort of consciousness is pure fancy, and that the sum of concrete realities which the word consciousness should cover deserves quite a different description" (James 1977 190).

4. As Livingston points out, so was A. N. Whitehead. In 1925, he was claiming in *Science and the Modern World* that the "modern epoch of philosophy lasted from 1637, when Descartes *Discourse on Method* appeared, to 1904 when James's essay ["Does Consciousness Exist?"] appeared" (Livingston 1994 258). Williams read Whitehead's book with attention on the steamer to Europe in 1927. He immediately responded with "a ten page thing called *Philosophy in Literature*" (September 30, 1927, *SL* 84–85), which I have not been able to identify. He immediately wrote Flossie about *Science and the Modern World*, urging her to read the book (September 27, 1927, *SL* 79). Whitehead's book was also one goad that provoked Wyndham Lewis's *Time and Western Man* (1927). Lewis discusses it in chapter 11 (156–61).

5. Burke noticed that Dewey was an economic determinist in the broad sense. Burke finds him similar in this regard to Marx. See *Permanence and Change* (1935), 38.

6. The text I am using is confected from the original *Individualism Old and New* (1930) for use in *Intelligence in the Modern World* (1939), a collection of Dewey's thought edited in collaboration with Dewey by Joseph Ratner, who contributed an introduction fully 241 pages long! A note at the beginning of the essay called "The Individual in Cultural Crisis" says that it is "from *Individualism Old and New*. The passages have been selected and arranged from all parts of the book. Ed." (Dewey 1939 405n).

7. For a strong reading of "The Wanderer" that stresses "Romantic idealism" in that poem, and in Williams's career generally, see Carl Rapp, *William Carlos Williams and Romantic Idealism* (Hanover: University Press of New England, 1984), esp. chap. 1.

8. Actually, this passage is quoted by Bloom from an unnamed essay by Thomas Frosch. Bloom finds his "lucid summary more concise than I have been able to be" (27; no source provided). This itself is an odd crossing of influence that Emerson had previously noted: "Observe, also, that a writer appears to more advantage in the pages of another book than in his own. In his own, he waits as a candidate for your approbation; in another's, he is a lawgiver." See Emerson, "Quotation and Originality," *Letters and Social Aims*, Riverside ed. (Boston: Houghton Mifflin, 1896), 156.

9. There are two slightly different versions of "The Wanderer." I am using the first version (*CP1* 27–36) because I assume that there the "Scene of Instruction" is less mediated by retrospection. The revision appeared in *Al Que Quiere* (1917) (*CP1* 108–17).

10. Williams seems to have regarded her as his English grandmother (*A* 60), Emily Dickinson Wellcome. With Harold Bloom's conception of "poetic misprision" in mind, we can, I think justifiably, disregard Williams's own repression (Bloom 1973 7).

11. Williams will often return in poems like "A Place (Any Place) to Transcend All Places" (*CP2* 163–66) or *Paterson* (for example, *P* 164) to the verticality of Manhattan as mirroring financial speculation. The city is, of course, a familiar scene for the specifically Modernist poem. "It could be argued that Modernist literature was born in the city and with Baudelaire—especially with his discovery that crowds mean loneliness" (G. H. Hyde 337), begins one typical essay. The importance of "The Wanderer" lies partly in its generic quality. The poem is just one more piece of evidence that something was importantly different in the modern period. I call it "corporate relations of production"; it has been called many other things. See G. H. Hyde, "The Poetry of the City," 337–48.

12. As "The Wanderer" was first published in *The Egoist* (March 1914) when T. S. Eliot was the editor, there is a real possibility of a direct influence.

13. There is considerable debate as to whether the poem is "complete" at the end of book 4. I would argue that, formally, *Paterson* was finished in 1951. Psychologically, it was obviously not finished—the unresolved struggle with Whitman goaded Williams to supplement the poem. Fragments of a sixth book were recovered after Williams's death in 1963.

14. See Henry Adams. History is "in essence incoherent and immoral, history had either to be taught as such—or falsified." In any case it must avoid the temptation of telling agreeable tales to "arouse sluggish-minded boys" (quoted in Diggins 483).

15. At least one reader, M. L. Rosenthal, did seem to recognize *Paterson* as a pragmatic poem even while dwelling on its "human-ecological mysticism" (Doyle 237).

16. *Dial* 67:6 (June 1920), 684–88. Williams read John Dewey all his life and responded to him more than once in essays. In 1933, Kenneth Burke complained that Williams's philosophical meditations in *The Embodiment of Knowledge* were too much informed by Dewey (Mariani 336). In that book, Williams openly suggests that Dewey and others should seek a solution to the problems of an American education in poetry (*EK* 7). His "basic affinity with Dewey's liberal philosophy" has been noted in his essay called "Revelation," printed in the *Yale Poetry Review* in 1947, which also shows the influence of William James (*SE* 268, Mariani 544). For a discussion of the profound effect that Dewey's essay had on Williams, see William Wasserstrom, "William Carlos Williams: The Healing Image," 40–53, especially 41.

17. September 17 was Williams's birthday.

18. My colleague David Rosenwasser knows a similar word game using the syllable "hob." Is "tut" a reference to King Tut, the Pharaoh Tutankhamen? If so, is this a self-consciously "africanized" word game? And created by whom? By Enall's friend? Or by Williams himself?

19. See note 6.

20. We find something similar in Burke's *Attitudes Toward History* (1937): "In

America, whatever resistance arose from local communities, could be obliterated by the unifying devices of abstract finance, which could control the destiny of the frontier (periphery) by controlling the organizing resources of the political center. The rationale of abstract finance served as a kind of smear that could be washed over the genius of particular localities, greatly obscuring the particular characteristics that might have developed as the result of geographical factors or racial tradition. This rationale provided the mould to shape the cultural mass poured from the "melting pot" (Burke 1937 146–47). Burke's description echoes Dewey's "Americanism and Localism," although in Burke's version, "abstract finance" plays the role of "Americanization." His critique is more pointed, and is informed, as Dewey's could not have been, by the experience of the Great Depression.

21. We could say that Pound never makes this move. In trying to make his poem relevant to the corporate age, he never wonders whether the new social conditions he has observed have created new kinds of people; *The Cantos* are populated entirely by peasants, politicians, artists, warriors, sages, all ancient archetypes standing by to renovate modernity. The worker as such, appears as he or she does in newspapers—as Other, far away, restless, and unhappy.

22. The Catholic Church as an institution is, of course, the original corporation and the object too of a certain strain of nativist paranoia within Populism—the Ku Klux Klan, for instance, has been a violently anti-Catholic organization.

23. It is very likely that these passages, which sound so much like those of Claude Bowers in his popular *Jefferson and Hamilton* (1925), were inspired by Bowers's book. The ideological connection is consistent; any direct influence, is, of course, only speculation.

24. See, for example, Pound, "The Economic Nature of the United States" (*SP* 139).

25. This characterization is apparently Thomas Edison's. Williams was working from antibank pamphlets put out by Alfredo and Clara Studer. (Conarroe says "Studa.") The pamphlet from which Williams excerpted the passage on page 74 of *Paterson* is called "Thomas Edison on the Money Subject." I gather, then, that Edison called the Federal Reserve System a "National Usury System" (see *P* 274, Conarroe 156).

26. This seems to be an echo of lines that satirically lamented the passing of the aesthete Mauberly from the scene in Pound's *Hugh Selwyn Mauberley* (1920):

Mouths biting empty air
The still stone dogs,
Caught in metamorphosis, were
Left him as epilogues [*Personae* 200]

27. For a sophisticated Freudian/Marxist reading of this passage, see Heinzelman, 234–75.

28. Henry Adams used the "dynamo" as the symbol of modernity in the *Education* (1914). Stuart Chase's popular *The Economy of Abundance* (1934) makes frequent references to "the power age" and symbolizes it with the turbine. Gorham Munson, who is probably in the back of Williams's mind in this passage, premises his *Aladdin's Lamp* (1945) on the concept of the turbine-driven "power age" (taken from a Federal Writer's Project Publication [*P* 272n]).

29. I notice that Munson uses a similar image in the prologue to *Aladdin's Lamp*, where he restates the tale of Aladdin as a parable of the Great Depression. In Munson's fable, an evil "Numerologist" leads Aladdin to a cave to fetch an old lamp. He is given a ring, inscribed with the word "debt" with which he may enter the cave and find the lamp. When Aladdin retrieves the lamp he wants the magician to help him out of the cave. The magician wants the lamp first. Alladin refuses. The magician then "invoke[s] a power named Mammon" and repeats a spell which sounded to Aladdin like "four clothes" [foreclose] (1). Immediately Aladdin is sealed in utter darkness underground. In his fright Aladdin summons the Genie and orders him to "Deliver me from this depression below the earth's crust" (Munson 2). The lamp is credit (Munson 211).

7: Overcoming Modernity: Representing the Corporation and the Promise of Pluralism

1. Pound's exposé of Zaharoff is concurrent with several others. According to Terrell, Pound based much of the canto on *The Man Behind the Scenes: The Career of Sir Basil Zaharoff* (London: n.p., 1929). *Merchants of Death: A Study of the International Armaments Industry*, published in New York in 1934 (the same year as Canto 38), by H. C. Engelbrecht and F. C. Hanighen, devotes a chapter to "The Supersalesman of Death." Zaharoff was a remarkable, even satanic, master of wheeling and dealing. As Pound suggests, Zaharoff knew how to play one side off against another. The story of his tricking Maxim, which Pound relates in Canto 18 (where Maxim is called Biers, 18:80–81) is corroborated by Engelbrecht and Hanighen (98–100). His probably apocryphal feats, such as staging his own death (compare 18:81), are matched by his supposed role as an undercover agent in the "Turpin Affair" (Engelbrecht and Hanighen 101). My point is that by focusing on such a colorful character, Pound's exposition by its method actually protects "the Vickers Octopus." See Engelbrecht and Hanighen illustrations 84–85.

2. Zaharoff was Russian Orthodox in religion (Engelbrecht and Hanighen 101). Pound's Metevsky is of indeterminate religion, but given the anti-Semitic tendency that is evident as *The Cantos* continue, Metevsky's Eastern European surname seems to suggest the Populist "jew," at least in the loose sense of the term, as Pound used it until the late 1930s.

3. Unities are always coercive because they are Absolutist, as Nietzsche points out in the "Preface" to *Beyond Good and Evil:* "The worst, most durable, and most dangerous of all errors so far was a dogmatist error—namely Plato's invention of the pure spirit and the godd as such" (Nietzsche 1886 3). And as James remarks in "The One and the Many": "Those who believe in the Absolute, as the all-knower is termed, usually say they do so for coercive reasons, which [they think] clear thinkers can not evade" (James 1977 411).

4. Overcoming this modern sense of helplessness is John Dewey's central theme, as it is Mussolini's, Pound's, and Williams's. A more recent endorsement of this reading of Modernity is its use as a premise by Jürgen Habermas in *The Philosophical Discourse of Modernity*, 1–22. See also Wyndham Lewis, *The Art of Being Ruled* (1926), especially 21–23, and Berman 7–8.

5. On the influence of "Futurism" on Pound, see Lawrence Rainey, "The Creation of the Avant-Garde: F. T. Marinetti and Ezra Pound," *Modernism/Modernity*

1:3 (September 1994), 195–219; Vincent Sherry, *Ezra Pound, Wyndham Lewis, and Radical Modernism* (Oxford: Oxford University Press, 1993).

6. Diggins recounts a letter that Dewey sent James in 1891, in which Dewey worried about how " 'class interests' can affect inquiry. It is not enough, concluded Dewey, that philosophical knowledge satisfy subjective needs; it must also 'secure the conditions of its objective expression' " (Diggins 140–41). Obviously it can do so only where there is freedom of the press, of speech and expression. In fact, newspaper censorship (in the United States) prompted Dewey to identify the problem.

7. Tim Redman concludes that Pound was a "Left-Fascist" and quotes the remarkable curriculum that Pound hoped to publish as a series of books during the brief duration of the Salo Republic: " '1. Upton Sinclair Letters to Judd. 2. Lenin: The teachings of Karl Marx. 3. Lenin: Imperialism. 4. Stalin: Leninism. 5. Stalin: Response to American Union Members. 6. Karl Marx: The England That We Fight (Chapter X of Kapital),' as well as works by Kitson, Overholser, Gesell and Douglas. He proposed to call the series 'Library of Political Culture, 2nd. Series, Parties of the Opposition' " (Redman 273). This proposal, dated March 28, 1945, shows that Pound was anything but an orthodox Fascist. See Redman's crucial chapter, "The Republic of Salo and Left-Wing Fascism" (233–74). Redman even speaks of Pound's "Jeffersonian fascism" (236).

8. Williams emphasized the importance of "the American idiom" in an interview with Mike Wallace, which is also part of *Paterson* (*P* 304n).

BIBLIOGRAPHY

Adams, Brooks. *The Law of Civilization and Decay.* New York: Macmillan, 1896.

Adams, Henry. *Novels, Mont St. Michel, The Education.* New York: Library of America, 1983.

Agresti, Olivia Rosetti. "Economics of Fascism." *Encyclopedia Britannica.* 14th ed. (1929), vol. 9, pp. 104–6.

Auden, W. H. *The Dyer's Hand.* New York: Vintage, 1968.

——. *Selected Poems.* Edited by Edward Mendelson. New York: Vintage, 1979.

Bailyn, Bernard. *The Ideological Origins of the American Revolution.* Cambridge, Mass.: Belknap Press, 1967.

Bataille, Georges. "The Notion of Expenditure" (1933). Translated by Allan Stoekl. *Raritan* 3:3 (1984): 62–79.

Baudrillard, Jean. *America.* London: Verso, 1989.

——. *For a Critique of the Political Economy of the Sign.* St. Louis: Telos, 1981.

——. *The Mirror of Production.* St. Louis: Telos, 1975.

Beard, Charles A. *Economic Interpretation of the Constitution of the United States* (1913). New York: Free Press, 1965.

Becker, Carl L. *The Declaration of Independence: A Study in the History of Political Ideas* (1922). New York: Vintage, 1958.

Beer, M. *An Inquiry into Physiocracy* (1939). New York: Russell and Russell, 1966.

Berman, Art. *Preface to Modernism.* Urbana: University of Illinois Press, 1994.

Bernstein, Michael André. *The Tale of the Tribe.* Princeton: Princeton University Press, 1980.

Berry, Wendell. *Home Economics.* San Francisco: North Point Press, 1987.

Bloom, Harold. "Agon: Revisionism and Critical Personality." *Raritan* 1:1 (1981): 18–47.

——. *The Anxiety of Influence.* London: Oxford University Press, 1973.

——. "Criticism, Canon-Formation, and Prophecy: The Sorrows of Facticity." *Raritan* 3:3 (1984): 1–20.

——. *Poetry and Repression.* New Haven: Yale University Press, 1976.

Booth, E. J. R. "A Commentary on 'The Mysteries of the Federal Reserve System' by Jerry Voorhis." *Paideuma* 11:3 (1982): 498–502.

Bowers, Claude G. *Jefferson and Hamilton: The Struggle for Democracy in America.* Boston: Houghton Mifflin, 1925.

——. *My Life*. New York: Simon and Schuster, 1962.

Bradbury, Malcolm, and MacFarlane, James, eds. *Modernism*. Harmondsworth, Essex: Penguin, 1976.

Brooke-Rose, Christine. *A ZBC of Ezra Pound*. Berkeley: University of California Press, 1971.

Bullert, Gary. *The Politics of John Dewey*. Buffalo: Prometheus Books, 1983.

Burke, Kenneth. *Attitudes Toward History* (1937). 3d ed. Berkeley: University of California Press, 1984.

——. *Counter-statement* (1931). Berkeley: University of California Press, 1968.

——. *A Grammar of Motives* (1945). Berkeley: University of California Press, 1969.

——. *Language as Symbolic Action*. Berkeley: University of California Press, 1966.

——. *Permanence and Change* (1935). 3d ed. Berkeley: University of California Press, 1984.

——. *The Philosophy of Literary Form* (1941). Berkeley: University of California Press, 1973.

——. *A Rhetoric of Motives* (1950). Berkeley: University of California Press, 1969.

Burnshaw, Stanley. *Robert Frost Himself*. New York: George Braziller, 1986.

Cappon, Lester J. *The Adams-Jefferson Letters*. Chapel Hill: University of North Carolina Press, 1959.

Carpenter, Humphrey. *Serious Character: The Life of Ezra Pound*. Boston: Houghton Mifflin, 1988.

Casillo, Robert. *The Genealogy of Demons: Anti-Semitism, Fascism, and the Myths of Ezra Pound*. Evanston: Northwestern University Press, 1988.

Cody, Thomas. "Adams, Mussolini, and the Personality of Genius." *Paideuma* 18:3 (1988): 77–103.

Conarroe, Joel. *William Carlos Williams' Paterson*. Philadelphia: University of Pennsylvania Press, 1970.

Conrad, Bryce. "The Deceptive Ground of History." *William Carlos Williams Review* 15:1 (Spring 1989): 22–40.

——. "Engendering History: The Sexual Structure of William Carlos Williams' *In the American Grain*." *Twentieth Century Literature* 35 (Fall 1989): 254–78.

——. *Refiguring America*. Urbana: University of Illinois Press, 1990.

Cord, Stephen B. *Henry George: Dreamer or Realist?* Philadelphia: University of Pennsylvania Press, 1965.

Coyle, Michael. " 'A Profounder Didacticism': Ruskin, Orage, and Pound's Reception of Social Credit." *Paideuma* 17:1 (Spring 1988): 7–28.

Croly, Herbert. *The Promise of American Life* (1909). Cambridge, Mass.: Belknap Press, 1965.

Cronon, William. *Changes in the Land*. New York: Hill and Wang, 1983.

Cushman, Stephen. *William Carlos Williams and the Meanings of Measure*. New Haven: Yale University Press, 1985.

Dasenbrock, Reed Way. *The Literary Vorticism of Ezra Pound and Wyndham Lewis*. Baltimore: Johns Hopkins University Press, 1985.

Davis, Earle. *Vision Fugitive*. Lawrence: University of Kansas Press, 1968.

Destutt de Tracy, Antoine-Louis-Claude. *Treatise on Political Economy* (1817). New York: August M. Kelley, 1970.

Dewey, John. "Americanism and Localism." *Dial* 68:6 (June 1920): 684–88.

———. *Freedom and Culture* (1939). *John Dewey: The Later Works 1938–1939*. Vol. 13. Edited by Jo Ann Boydston. Carbondale: Southern Illinois University Press, 1988.

———. *Individualism Old and New* (1930). New York: Capricorn, 1962.

———. *Intelligence in the Modern World*. New York: Milton, Balch, 1939.

———. *Philosophy and Civilization*. New York: Milton, Balch, 1931.

———. *Reconstruction in Philosophy* (1920). Boston: Beacon Press, 1957.

Diggins, John Patrick. *The Promise of Pragmatism*. Chicago: University of Chicago Press, 1994.

Douglas, C. H. *Credit Power and Democracy*. London: Cecil Palmer, 1920.

———. *Economic Democracy* (1919). London: Institute of Economic Democracy, 1979.

———. *The Monopoly of Credit*. London: Chapman and Hall, 1931.

———. *Social Credit* (1924 rev. 1933). Vancouver: Institute of Economic Democracy, 1979.

Doyle, Charles, ed. *William Carlos Williams: The Critical Heritage*. London: Routledge and Kegan Paul, 1980.

Eliot, T. S. *The Complete Poems and Plays*. New York: Harcourt Brace, 1962.

———. *The Use of Poetry and the Use of Criticism*. Cambridge, Mass.: Harvard University Press, 1933.

Elkins, Stanley, and McKitrick, Eric. *The Age of Federalism*. New York: Oxford University Press, 1993.

Emerson, Ralph Waldo. *Essays and Lectures*. New York: Library of America, 1983.

Faulkner, William. *The Sound and the Fury*. Norton Critical Ed. New York: W. W. Norton, 1987.

Federal Reserve, Board of Governors. *The Federal Reserve System*. Washington, D.C.: GPO, 1963.

Ferguson, Charles. *The Great News*. New York: Mitchell and Kennerly, 1915.

Ferkiss, Victor C. "Ezra Pound and American Fascism." *Journal of Politics* 17 (May 1955): 173–97.

———. "Populist Influences on American Fascism." *Western Political Quarterly* 10 (June 1957): 350–73.

Flory, Wendy Stallard. *The American Ezra Pound*. New Haven: Yale University Press, 1989.

———. *Ezra Pound and the Cantos: A Record of Struggle*. New Haven: Yale University Press, 1980.

Fox-Genovese, Elizabeth. *The Origins of Physiocracy*. Ithaca: Cornell University Press, 1976.

Frail, David. " 'The Regular Fourth of July Stuff': William Carlos Williams' Colonial Figures as Poets." *William Carlos Williams Review* 6:2 (1980): 1–14.

Freud, Sigmund. *Civilization and Its Discontents* (1930). New York: W. W. Norton, 1961.

———. *Totem and Taboo* (1913). New York: W. W. Norton, 1950.

Frost, Robert. *The Poetry of Robert Frost*. New York: Holt, Rinehart and Winston, 1969.

Galbraith, John Kenneth. *American Capitalism*. Boston: Houghton Mifflin, 1956.

———. *Economics in Perspective*. Boston: Houghton Mifflin, 1987.

———. *The Great Crash 1929* (1954). Boston: Houghton Mifflin, 1988.

Gentile, Emilio. "The Conquest of Modernity: From Modernist Nationalism to Fascism." Translated by Lawrence Rainey. *Modernism/Modernity* 1:3 (September 1994): 55–87.

George, Henry. *A Perplexed Philosopher* (1892). New York: Robert Schalkenbach Foundation, 1965.

———. *Progress and Poverty (1879)*. *New York: Robert Schalkenbach Foundation, 1987.*

———. *Protection or Free Trade* (1886). New York: Robert Schalkenbach Foundation, 1941.

———. *Social Problems* (1883). Vol. 11, *Complete Works of Henry George*. Garden City, N.Y.: Doubleday, Page and Co., 1911.

Gesell, Silvio. *The Natural Economic Order*. Translated by Phillip Pye. San Antonio: Free-Economy, 1936.

Goldman, Eric F. *Rendevous with Destiny*. New York: Vintage, 1977.

Goodwyn, Lawrence. *The Populist Moment*. Oxford: Oxford University Press, 1978.

Goux, Jean-Joseph. *Symbolic Economies*. Ithaca: Cornell University Press, 1990.

Graves, Robert. *The White Goddess*. Enlarged ed. New York: Noonday, 1966.

Green, Timothy. "From a Pawnshop to a Patron of the Arts in Five Centuries." *Smithsonian* 22:4 (July 1991): 59–69.

Greider, William. *Secrets of the Temple: How the Federal Reserve Runs the Country*. New York: Simon and Schuster, 1987.

Grusin, Richard A. " 'Put God in Your Debt': Emerson's Economy of Expenditure." *PMLA* 103:1 (1988): 35–44.

Guillory, John. *Cultural Capital: The Problem of Literary Canon Formation.* Chicago: University of Chicago Press, 1993.

Habermas, Jürgen. *The Philosophical Discourse of Modernity.* Cambridge, Mass.: MIT Press, 1987.

Hamilton, Alexander. *The Works of Alexander Hamilton.* Edited by Henry Cabot Lodge. Vols. 1, 4. New York: Haskell House, 1971.

Hamilton, Alexander, Jay, John, and Madison, James. *The Federalist Papers* (1787–88). Edited by Clinton Rossiter. New York: New American Library, 1961.

Harvey, David. *The Condition of Post-Modernity.* Oxford: Blackwell, 1990.

Harvey, W. H. *Coin's Financial School.* Chicago: Coin Publishing, 1894.

——. *A Tale of Two Nations.* Chicago: Coin Publishing, 1894.

——. *Up to Date: Coin's Financial School Cont[inued].* Chicago: Coin Publishing, 1895.

——, ed. *Coin's Financial Series.* Vol. 8. Chicago: Coin Publishing, 1895.

Heidegger, Martin. *Basic Writings.* San Francisco: Harper Collins, 1977.

——. *Poetry, Language, Thought.* New York: Harper and Row, 1971.

Heilbroner, Robert L. *Behind the Veil of Economics.* New York: W. W. Norton, 1988.

——. *The Economic Transformation of America.* New York: Harcourt, Brace, Jovanovich, 1977.

——. *The Nature and Logic of Capitalism.* New York: W. W. Norton, 1985.

Heinzelmann, Kurt. *The Economics of the Imagination.* Amherst: University of Massachusetts Press, 1980.

Henault, Marie, ed. *Studies in the Cantos.* Columbus: Charles E. Merrill, 1971.

Hobbes, Thomas. *Leviathan* (1651). New York: Penguin, 1981.

Hoffman, Daniel, ed. *Ezra Pound and William Carlos Williams.* Philadelphia: University of Pennsylvania Press, 1983.

Hofstadter, Richard. *The Age of Reform.* New York: Vintage, 1955.

——. *The American Political Tradition* (1948). New York: Vintage, 1974.

——. *The Idea of a Party System.* Berkeley: University of California Press, 1969.

——. *The Paranoid Style in American Politics* (1952). New York: Vintage, 1967.

——. *The Progressive Historians.* New York: Alfred A. Knopf, 1968.

Hyde, G. H. "The Poetry of the City." In *Modernism.* Edited by Malcolm Bradbury and James McFarlane. Harmondsworth, Essex: Penguin, 1976.

Hyde, Lewis. *The Gift: Imagination and the Erotic Life of Property.* New York: Vintage, 1990.

James, William. *Writings, 1902–1910.* New York: Library of America, 1987.

——. *The Writings of William James.* Edited by John J. McDermott. Chicago: University of Chicago Press, 1977.

Jarrell, Randall. *Kipling, Auden, and Company.* New York: Farrar, Straus, Giroux, 1980.

——. *Poetry and the Age* (1953). New York: Ecco, 1980.

Jefferson, Thomas. *Writings.* New York: Library of America, 1984.

Jehlen, Myra. *The American Incarnation.* Cambridge, Mass.: Harvard University Press, 1986.

Jelley, S. M., ed. *The Voice of Labor.* Philadelphia: n.p., 1888.

Kayman, Martin A. "Ezra Pound: The Color of His Money." *Paideuma* 15:2–3 (1985): 39–52.

Kearns, George. *The Cantos.* Cambridge: Cambridge University Press, 1989.

——. *Guide to Ezra Pound's Selected Cantos.* New Brunswick: Rutgers University Press, 1980.

Kenner, Hugh. *The Pound Era.* Berkeley: University of California Press, 1971.

Kitson, Arthur. Correspondence with Ezra Pound. YCAL 43. Beinecke Library, Yale University, New Haven, Conn.

——. *Unemployment.* London: n.p., 1921.

Kuczynski, Marguerite, and Meek, Ronald L., eds. *Quesnay's "Tableau économique."* London: Macmillan, 1972.

Langer, Susanne K. *Philosophy in a New Key.* Cambridge, Mass.: Harvard University Press, 1979.

Lears, T. J. Jackson. *No Place of Grace.* New York: Pantheon, 1982.

Lentricchia, Frank. *Ariel and the Police.* Madison: University of Wisconsin Press, 1988.

——. *Criticism and Social Change.* Chicago: University of Chicago Press, 1985.

Lewis, Wyndham. *The Art of Being Ruled* (1926). Edited by Reed Way Dasenbrock. Santa Rosa: Black Sparrow, 1989.

——. *Time and Western Man* (1927). Boston: Beacon Press, 1957.

Lindberg, Kathryn V. *Reading Pound Reading.* New York: Oxford University Press, 1987.

Littlefield, Henry M. "*The Wizard of Oz:* Parable of Populism." *American Quarterly* 16:1 (Spring 1964): 47–58.

Livingston, James. *Origins of the Federal Reserve System: Money, Class, and Corporate Capitalism, 1890–1913.* Ithaca: Cornell University Press, 1986.

——. *Pragmatism and the Political Economy of Cultural Revolution, 1850–1940.* Durham: University of North Carolina Press, 1994.

——. "The Social Analysis of Economic History and Theory: Conjectures on Late Nineteenth-Century Development." *American Historical Review* 92:1 (February 1987): 69–95.

Lloyd, Margaret Glynne. *William Carlos Williams' Paterson.* Rutherford: Fairleigh Dickinson University Press, 1980.

Longenbach, James. *Wallace Stevens: The Plain Sense of Things*. Oxford: Oxford University Press, 1991.

Mairet, Philip. *The Douglas Manual*. London: Stanley Nott, 1934.

Makin, Peter. *Pound's Cantos*. Baltimore: Johns Hopkins University Press, 1992.

Marcuse, Herbert. *Eros and Civilization*. New York: Vintage, 1955.

Mariani, Paul. *William Carlos Williams: A New World Naked*. New York: W. W. Norton, 1981.

Mark, Jeffrey. *The Modern Idolatry: Being an Analysis of Usury and the Pathology of Debt*. London: Chatto and Windus, 1934.

Marsh, Alec. "Poetry and the Age: Pound, Zukofsky, and the Labor Theory of Value." In *Upper Limit Music: The Writings of Louis Zukofsky*. Edited by Mark Scroggins. University of Alabama Press, 1997.

Marx, Karl. *Capital*. Vol. 1 (1867). New York: Vintage, 1977.

———. *Early Writings*. New York: Vintage, 1975.

Marx, Karl, and Engels, Friedrich. *The Communist Manifesto* (1848). New York: Penguin, 1967.

Marx, Karl, Engels, Friedrich, and Lenin, Vladimir Ilyich Ulyanov, *The Essential Left*. New York: Barnes and Noble, 1961.

Matthews, Richard K. *The Radical Politics of Thomas Jefferson*. Lawrence: University Press of Kansas, 1984.

Mauss, Marcel. *The Gift (Essai sur le don, forme archaique de l'échange)* (1925). New York: W. W. Norton, 1967.

McCoy, Drew R. *The Elusive Republic: Political Economy in Jeffersonian America*. New York: W. W. Norton, 1980.

McDonald, Forrest. *Alexander Hamilton*. New York: W. W. Norton, 1979.

———. *The Presidency of Thomas Jefferson*. Lawrence: University Press of Kansas, 1976.

McLellan, David. *Friedrich Engels*. New York: Penguin, 1978.

———. *Karl Marx*. New York: Penguin, 1976.

Meek, Ronald L. *The Economics of Physiocracy*. Cambridge, Mass.: Harvard University Press, 1963.

———. *Studies in the Labor Theory of Value*. 2d ed. New York: Monthly Review Press, 1975.

Meisel, Perry. *The Myth of the Modern*. New Haven, Conn.: Yale University Press, 1987.

Michaels, Walter Benn. *The Gold Standard and the Logic of Naturalism*. Berkeley: University of California Press, 1987.

Miller, James E., Jr. *The American Quest for a Supreme Fiction*. Chicago: University of Chicago Press, 1979.

Miller, J. Hillis. *The Linguistic Moment*. Princeton: Princeton University Press, 1985.

Miller, Tyrus. "Pound's Economic Ideal: Sylvio Gesell and *The Cantos*." *Paideuma* 19:1–2 (1989): 169–80.

Munson, Gorham. *Aladdin's Lamp.* New York: Creative Age, 1945.

Murray, David. "Pound-Signs: Money and Representation in Ezra Pound." *Ezra Pound: Tactics for Reading.* Edited by Ian F. A. Bell. London: Vision, 1982.

Mussolini, Benito. *The Corporate State.* Firenze: Vallecchi Editore, 1936.

———. *Fascism: Doctrine and Institutions* (1935). New York: Howard Fertig, 1968.

Nelson, Benjamin. *The Idea of Usury: From Universal Brotherhood to Universal Otherhood.* Chicago: University of Chicago Press, 1969.

Nicholls, Peter. *Ezra Pound: Politics, Economics, and Writing.* London: Macmillan, 1984.

Nietzsche, Friedrich. *Beyond Good and Evil* (1886). Translated by Walter Kaufman. New York: Vintage, 1966.

Oderman, Kevin. *Ezra Pound and the Erotic Medium.* Chapel Hill: Duke University Press, 1986.

Parker, Andrew. "Ezra Pound and the 'Economy' of Anti-Semitism." *Boundary 2* 11:2 (1982–83): 103–28.

Parrington, Vernon Louis. *Main Currents in American Thought.* New York: Harcourt, Brace, 1927.

Penty, Arthur J. *Protection and the Social Problem.* London: Methuen, 1926.

Poirier, Richard. *Poetry and Pragmatism.* Cambridge, Mass.: Harvard University Press, 1992.

———. *The Renewal of Literature.* New York: Random House, 1987.

———. *Robert Frost: The Work of Knowing.* New York: Oxford University Press, 1977.

Polanyi, Karl. *The Great Transformation* (1944). Boston: Beacon Press, 1957.

Pound, Ezra. *The ABC of Reading.* New York: New Directions, 1960.

———. *The Cantos.* New York: New Directions, 1989.

———. *The Collected Early Poems of Ezra Pound.* New York: New Directions, 1976.

———. *The Confucian Odes* (1954). New York: New Directions, 1959.

———. *Confucius.* New York: New Directions, 1969.

———. *"Ezra Pound Speaking": Radio Speeches of World War II.* Edited by Leonard W. Doob. Westport: Greenwood Press, 1978.

———. *Gaudier-Brzeska* (1916). New York: New Directions, 1970.

———. *Guide to Kulchur.* New York: New Directions, 1970.

———. *Jefferson and/or Mussolini* (1935). New York: Liveright, 1970.

———. Pound to John Dewey. November 13, 1934. YCAL 43. Beinecke Library, Yale University, New Haven, Conn.

———. Pound to C. H. Douglas. May 15, 1940. YCAL 43. Beinecke Library, Yale University, New Haven, Conn.

———. *Literary Essays of Ezra Pound* (1935). Edited by T. S. Eliot. New York: New Directions, 1968.

———, ed. *Populism: Nostalgic or Progressive?* New York: Rand McNally, 1964.

Van Buren, Martin. *The Autobiography of Martin van Buren* (1918). Reprint. New York: Chelsea House, 1983.

Veblen, Thorstein. *The Theory of the Leisure Class* (1899). New York: Modern Library, 1931.

Vendler, Helen. *On Extended Wings: Wallace Stevens' Longer Poems.* Cambridge, Mass.: Harvard University Press, 1969.

Voorhis, Jerry. "The Mysteries of the Federal Reserve System." *Paideuma* 11:3 (1982): 488–97.

Wasserstrom, William. "William Carlos Williams: The Healing Image." *Bennington Review* 10 (April 1981): 40–53.

Weaver, William. *William Carlos Williams: The American Background.* Cambridge: Cambridge University Press, 1977.

White, Horace. *Coin's Financial Fool.* New York: J. S. Ogilvie, 1895.

Whitman, Walt. *Complete Poetry and Collected Prose.* New York. Library of America, 1982.

Wiebe, Robert H. *The Search for Order, 1877–1920.* New York: Hill and Wang, 1967.

Wilhelm, James J. *The American Roots of Ezra Pound.* New York: Garland, 1985.

Williams, William Carlos. *Autobiography.* New York: New Directions, 1970.

———. *The Collected Poems of William Carlos Williams, Vol. 1, 1909–1939.* New York: New Directions, 1986.

———. *The Collected Poems of William Carlos Williams, Vol. 2, 1939–1962.* New York: New Directions, 1986.

———. *The Embodiment of Knowledge.* New York: New Directions, 1974.

———. *Imaginations.* New York: New Directions, 1970.

———. *In the American Grain.* New York: New Directions, 1956.

———. *In the Money.* New York: New Directions, 1940.

———. *I Wanted to Write a Poem.* New York: New Directions, 1978.

———. Williams to Sherry Mangan. N.d. [1934?]. YCAL 43, Box 49. Beinecke Library, Yale University, New Haven, Conn.

———. *Paterson.* Edited by Christopher MacCowan. New York: New Directions, 1992.

———. *A Recognizable Image: William Carlos Williams on Art and Artists.* Edited by Bram Dijkstra. New York: New Directions, 1978.

———. *Selected Essays.* New York: New Directions, 1969.

———. *The Selected Letters of William Carlos Williams.* Edited by John C. Thirwall. New York: New Directions, 1984.

———. *Something to Say: William Carlos Williams on Younger Poets.* Edited by James E. B. Breslin. New York: New Directions, 1985.

Williams, William Eric. "Money." *William Carlos Williams Review* 9:1–2 (1983): 42–44.

Wilson, Edmund. *Shores of Light*. New York: Farrar Straus and Young, 1952.

Wilstach, Paul, ed. *Correspondence of John Adams and Thomas Jefferson, 1812–1826*. New York: Kraus Reprint, 1972.

Wiltse, Charles M. *The Jeffersonian Tradition in American Democracy*. New York: Hill and Wang, 1960.

Wood, Gordon S. *The Creation of the American Republic, 1776–1787*. New York: W. W. Norton, 1969.

Zukofsky, Louis. *A*. Berkeley: University of California Press, 1978.

———. *Complete Short Poetry*. Baltimore: Johns Hopkins University Press, 1991.

INDEX

ABOUT THE AUTHOR

Alec Marsh is Assistant Professor of English at Muhlenberg College, Allentown, Pennsylvania. He received his bachelor's degree from Bennington College, and his master's and doctorate from Rutgers University.